CAMBRIDGE LI

Books of end

MW00791819

Medieval History

This series includes pioneering editions of medieval historical accounts by eye-witnesses and contemporaries, collections of source materials such as charters and letters, and works that applied new historiographical methods to the interpretation of the European middle ages. The nineteenth century saw an upsurge of interest in medieval manuscripts, texts and artefacts, and the enthusiastic efforts of scholars and antiquaries made a large body of material available in print for the first time. Although many of the analyses have been superseded, they provide fascinating evidence of the academic practices of their time, while a considerable number of texts have still not been re-edited and are still widely consulted.

Yorkshire Deeds

Published between 1909 and 1955, this ten-volume collection contains deeds relating to all of Yorkshire, from the twelfth to the seventeenth century. The deeds are of local historical interest, and provide topographical, philological and genealogical information, as well as insights into daily life. The majority of the records here are presented as abstracts, while documents in the vernacular that are of greater interest or importance are printed in full. Where possible, the documents are dated. Thorough background information and discussion of the deeds is included, as are notable physical descriptions, in particular of the seals. Each volume concludes with an index of people and places. Published in 1955, Volume 10 was edited by M.J. Stanley Price (formerly M.J. Hebditch) and is compiled largely from documents held by the Yorkshire Archaeological Society. It also contains many miscellaneous documents included to complete collections published elsewhere in the ten volumes.

Cambridge University Press has long been a pioneer in the reissuing of out-of-print titles from its own backlist, producing digital reprints of books that are still sought after by scholars and students but could not be reprinted economically using traditional technology. The Cambridge Library Collection extends this activity to a wider range of books which are still of importance to researchers and professionals, either for the source material they contain, or as landmarks in the history of their academic discipline.

Drawing from the world-renowned collections in the Cambridge University Library and other partner libraries, and guided by the advice of experts in each subject area, Cambridge University Press is using state-of-the-art scanning machines in its own Printing House to capture the content of each book selected for inclusion. The files are processed to give a consistently clear, crisp image, and the books finished to the high quality standard for which the Press is recognised around the world. The latest print-on-demand technology ensures that the books will remain available indefinitely, and that orders for single or multiple copies can quickly be supplied.

The Cambridge Library Collection brings back to life books of enduring scholarly value (including out-of-copyright works originally issued by other publishers) across a wide range of disciplines in the humanities and social sciences and in science and technology.

Yorkshire Deeds

VOLUME 10

EDITED BY M.J. STANLEY PRICE

CAMBRIDGE
UNIVERSITY PRESS

CAMBRIDGE UNIVERSITY PRESS

Cambridge, New York, Melbourne, Madrid, Cape Town,
Singapore, São Paolo, Delhi, Mexico City

Published in the United States of America by Cambridge University Press, New York

www.cambridge.org
Information on this title: www.cambridge.org/9781108058490

© in this compilation Cambridge University Press 2013

This edition first published 1955
This digitally printed version 2013

ISBN 978-1-108-05849-0 Paperback

This book reproduces the text of the original edition. The content and language reflect the beliefs, practices and terminology of their time, and have not been updated.

Cambridge University Press wishes to make clear that the book, unless originally published by Cambridge, is not being republished by, in association or collaboration with, or with the endorsement or approval of, the original publisher or its successors in title.

YORKSHIRE DEEDS

VOL. X

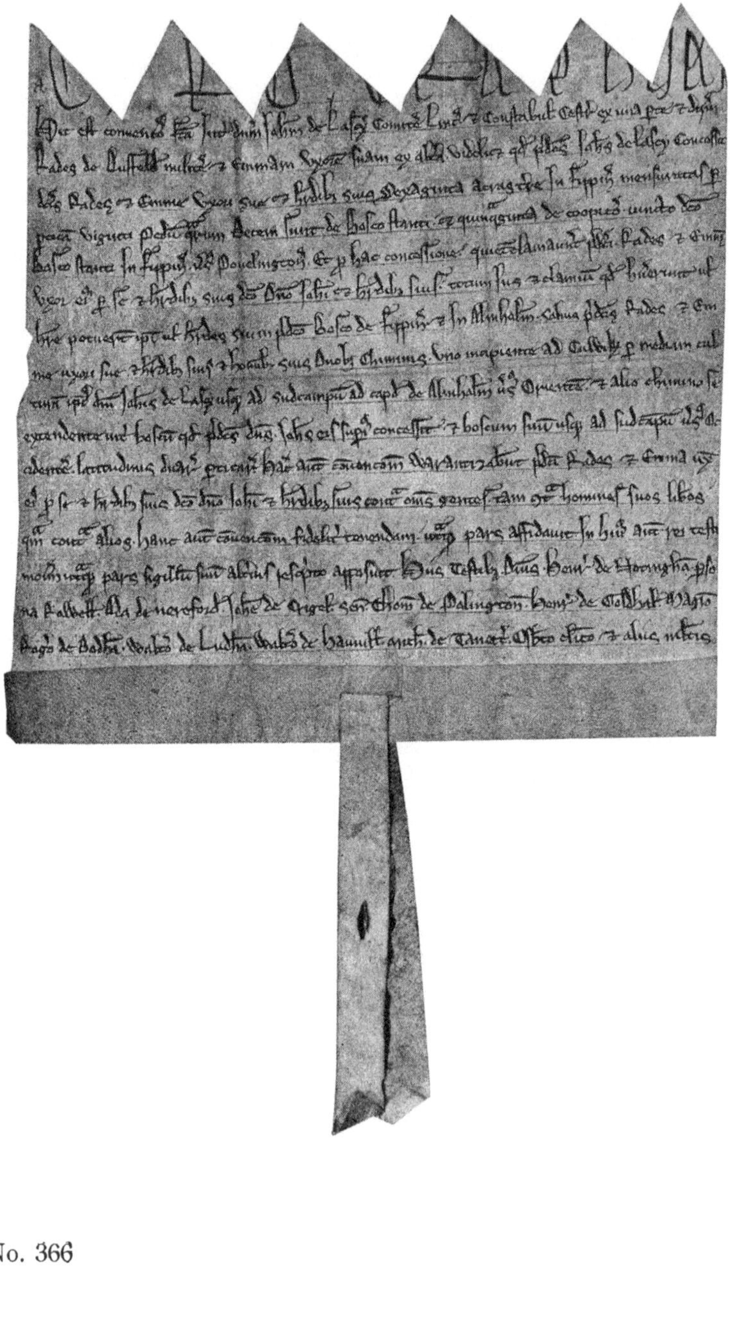

No. 366

THE YORKSHIRE
ARCHÆOLOGICAL SOCIETY

FOUNDED 1863 INCORPORATED 1893

RECORD SERIES

VOL. CXX

FOR THE YEAR 1953

YORKSHIRE DEEDS

VOL. X

EDITED BY

M. J. STANLEY PRICE, M.A.

PRINTED FOR THE SOCIETY

1955

Printed by
THE HERALD PRINTING WORKS,
YORK AND LONDON.

CONTENTS

ILLUSTRATION

INTRODUCTION

The ownership of the documents printed in this volume is as follows:

Archer-Houblon MSS. (in the custody of the Y.A.S.), Nos. 41–69.

Cartwright Memorial Hall, Bradford, Nos. 25–40, 86–88, 136, 148–150, 333.

Lady Galway (Serlby Hall Muniments), Nos. 70–72, 82, 102, 109, 116–125, 157, 210, 248-255, 261-280, 288–293, 295–297, 302–308, 327, 405, 416, 417.

Major le G. G. W. Horton-Fawkes (Farnley Hall Muniments, in the custody of the Y.A.S.), Nos. 194-206, 218, 239–246, 260, 330–332, 334, 346–348, 368-370, 525.

N. G. Hyde, Esq., 19 Foregate Street, Worcester (in the custody of the Y.A.S.), Nos. 126–135, 142, 156, 217, 301, 364, 365, 406, 407.

Roger Lee, Esq., Roseberry Cottage, Glan Conway, North Wales), Nos. 238, 287, 299, 337–345, 352, 355–362, 510–513, 524.

Dr. E. G. Millar, 28 Holland Park Road, London, Nos. 75, 76, 101, 111, 140, 143, 144, 219, 220, 259, 281–286, 366, 412, 414.

Newburgh Priory Muniments (in the custody of the Y.A.S.), Nos. 89, 97, 100, 160–162, 247, 300, 325, 326, 371, 408–411.

J. B. Payne, Esq., Kalgar, Welwyn, Herts., Nos. 74, 329, 437–441.

Lord Scarbrough, Sandbeck Hall, Nos. 442–472.

G. T. Schofield, Esq., 54 Gamble Lane, Farnley, Leeds, Nos. 163–193.

E. Stanley Jones, Esq., Malton (in the custody of the Y.A.S.), Nos. 153–155, 207–208, 222–237, 328.

H. Wrigley, Esq., Ganton Hall (in the custody of the Y.A.S.). Nos. 211–216.

The Yorkshire Archaeological Society, Nos. 1–25, 73, 77–81, 83–85, 90–96, 98, 99, 103–108, 110, 112–115, 137–139, 141, 145–147, 151, 152, 158, 159, 209, 221, 256–258, 294, 298, 309–324, 335, 336, 349–351, 353, 354, 363, 367, 372–404, 413, 415, 418–436, 473–509, 514–523.

The present volume contains a representative collection of documents, which covers all parts of Yorkshire and ranges from the twelfth to the sixteenth century, as in the previous nine volumes. Here there are slightly more from the southern part of the county due to the two collections relating to Tickhill and Hemsworth which have been printed through the kindness of Lord Scarbrough and Lady Galway.

Also included are further documents from the large Dawnay collection which cover Snaith and District. Many from this series which were a gift to the Yorkshire Archaeological Society from Dr. E. Millar, were printed in the preceding volume, but the present selection is from transcripts made by Mr. C. T. Clay from deeds still in Dr. Millar's possession. The Pollington deed illustrated in the frontispiece is reproduced here through his kindness.

The collection of Mr. E. Stanley Jones, now deposited with the Y.A.S., supplied an interesting series from Gristhorpe, and Mr. N. G. Hyde has also deposited at Park Place those documents relating to Cawton, Polkthorpe, etc., which he had previously lent for transcription. Among these is an almost identical duplicate (No. 126) of a charter already printed by Mr. Clay, which accounts for the different reference numbers. Mr. Clay gives his example as Y.A.S. DD 65/1.

A further 33 deeds from the Farnley Hall Muniments are printed. This very large collection provides a remarkable example of the durability of such records despite adverse conditions. They escaped destruction narrowly, and after being relegated to a potting shed for many years, were rescued by the present owner, found to be in almost perfect condition and placed in the safe custody of the Y.A.S.

It will be noticed that there are many single documents relating to separate places. These were included in order to complete the medieval sections of certain collections not printed in their entirety in earlier volumes. Among them is the remainder of the Acaster Chartulay (Nos. 1–24), of the Archer-Houblon Collection (Nos. 41–69); Y.A.S. MD 59/19 and 59/24, etc. This completes the printing of all suitable medieval deeds preserved at Park Place up to 1950.

Once again it is possible to add to the history of many Yorkshire manors whose names may be found here, notably, Gristhorpe, Farnley (Otley), Kirkby Fleetham, Pinchingthorpe and Farnley (Leeds). The series relating to Farnley, near Leeds, were kindly lent by Mr. G. T. Schofield, and perhaps the most interesting is No. 171, where Sir Robert de Neville transfers all cattle, corn, hay and other profits from all his lands to his uncle for the support of Sir Robert's wife and children, possibly to provide for them while he was absent in the King's forces in France. Nos. 177, 179, 186, 187, relate to certain smithies and their maintenance, at Farnley and Tong.

There are few unusual words to be found in this volume, but 'soers' is not common, and may mean sisters, while St. Eigne could be a curious form of St. Agnes.

One small point of interest may be noted. No. 7 is a grant from John Fairfax to his nephew Richard, not only of his manors, lands, etc., but also of the name and arms of Malbys, and in default of issue remainder of the same to Thomas, son of Robert de Rouclif. Such grants must surely spring traps for the unwary genealogist.

The thanks of the Record Series Committee are due to all those owners of deeds who have so kindly lent their documents and have allowed them to be transcribed and printed. The thanks of the editor is most gratefully given to Miss Foster for her help, and in particular to Mr. C. T. Clay for his patience in checking proofs and for assisting at every stage in the rather protracted work on this volume.

M. J. STANLEY PRICE.

YORKSHIRE DEEDS

Acaster Malbis.

1. Grant by Robert Holdebord to William son of John de Cuniggeston, citizen of York, of the following annual rents, namely, 1*d.* at All Saints from Robert son of Gene de Acastre, with wards, reliefs and escheats from 2½ acres of land in the fields of Thorp' which he holds of the grantor; 1*d.* at All Saints from John son of Agatha de Drengehuses for 6 acres of land in the fields of Thorp'; 1*d.* from Slethman of York at the Nativity for 3 acres of land; 1*d.* from Sir John le Beck at the Nativity for 5 acres of land and 4 acres of meadow in the fields of Thorp'; 1*d.* at Whitsuntide from the heirs of Gace de Chaumunt, once citizen of York, for 2 acres of land in the fields of Acastre, less one rood; 1*d.* from Peter Noel and his heirs and assigns, at the Nativity, for 3 acres of land in the fields of Thorp'; the rent of an arrow from John de Fytling at St. John the Baptist for 1½ acres of land; a pepper-corn at the Nativity from Robert the chaplain of Thorp' for 1½ acres of land; ½*d.* from John de Sutton and William the forester, citizens of York, for 2 bovates of meadow in the fields of Thorp'; to hold to William, his heirs and assigns, with all appurtenances, wards, reliefs and escheats within and without the vill of Thorp', and with all other services, of the grantor and his heirs, freely and peacefully as held by the grantor, and paying yearly to him a rose at the Nativity of St. John for all secular services, exactions and demands. Warranty. Witnesses: John de Seleby, mayor of York[1], William de Ackum, John Speciaria, Thomas Bustard of Thorp', John Malecak of Acastre, Richard son of Hugh of the same, John de Fytling, John de Marston', Ralph de Ackum, Wydone de Appelton'. (*Y.A.S.*, Md. 2. No. 1).

2. Dec. 9, 13 Edward III [1339]. Indenture whereby Henry son of Alan Ercedeken of Acastre grants to William de Aula of Scalton and Isabel, his wife, 2 tofts and 4 acres of arable land in Oueracastre, which tenement once came to John, the grantor's brother, after the death of Alan, their father; to hold to William and Isabel for the term of their lives or for the lifetime of the survivor, of the grantor for the term of his life, paying yearly for the term of the grantor's life, 8*s.* of silver at Whitsuntide and Martinmas in equal portions and performing the due and accustomed services; should the rent be in arrears either wholly or in part for so long as 15 days, power to the grantor or his attorney to enter and distrain on all the lands, buildings, goods and chattels until the said rent be paid

[1] John de Seleby was mayor of York in 1252 and 1263.

doubly to cover the cost of damages and delays. After the death of William and Elizabeth remainder to Henry, son of Isabel, and his lawfully begotten heirs for the term of the grantor's life, and in default of issue to the heirs of William and Elizabeth, and after the grantor's death reversion to his heirs. Warranty. Sealing clause. Witnesses: John Malbys, Henry de Coupmanthorp', Laurence his brother, Roger Bakester, John Joukyn. At Acastre. (*Ibid.*, No. 2).

3. Vigil of the Nativity, 32 Edward III [Dec. 24, 1358]. Grant by William Malbys, knt., and Walter Malbys, son of Sir William, to William del Hall of Acastre, of 2 acres and half a rood of meadow in the south meadows of Acastre, lying next to the meadow of the abbot and convent of Rievall' on the south; to hold to William del Halle for the term of his life. Warranty. Sealing clause. At Skalton. (*Ibid.*, No. 3).

4. Aug. 5, 1365. Indenture[1] between Sir William de Seint Quintyn and Sir Walter Malbys stating that whereas Sir Walter has brought several suits against Sir William and Dame Elizabeth, his wife, in respect of the manors of Acastre Malbys, Coupmanthorp and divers other lands with appurtenances which lately belonged to William Malbys, now with God, which lands the said Sir William had entered upon by right heritage of his wife, believing it to be the truth that Sir Walter was deceased in foreign parts; now it is agreed that no further action shall be taken in respect of the said suits, which shall be delayed (*mis en suspense*) in the following manner, namely, that they shall be held up with this intent, that there shall be no move made either by one party or by the other until the affair comes before Mag. Thomas de Bukton between the date of these presents and the 20th day of Christmas next following. And should it happen that during this time of peace that the parties direct themselves, each by the advice and counsels of their friends, but without any desire for fraudulent delay, to discuss the cause of their quarrel in true amity, through six persons speaking on behalf of each party, or by any other method the parties or their advisers contrive, it shall be allowed, and if the said Mag. Thomas does not come in peace during the said 20 days of Christmas, or if certain news comes that he cannot appear or is deceased, then the parties shall proceed to their agreement in the manner aforesaid. And Sir William and his wife loyally promise a reasonable restitution to Sir Walter of the lands with all reliefs and whatsoever profits they have or may receive from the lands entered upon, and admit without argument, rancour or discussion the truth, if the right was judged to be Sir Walter's by the advisers of both parties, to the end that they may accord damages as well as the lands. And as there are many other lands also of the Malbys inheritance which Sir William had not entered upon and which are not in the possession of Sir Walter, to which the said Sir William and his wife claim a similar title, as well as to

[1] In French.

those which they entered, the said Sir Walter in truth and honesty has loyally promised that he will make restitution to Sir William and his wife of all that he has received and taken and of all that he may receive from these said lands and appurtenances, without argument, rancour or contradiction, if Elizabeth's right to the lands is proved by the decision of the friends, as above said. And it is agreed that neither party nor their supporters shall by any means, from any cause hereafter arising, cause any suit to be instigated either peacefully or otherwise, by persuasion, gift or promise, against the other party without inviting the other to a discussion where he may personally or by his agents ask and discover whatsoever is necessary for his information concerning his rights in the matter. Wherefore the said Sir William and Sir Walter shall not institute any act of alienation or demise any or all of the said lands and tenements once belonging to William Malbys, in respect of the lordship or in any matter which might be prejudicial or cause damage to those who ought by rightful title firstly and entirely, to enjoy the possession of the said lordship as held on the day of the decease of William Malbys . . .[1] observe the truth as decided by the friends of both parties in the manner and form above written. And Sir William and Elizabeth shall not bring any [action] . . . against Sir Walter relating to the lands which Sir Walter occupies on the day of the making of these indentures until the business is discussed . . . good and reasonable agreement, nor shall anything be undertaken between the parties . . . within the said 20 days of Christmas. And each of the parties shall hold faithfully to the terms of these indentures . . . and in the presence of the following witnesses have placed their seals: Sirs W . . . Thomas de Musgraue, Ralph de Hastyngs, Thomas Ughtred, Thomas de Metham, Marmaduke de Lou . . . , Marmaduke de Conestable, Robert Hawley, John Bygot, Roger de Lascelles, Brian de Rouclif, Simon de Hes[lyngton], William de Acclom, William de Aldeburgh, knts., Thomas de Mawley, John de Langton of York, Hamo de Hessay, John de Bentelay, William Fayrefax. At York. (*Ibid.*, No. 4).

5. St. Mark the Evangelist, 42 Edward III [April 25, 1368]. Grant by William de Sancto Quintino, knt., to William Fairfax, his heirs and assigns, of his capital messuage, 5 tofts, 8 bovates and 40 acres of land, 16 acres of meadow and a rent of 10*d*., a pound of pepper, 2 pounds of cummin and a rose, in Acastremalbys, also all the lands and tenements, rents and services with appurtenances which the grantor has and which once belonged to John Sampson, knt., in the same vill; to hold to William Fairfax, with all rights and easements, of the chief lords of the fee, in perpetuity. Warranty. Sealing clause[2]. Witnesses: John Chaumont, Henry Gramary, William de Aclom, knts., John de Langeton of York, Richard de

[1] Deed blurred and illegible.

[2] Part of a seal of brown wax; a shield of arms couchée below a helm; a chevron . . .

Aske, John de Laisingtoft, John de Kirkeby of Wyginthorp'. At Acastremalbys. (*Ibid.*, No. 5).

6. Dec. 10, 42 Edward III [1368]. Appointment by Thomas Ughtred, knt., of John Scott of Acastre Malbys as his attorney to deliver se sin to Thomas Lastyngham, of a messuage and 2½ acres of land and appurtenances in the vill of Acastre Malbys, in accordance with his charter of feoffment. Sealing clause[1]. At Kexby. (*Ibid.*, No. 6).

7. Monday after All Saints, 43 Edward III [Nov. 4], 1369. Tripartite indenture whereby John Fairfax, rector of Gillyng in Ridale, grants to Richard son of William Fairfax, his brother, all his manors of Scalton, Acastremalbys, and Coupmanthorp' with all appurtenances as well in lands, dwellings, woods, meadows, mills and waters, as in reversions, rents, and services of villeins and freemen, without reservation, and with the name and arms of Malbys, fully and completely as held by the grantor; to hold the said manors and appurtenances to Richard and his male heirs lawfully begotten, of the grantor, by the service of a knight's fee, and paying yearly to the grantor and his heirs, namely, for the first six years after the date of these presents 100 marks at Martinmas and Whitsuntide in equal portions, and thereafter a rose at the Nativity of St. John the Baptist if demanded, and performing for the grantor the services due and accustomed to the chief lords of the fee. Should Richard die without lawful male issue, remainder to Thomas son of Robert de Rouclyf, knt., and his lawfully begotten heirs male on the same terms, and in default of such issue reversion to the grantor and his heirs, without reservation. Alternate seals and the several parts of the indenture to remain with Richard, Thomas and the grantor. Witnesses: Brian de Stapilton, John Chaumont, knts., John de Langeton of York, Thomas de Etton, Robert de Sproxton, William Dayuill, Richard Basy, John de Laysingtoft, Robert de Flaynburgh. At Scalton. (*Ibid.*, No. 7).

8. June 12, 10 Richard II [1387]. Grant by Robert de Acastre, chaplain, to Margaret daughter of John de Camsall of Acastre, of a messuage, one acre of land and half an acre of meadow in the vill and territory of Acastre Malbys, which messuage lies near the highway called Dousgayle on the south and the tenement of John Joukyn' on the north, and the acre of land lies in the north field of Acastre Malbys between the land of Richard Malbys, lord of Acastre Malbys on the north and the land of the said John Joukyn on the south, and the said half acre of meadow lies in the north meadow of Acastre Malbys between the meadow of the said Richard on the south and the meadow once belonging to Roger Chaumbirlayn

[1] There is a note in a later hand to the effect that the seal bore a cross flory

on the north; to hold with all appurtenances to Margaret and her lawfully begotten heirs, and in default of issue to John de Camsall and his heirs, freely, quietly and in peace, of the chief lords of the fee by the due and accustomed services, and also paying yearly 12*d*. of silver for a candle to burn in the church of the Holy Trinity in Acastre Malbys. Warranty. Sealing clause. Witnesses: Dom Richard de Gram . . . , vicar of Acastre, Thomas Nanson', John Joukyn, John de Couton', Thomas Hudson, William Casgoigne. At Acastre Malbys. (*Ibid.*, No. 8).

9. Monday after St. Peter in cathedra,[1] 12 Richard II [Feb. 22, 1388-9]. Grant by Margaret Coke, widow of Thomas Coke of York, son and heir of Simon Gouke, once citizen and merchant of York, to John Betenson of Acastre Malbys, of 3 tofts and 7 acres and 3 roods of land with appurtenances in the vill and territory of Acastre Malbys which the grantor recently had of the gift and feoffment of Dom William Malbys, chaplain; to hold to John Betonson, his heirs and assigns, freely and peacefully, of the chief lords of the fee. Warranty. Sealing clause. Witnesses: Thomas Fayrefax, Thomas Thurkill, William Pawmes, Nicholas de Northfolk, William Sampson. (*Ibid.*, No. 9).

10. Thursday after the Invention of the Cross, 12 Richard II [May 6, 1389]. Grant by John Betonson of Acastre Malbys to Richard Malbys, of 3 tofts and 7 acres and 3 roods of land with appurtenances, which the grantor recently had of the gift and feoffment of Margaret Coke, widow of Thomas Coke, son and heir of Simon Gouke, once citizen and merchant of York; to hold to Richard, his heirs and assigns, freely and in peace, of the chief lords of the fee. Warranty. Sealing clause. Witnesses: Thomas Fayrefax, Thomas Thurkill, William Pawmes, Nicholas de Northfolk, William Sampson, Richard Gyffon, Philip de Cornubia, clerk. At Acastre Malbys. (*Ibid.*, No. 10).

11. Nativity of the B.V.M., 13 Richard II [Sept. 8, 1389]. Grant by John Clerkson of Coupmanthorp to Roger de Celer, his heirs and assigns, of all the rents and services, lands and tenements which he has in the vill and territory of Acastre Malbys, and which belonged to Walter son of John de Coupmanthorp; he also grants half an acre of meadow in the fields of Acastre Malbys, between the meadow of the vicar of Acastre on one side and the meadow of Richard Malbys on the other and which abuts on the highway in front and on the water of the Use at the back; to hold to Roger, his heirs and assigns, of the chief lords of the fee. Quitclaim of the same and warranty. John Clerkson also wishes and grants for himself and his executors that should any claim be made on the said lands, Roger, his heirs and assigns shall be paid 100*s*. of lawful

[1] In 1389 February 22 was a Monday.

English money without delay. Sealing clause. Witnesses: John de Burton, clerk and vicar, Thomas de Brunby, Geoffrey Bacster. At York. (*Ibid.*, No. 11).

12. March 16, 1393 [-4], 17 Richard II. Grant by Stephen de Girlyngton of York, *littester*, to John Betenson of Acastre Malbys, of 2 tofts with appurtenances which he had of the gift and feoffment of John de Catton of York, baker, in the vill of Acastre Malbys; to hold to John, his heirs and assigns, freely and in peace of the chief lords of the fee. Warranty. Sealing clause. Witnesses: Thomas Fayrefax, Richard Malbys, Richard Basy, Nicholas de Northfolk, William Fraunkelayn. At Acastre Malbys. (*Ibid.*, No. 12).

13. Aug. 15, 1408, 9 Henry IV. Grant by John Joukyn of Acastre Malbys to William Joukyn, his son, of all his lands and tenements which he has in the vill and territory of Acastre Malbys; to hold to William and his lawfully begotten heirs, freely and in peace of the chief lords of the fee, and in default of issue, remainder to the right heirs of the grantor. Warranty. Sealing clause.[1] Witnesses: William Langton, John Catton, Richard Caterton, John Betonson, now John Aldwerk of Acastre Malbys. At Acastre Malbys. (*Ibid.*, No. 13).

14. Dec. 4, 5 Henry VI [1426]. Grant by Richard Fayrfax to Sirs Henry Percy, earl of Northumberland, Roger Chaums, John Salwan, knts., Guy Fayrfax, William Fayrfax, the grantor's son, William Fulthorp, John Fayrfax, Thomas Fayrfax, Henry Daywell and Edmund Wodcok, of his manor of Acastre Mallbys, with all his other lands and tenements in Thorparch, co. York; to hold to the grantees, their heirs and assigns, of the chief lords of the fee. Warranty. Sealing clause. Witnesses: Ralph Graystok, William Normanwile, knts., Henry Wauasour, Alexander Neuyll', William Midilton, Thomas Pallmys, esqs., William Ogylsthorp, John Martell, vicar of Thorparch, William Sigraue. At Thorparch. (*Ibid.*, No. 14).

15. Nov. 5, 6 Henry VI [1427]. Grant by John Campsalle of Acastre Malbys and Joan, his wife, to Thomas Campsalle of Acastre Malbys, his brother, of that messuage and 2½ acres with appurtenances which the grantor once had of the gift and feoffment of Robert de Acastre, chaplain, in the vill and territory of Acastre Malbys, which messuage lies between the ground of Richard Farefax on the west and a certain place called Lumbygayle on the east, and the 2½ acres lie in Fosseryddyng between the land of the said Richard Farefax on the east and the land once of Simon Gouke on the west; to hold to Thomas with all appurtenances, freely and in peace of the chief lords of the fee. Warranty. Sealing clause.[2]

[1] Fragment of small seal of red wax.
[2] Two small seals of black wax; (1) a rose; (2) a heart pierced by an arrow.

Witnesses: Thomas Palmes of Naburn, John Northfolk of the same, Nicholas Chapman of the same, Thomas Sampson of Appilton, William Jowkyn of Acastre malbys. At Acastre Malbys. (*Ibid.*, No. 15).

16. Feb. 12, 9 Henry VI [1430-1]. Grant by Robert Jacob of London, *Draper*, and Elizabeth his wife, to Richard Fayrfax esq., Brian Fayrfax, clerk and Guy Fayrfax, their brother, of all their lands and tenements in the vill and territory of Acastre Malbys in co. York; to hold to Richard, Brian and Guy, their heirs and assigns, of the chief lords of the fee. Warranty. Sealing clause. Witnesses: William de Ryther, knt., Brian Dayuyll, William Thwaytes, Richard Bank, Thomas Sampson. (*Ibid.*, No. 16).

17. March 25, 24 Henry VI [1446]. Grant[1] by Richard Carnaby of Carnaby[2] on Waldam, to William Jowkyn of York, his heirs and assigns, of a messuage and 2 bovates of land and meadow in the vill and fields of Acastre Malbys. Warranty. Sealing clause. Witnesses: William Fayrefax, William Wayte, William Sparowe, Thomas Wawan, Nicholas Chapman of Naburn'. (*Ibid.*, No. 17).

18. Sept. 28, 27 Henry VI [1448]. Grant by Thomas Campsalle of Acastre Malbys to John Joukyn of the same, of a certain waste piece of ground (*fundum*) lying between the messuage of the said John in front and the common way at the back; to hold with appurtenances to John, his heirs and assigns, freely and in peace, of the chief lords of the fee, paying yearly to the grantor and his assigns during his lifetime 12*d.* at the Nativity, and yearly in perpetuity after his death, 12*d.* to the church of the Holy Trinity at Acastre Malbys, for the maintenance of a candle to burn before the high altar in the said church at the time of the elevation of the Host. Warranty. Sealing clause. Witnesses: Robert Leper, William Wayte, William Carter. At Acaster Malbys. (*Ibid.*, No. 19).

19. Aug. 4, 5 Edward IV [1465]. Quitclaim by Robert Marsshall of Foulesutton in co. York, *yoman*, and Joan his wife, daughter of John Carnaby and Marjory his wife, once of Carnaby in the parish of Bridelyngton, to William Jowkyn of Acastre Malbys in Aynsty in the county of the city of York, and his heirs and assigns, of all right in a messuage and 2 bovates of land and meadow with appurtenances in the vill and fields of Acastre, which William Jowkyn, recently of York, and father of the said William, had of the gift and feoffment of Richard Carnaby of Carnaby, brother of the said Joan, the grantor's wife. Warranty. Sealing clause.

[1] Also quitclaim of the same to the same dated April 6, 1446. (*Ibid.*, No. 18).

[2] In the parish of Bridlington.

Witnesses: Richard Moyse, John Betenson of Acastre Malbys, Thomas Grissop, citizen and merchant of York. (*Ibid.*, No. 20).

20. April 8, 6 Henry VII [1491]. Grant by John Nassyngton of York, gentleman, son and heir of Richard Nassyngton, son and heir of John Nassyngton, senior, of York gentleman, now deceased, to Richard Beilby and John Askewith, chaplain, of a messuage, 2 gardens and 9½ acres of land and 1½ acres of meadow with appurtenances in Acastre Malbysshe in the county of the city of York, which lately belonged to John Nassyngton, senior; to hold to Richard and John, their heirs and assigns, of the chief lords of the fee. Warranty. Appointment of John Beilby and Robert Wilkynson as his attorneys to enter the said lands and take seisin on his behalf and thereafter to deliver seisin of the same to the grantees. Sealing clause. Witnesses: Seth Snawsell, Thomas Stillyngton, John Bulmer, Henry Vauasour, Hugh Beswyk.[1] (*Ibid.*, No. 21).

21. Feb. 22, 8 Henry VII [1492-3]. Note that since John Askewith, chaplain was recently enfeoffed in trust together with Richard Beilby, of a messuage, 9½ acres of land and 1½ acres of meadow with appurtenances in Acastremalbyssh, to the use of the said Richard Beilby and his heirs, now John, at Richard's request quitclaims to him, his heirs and assigns, all right in the said lands. Warranty. Sealing clause. (*Ibid.*, No. 22).

22. May 2, 18 Henry VII [1503]. Grant[2] by John Beilby to William Neleson, alderman of the city of York and William Cokan, chaplain, of a messuage, a toft, a croft and a garden, 24 acres of arable land and 4 acres of meadow with appurtenances in Acastre Malbysshe in the county of the city of York, which lands the grantor had with Thomas Fairfax, son of Guy Fairfax, knt., deceased, and John Bolton; to hold to William and William, of the chief lords of the fee in perpetuity. Appointment of Richard Broun and John Armeley as his attorneys either severally or together, to deliver full and peaceful seisin to the grantees, their heirs and assigns, in accordance with the form of this charter. Sealing clause. (*Ibid.*, No. 23).

23. Nov. 13, 23 Henry VIII [1531]. Quitclaim by John Harvy, gentleman, executor of the last will and testament of John Yellyn of London, mercer, to Nicholas Faierfaux, knt., son and heir of Thomas Faierfaux, knt., of all right in the manor of Acastre Malves and in all the other manors, lands and tenements recently belonging

[1] Signature of John Nassyngton on the bottom of the deed.

[2] Quitclaim of the same to the same, dated May 20, with the further information that the lands came to the grantor, Thomas Fairfax and John Bolton of the gift of John Joukyn, son and heir of John Joukyn of York, *shipman*. (*Ibid*, No. 24)

to Thomas Faierfaux, as well in the county of the city of York as in co. Yorks. Warranty. Sealing clause.[1] (*Ibid.*, No. 25).

24. Oct. 21, 36 Henry VIII [1544]. Bargain and sale by Thomas Vavasor of Copmanthorp in the county of the city of York, gent., to Sir Nicholas Fairfax in return for a sum of money, of a messuage with appurtenances in Acastre Malbis, and a bovate of arable land containing 9 acres and 1½ acres of meadow in Acastre, with all his lands and tenements, meadows and pastures in the territory of Acastre and now in the occupation of Agnes Tomson, widow; to hold to Nicholas, his heirs and assigns, of the chief lords of the fee. Warranty. Appointment of Miles Fairfax and John Redman as his attorneys to deliver seisin in accordance with the form of this charter. Sealing clause.[2] (*Ibid.*, No. 26).

Dorso: Season and Possescon taken the vi[th] day of November in the xxxvi[th] yere of the reign of oure soveraign lord Kyng Henry the viii[th] by Sir Jhon Browle clerke to the use of Sir Nycholas Fayreffax knyght. Witnessid: William Rede, Robert Salton, George Francland, Ottewell Jake, with others.

Addingham.

25. Confirmation by Adam de Breretun to Sir John Vauasor of 5 acres with appurtenances in Addingham,[3] that is, half an acre which lies above Lobewicslehte and extends towards Lobewic, one rood in the same field which lies within Smaledales and extends above Heselwodegile, and one rood in the same field which lies within Overwralandes, one rood in Nehtherwra, and one and a half roods above Mikeldales, half a rood above Aftwaldes, and one rood in the field of Norhfeld which lies in Byurbladethyart, one and a half roods which lie in Geoffrey's assart, and one rood in the same field which extends above that assart, one rood which lies above Heselheued, one rood which lies above Grettilandes, half an acre in a culture which is called Breretunholm between the grantor's land and the water, one rood in a culture which is called Havenham, half an acre in Suhfeld, on the east side, which extends towards Scalegile, half an acre in the same field which extends to Henry's cross, half a rood in a culture which is called Ricardecroft which extends towards the land of Richard Queinte; to hold to the said John and his heirs freely and hereditarily [*etc.*], with all liberties and easements pertaining to the said lands, paying yearly to the grantor and his heirs a pair of white gloves at Christmas for all services. Warranty. Sealing clause.[4] Witnesses: Sir John de

[1] Seal of red wax: a hare between the letters T W Signature of John Harvy

[2] Signature of Thomas Vavasor

[3] One of the deeds in this series has been printed in *Early Yorkshire Charters*, vol. VII, No. 107.

[4] An oval seal of black wax, 1¼ in. × 1 in.; legend: S: ADE . . BRERET' Endorsed: Adigham, in early hand; in later hand, Dns. Johannes Vauasur.

Horneby, William Maloleporar', Nigel de Nescefeld, Robert de Farnhil, John his son, Roger de Oterington, Simon de Burg', Adam de Walpol, Adam Sorheles, Jordan the hunter (*uenator*), Gilbert his son, Richard Callid, Richard Poer, clerk. (*Cartwright Memorial Hall, Bradford*).

26. Quitclaim by Adam de Breretun to Sir John Vauasor and his heirs, of all right which he has in all the land, with appurtenances, and rent which Agnes wife of Ralph the smith (*fabri*) once held of him; to hold to him and his heirs freely and peacefully. Warranty. Sealing clause. Witnesses: Walter de Haulay, Thomas de Osebalton, Robert de Fernhill, Nigel de Nescefeud, Adam Sorheles, Jordan the Hunter, Thomas Gilur, Richard Poer. (*Ibid.*).

27. Quitclaim by Richard son of Richard de Brereton to Sir John le Vauasur and his heirs or assigns, for a certain sum of money, of all right and claim in half a carucate of land with appurtenances, which Adam de Brereton held of the grantor in Addingham, with his homage and service and 8*s.* rent which Adam was accustomed to pay to the grantor, with all escheats and other things pertaining. He releases for himself and his heirs all right in the said land. Warranty. Sealing clause. Witnesses: Sir Peter de Percy, Sir Mauger le Vauasur, Sir Eudo de Boyvill, Sir Godfrey de Autriff, Thomas de Lellay, constable of Scippton, Robert de Plumton, William Maulever', Robert de Fernill, William de Marton, William de Trammayr, William de Hertellington, Roger de Otterington, Henry de Stutton. (*Ibid.*).

28. Confirmation by Agnes Gillur of Adyngham in her own proper right to Dame Alice la Vauasur, widow of Sir John le Vauasur, knight, of all the land which she has in Adyngham; namely one toft and two bovates, also le Langerydyng, Wrarydyng and Northrydyng, with all the lands and assarts granted by Robert le Vauasur to her ancestors, that is, all land formerly belonging to Gamellus son of Kerlyng; to hold to Alice and her heirs freely and in perpetuity, with all rights within and without the vill of Adyngham which pertain to the same land, in wood and plain, meadows and pasture, ways and paths, collecting nuts (*nucibus*), and pasturing pigs without payment of pannage; rendering to the chief lords of the fee the due and accustomed services. Warranty. Sealing clause. Witnesses: Sir Robert de Plumton, knt., Sir Robert de Stiveton, knt., John de Farnhyl, William Counel of Sylesden, Richard de Beurepayr, William de Scalwra, Peter Ayre of Adyngham, Robert the clerk of [B]ilton.[1] (*Ibid.*).

29. Demise and quitclaim by Edmund de Meresthowe, junior, and Edmund Forestar, chaplain, to Richard Robynson of Adyngham

[1] Endorsed: in an early hand, Adyngham; in a later hand, Addingham langeriding, wrayrydyng, Northrydyng.

and Thomas, his son, of all right which they have in a messuage and 15 acres of wood and meadow with appurtenances in a place which is called Gyldusbergh, which they had as a gift from John Caudray. The grantors renounce all claim to the land for themselves and on their behalf and no law suit to be brought against them. Warranty. Sealing clause. Witnesses: John de Coppelay, John de Scardebugh.[1] (*Ibid.*).

30. Confirmation by Peter son of Paul the Carpenter (*carpentarii*) of Adingham, to William son of Thomas de Scalwra, his heirs and assigns, of a bovate, with an assart containing 3 acres, which lies under Lobuic and extends in length from Wodestory Bec to Dinandekelde and in width from the ditch of Lobwic to the assart which William Disspensator once held in Adingham; to hold to him and his heirs, of Sir William le Vauasur and his heirs in fee and hereditarily freely [*etc.*]; paying 6*d.* at Martinmas and 6*d.* at Whitsuntide, doing forinsec service due from one bovate. Warranty. Sealing clause. Witnesses: Sir Robert de Plumton, knt., John de Farnehil, Richard de Halton, Walter son of Osbert, Richard Snaubal, Simon the smith (*fabro*) of Gildehus, Beret. (*Ibid.*).

31. Martinmas [Nov. 11], 1311. Lease by William le Vauasour to Ralph the carpenter of a toft, 2 bovates and 2 acres with appurtenances in Adingham which Benedict de Schalwra and Robert Autim [*sic*] held of the grantor; to hold to Ralph and his assigns of the grantor and his heirs for the term of 15 years, paying yearly 9*s.* sterling in equal portions at Whitsuntide and Martinmas and rendering the due and accustomed services. The toft and land to be returned at the end of the term in as good or better condition than when received. Warranty. Alternate seals. At Herewod.[2] (*Ibid.*).

32. Lease by William le Vauasour to William de Rancest for the term of his life, for his service and an annual rent of two marks to be taken yearly from the manor and tenants of Adingham in equal portions at Whitsuntide and Martinmas; to hold of the grantor and his heirs for the term of the life of the grantee. Power to distrain for non payment of rent. Grantee to have power to distrain on villeins if they do not pay rent. Warranty. Sealing clause. Alternate seals. Witnesses: Dom. John, Prior of Boulton, William de Stopham, Thomas de Alta Rypa, knts., Walter de Middelton living in Burley, John de Boulton, Edward Maunseil. (*Ibid.*).

33. Martinmas [Nov. 11], 1313. Lease for ten years from Sir Walter Vauasour to Robert, son of Thomas de Adingham, of a toft

[1] Endorsed: Adyngham, in an early hand; locus dictus Gildusberg, in a later hand.

[2] Endorsed in an early hand: Adyngham, and in a later hand: A lease for 15 years of some small parcells of lande.

with a building on it, 2 bovates of land and meadow, 2 acres, 3½ roods of land and meadow of Forland with appurtenances in the vill and territory of Adingham; that toft and building and 2 bovates of land and meadow with the forland which John Bischope once held at farm (*ad firmam*); to hold by paying yearly to Walter his heirs and assigns, 8*s.* 3*d.*, half at Pentecost and half at Martinmas, and by performing the same works as William de Mora, Richard son of Margote and the other free tenants of the vill. Robert to be responsible for the upkeep of the house and the state of repair to be decided by neighbours. Warranty. Alternate seals. Witnesses: Henry de Hertelington, John de Stiveton, knts., Robert de Farnhill, Robert Buck, Robert Cokebayn, Thomas Revel, Adam de Berewike, Adam Fauvel, Robert de Bentley, William Bremham. (*Ibid.*).

34. Sunday, St. Augustine, 17 Edw. II [May 27, 1324]. Confirmation by William, son of Thomas de Scalwra, to Richard son of Robert son of Thomas de Harewod, and Marjory daughter of the grantor, of a toft and croft, a bovate, with appurtenances, in Adingham, with an assart containing three acres in the same vill; which assart lies under Lobwych, and extends in length from Westorthbeck to Dynandkeld, and in breadth from the ditch (*fossato*) of Baliwych to the assart which William Dispensator once held in Adingham; which toft, croft, bovate and assart William had of the gift and feoffment of Peter son of Paulinus the carpenter; to hold freely to them, their heirs and assigns, with all liberties and easements, of the chief lords of the tenement. Warranty. Sealing clause. Witnesses: Robert de Farnhill, Robert Buck, Robert Crobchayn, Elia Buck, Robert Counell. At Adingham. (*Ibid.*).

35. Sunday before St. George the Martyr [April 19], 1360. Lease by Henry Spenser of Ilklay and Matilda, his wife, to Dom. William son of Richard de Adyngham, chaplain, of a messuage lying in Adyngham with 11 acres of arable land which they had of the gift of the said William; to hold the messuage and land of Henry and Matilda in return for a certain sum of money, of the chief lords of the fee by due and accustomed services for a term of ten years, to begin at the Martinmas, 1360. Warranty. Alternate seals. Witnesses: Dom. William de Spayngs, rector of the church of Ilklay, Dom. Thomas de Neuton, chaplain of the parish of Ilklay, Thomas de Grene of Adyngham, John Stedman of the same, Peter de Scalwray of the same. (*Ibid.*).

36. Saturday, 16 October, 35 Edw. III [1361]. Demise by Robert de Roos of Ingmanthorpe, knt., William de Ergum, knt., Hugh de Cressy of Selston and John de Herthill, chaplain, to William Vauassour, son of Henry Vauassour, knt., and Elizabeth his wife, daughter of Hugh de Cressy, knt., of the manor of Adyngham, with the advowson of the church of Adyngham, also all lands, tenements,

rents and services and the reversion of all manner of tenants, and villeins and their chattels and offspring, with all their appurtenances, which the grantors had of gift of the aforesaid William Vauassour in Adyngham and Ilkelay or anywhere else in the wapentakes of Stayinclif and Skyreck; they also demise all lands, rents, tenements, services and reversions, etc., which they had of the gift of William Vauassour in Stutton near Tadcaster; also all lands, etc., which they held, by the demise of Thomas de Spaygne and William de Calthorn for the term of the life of William de Bolteby, and later in fee simple, by confirmation of William Vauassour in Stutton and Cokesfyrd; to hold all the lands [*etc.*] for the lives of William and Elizabeth, of the chief lords of the fee. Sealing clause. Witnesses: William de Plumpton, knt., Thomas de Midilton, knt., James Vauassour, Thomas de Nesfeld and Thomas de Spayn. At Heslewode. (*Ibid.*).

37. 24 Oct., 35 Edw. III [1361]. Recites that whereas Robert de Roos of Ingmanthorpe, knt., William de Ergham, knt., Hugh de Cressy of Selston, and John de Herthill, chaplain, granted to William Vauasour son of Henry Vauasour, knt., and Elizabeth his wife, daughter of Hugh de Cressy, knt., the manor of Adyngham, with appurtenances, with the advowson of the church of Adyngham, also all the lands and tenements, rents and services, reversions of all manner of tenants, villeins with their chattels and offspring, with all their appurtenances whatsoever, which the grantors had of the gift of the said William Vauasour in Adyngham, Ilklay, or elsewhere in the Wapentakes of Staynclif and Skyreik and in Stutton near Tadcaster, and also of the gift of Thomas de Spaygne and William de Calthorn, and of the confirmation of the said William Vauasour, in Stutton and Cokkesforth; to hold to the said William and Elizabeth Vauasour for the term of their lives.

The grantors now release to William son of William and Elizabeth remainder of all the above specified lands, tenements [*etc.*], which on the death of William and Elizabeth ought to revert to the grantors; to hold to him and the heirs of his body, of the chief lords of the fee by the due and accustomed services. Remainder in default of issue to William son of Henry Vauasour, his heirs and assigns in perpetuity. Sealing clause. Witnesses: William de Plumpton, knt., Thomas de Midylton, knt., James Vauasour, Thomas de Nessefeld and Thomas de Spaygne. At Hesilwode. (*Ibid.*).

38. . . . August, 21 Richard II [1397]. Elizabeth[1] wife of the late William Vauasor, who holds the manor of Adingham for the term of her life with reversion after her decease to Henry Vavasor, son and heir of the said William, surrenders to Henry, the said manor with appurtenances on condition that if Henry dies before Elizabeth,

[1] In French.

it shall be lawful for her to hold the said manor for the term of her life. Alternate seals.[1] At Hesilwood. (*Ibid.*).

39. 3 Jan., 21 Richard II [1397-8]. Grant[2] by Elizabeth, wife of the late William Vavasor to Henry Vavasor, her son, of the manor of Adyngham with appurtenances, for the term of 40 years, paying 1*d*. at Easter. Alternate seals.[3] At Adyngham. (*Ibid.*).

20 October, 10 Henry IV [1408]. Grant and confirmation by Henry Vauasour, knt., to Master John Neweton, treasurer of the Cathedral Church of St. Peter, York, William Anthorp, parson of the church of Dyghton near Wetherby, John de Skipwith son of William de Skipwith, knt., Richard de Norton, John de Ask, son of John de Ask, Nicholas Gascoigne, Robert Barry and Robert Rawedon of Abyrford, of his manor of Adyngham with the advowson of the church of Adyngham, with all lands, tenements, rents and services and their appurtenances, as well in lordships and services as in demesnes and reversions; to hold the said manor and advowson to the above persons, their heirs and assigns, freely and peacefully, of the chief lords of the fee. Warranty. Sealing clause. Witnesses: Richard Redeman, Nicholas de Middelton, William Ryther, knt., Thomas Skargyll, Richard Fayrefax, Henry de Meleton, Robert Malyverer. (*Ibid.*).

10 Feb., 13 Henry IV [1411-12]. Grant and confirmation by Robert Bucktrowt of Nesfeld in Qwhorfdale to Henry Vauasor, knt., and his heirs, of a toft with appurtenances in the vill of Adingham, which formerly belonged to Thomas de Ilkelay. Warranty. Witnesses: Nicholas de Medilton, Richard Tempest, knts., John Vauasor, John Faukes, John Wayte. At Adingham.[4] (*Ibid.*).

40. Recites that whereas John de Ryther and Alianora his wife hold the manor of Adingham and of Wodehale near Wetherby, and the advowson of the manor of Adingham with appurtenances, by reason of a fine made in the Court of Common Pleas before William de Berford and his colleagues, to the said Alianora and Walter her late husband, and the heirs of their bodies; and if the said Walter died without heirs by Alianora, the manor of Adingham and advowson to go to right heirs of Walter, and Walter having so died, the manor and advowson have reverted to Robert, brother and heir of Walter. Robert wishing to better the state of the said John de Ryther, grants and confirms the said manor and advowson of Adingham as well in demesne as in services, except the moiety of the whole rent of Sicklynghale, after the death of Alianora; to hold for the life

[1] Round seal of red wax; a shield of arms, a fess dancetty (Vavasur)

[2] In French.

[3] Fragment of a small round seal of red wax, as to No. 38.

[4] Small fragment of brown seal.

of the said John, of the chief lords of that fee by the service pertaining to the manor. Warranty. John to be allowed to treat the lands as he wishes (*volo et concedo pro me et heredibus meis quod predictus Johannes in predictis maneriis cum suis pertinenciis tota vita sua licite commodum suum facere possit, et se appruare in boscis et omnibus aliis locis*) and to improve the land, but Robert to be quit of all action of waste and destruction brought against John, except in the case of houses, large oaks, and the expulsion (*exilio*) of villeins. If it should happen that after the death of Alianora, Robert or his heirs should disseise John of these manors, or if it should happen that John, through Robert or his heirs being impleaded should lose the manors by a judgement, then he binds himself and his heirs in a sum of a thousand pounds to be paid to John. Reversion on the death of John and Alianora to Robert and his heirs. Alternate seals. Witnesses: Sir Richard le Waleys, knt., Geoffrey le Scrope, William de Byngham, Richard de Aldeburgh, Thomas Dayvile, Walter Faukunberg. At Doncaster. (*Ibid.*).

Adlingfleet.

41. Monday after St. Gregory the Pope, 15 Edward II [March 15, 1321-2]. Quitclaim by John de Eyuill, knt., to Thomas de Egmanton of Folquardby[1], his heirs and assigns, of all right which he has in a messuage and half a bovate of land, with meadows, moors and all other appurtenances, suit of court and forinsec service in the vill and territory of Adelingflet, which Emma Augrim and Richard, her son, held of John, saving to the said John, 10*s.* yearly from the said tenements; to hold by the service of the 10*s.* which John had assigned to his son, Robert, and Robert's wife, Margaret. Warranty. Sealing clause [2] Witnesses: William de Hustwayt, William de Waterton, William Gaterist, John de Ousflet, Thomas de Slengesby, Stephen de Celer, William Gouk. At Burtonstayer. (*Archer Houblon MSS.*, No. 30).

42. Morrow of St. Michael [Sept. 30], 1322. Grant by William del Bour of Athelingflet to Alan de Celar of the same vill, his heirs and assigns, of all right in a rood of land which extends from the garden of the said Alan to a ditch called Crostdyk, and which was the dower of Alice de Slengesby, formerly the wife of John del Bour. This grant is to take effect after William Gouk's term comes to an end, namely, two years after the date of this grant; to hold after the said term, for the lifetime of Alice, of the chief lords of the fee. Sealing clause. Witnesses: William de Hustwayt, Thomas de Slengesby, John de Useflet, Thomas Graunt, Stephen de Celar, Robert Utyng, Hugh de Burton. At Athelingflet. (*Ibid.*, No. 31).

[1] Fockerby or Foccarby.

[2] Seal of brown wax, broken.

43. Tuesday, St. Peter in cathedra, 16 Edward II [Feb. 22, 1322-3]. Quitclaim by William de Camera of Athelyngflet to William Gouk and his heirs, of 60*s*. rent with appurtenances which the said William is bound to pay to the grantor by virtue of an indenture between the latter and John Gouk, father of William Gouk, whose heir he is, and Alice, his wife, in respect of certain lands and tenements in Athelyngflet. Sealing clause. Witnesses: William de Hustwayt, Thomas de Egmanton, John de Usflet, John Russel. At Athelyngflet. (*Ibid.*, No. 32).

44. Sunday after the Purification of the B.V.M., 10 Edward III [Feb. 4, 1335-6]. Grant and confirmation by Alan de Wolsy of Athelyngflet to Robert son of William del Celer of Athelyngflet, his heirs and assigns, of 2 acres of meadow with appurtenances in Athelyngflet, which the grantor had of the gift of William del Celer; to hold of the chief lords of the fee in perpetuity. Warranty. Sealing clause. Witnesses: William de Hustwayt, John de Useflet, William Gouk, Thomas de Slengesby, Thomas Russel. At Athelyngflet. (*Ibid.*, No. 33).

45. St. Nicholas [Dec. 6], 1342. Grant by John Nelle of Athelingflete to William Gouk of the same, his heirs and assigns, of his messuage and croft which lie in length and breadth between the messuage and croft of Thomas Russell on the one side and the house of John Watreton on the other, and of a strip of land lying in the field called les Resshcroftlandes between the land of John de Slengesby on the one side and the land of Nicholas de Hustwayt on the other; also half a rood of moor with a piece of ground (*cum fundo*) lying in the moors of Athelingflete in breadth between the moor of Thomas Russell and the moor which formerly belonged to William de Hustwayt, and in length so far as the moor of Athelingflete extends (*quantum mora de Athelingflete durat*); to hold of the chief lords of the fee. Warranty. Sealing clause.[1] Witnesses: Dom. John de Celar, John de Usflete, Nicholas de Hustwayt, John de Slengesby, Thomas Russell of Athelingflete. At Athelingflete. (*Ibid.*, No. 34).

46. Monday before the Circumcision [Dec. 30], 1342. Grant by James de Eyuill of Athelingflete to William Gouk of the same, and his lawfully begotten heirs of a strip of land called Mideldaile, lying in the east field of Athelingflete between the land of Dom. John de Celar, chaplain and that of Alan de Watreton; to hold freely and in peace in perpetuity, paying yearly a rose at the Nativity of St. John the Baptist for 10 years for all services and thereafter an annual rent of 10*s*. of silver at Michaelmas. Power to re-enter if the rent is in arrears either in part or whole. Warranty. Alternate seals. Witnesses: Dom. John de Celar, chaplain, John de Usseflete, Nicholas de Hustwayt, John de Slengesby and Thomas Russell. At Athelingflete. (*Ibid.*, No. 35).

[1] Seal of yellow wax, diam 1 in , an animal; legend blurred

47. Thursday, Corpus Christi, 17 Edward III [June 12, 1343]. Grant by John, son of William de Wat[er]ton of Athelyngflet, chaplain, to William Gouk and the heirs of his body, for ever, of the remainder in a strip of land called Croft in Atthelyngflet which lies between the croft of Adam Nisaund and the croft which once belonged to William del Boure, and which is held by Cecily, the grantor's mother, for the term of her life, and which should revert to the grantor and his heirs after Cecily's death; to hold of the chief lord of the fee by the due and accustomed services. Warranty. Sealing clause.[1] Witnesses: Dom. John de Celar, chaplain, John de Useflet, Nicholas de Hustewayte, Robert Cortewyse, Thomas Russell. At Athelingflet. (*Ibid.*, No. 36).

48. July 22, 17 Edward III [1343]. Writ of Edward III to Thomas Gouk summoning him with other merchants to a council at Westminster on *d . . . ne*[2] after the Assumption of the B.V.M. next following, to treat of matters concerning the king, the merchants and all the people of the kingdom. At Claryngdon. (*Ibid.*, No. 37).

49. Sunday before St. Martin, 17 Edward III [Nov. 9, 1343]. Lease by William Gowke of Athelingflet to John de Waterton, chaplain, of the messuage in Athelingflet and 4 strips of land and a rood in le Southfeld, and a rood of moor in the same vill, which the said William had of the gift and feoffment of John; to hold during the lifetime of Cecily, mother of John, paying yearly 1*d.* at Whitsuntide and performing for the said William, the due and accustomed services. Alternate seals. Witnesses: John Deyuill, Nicholas de Ustewat, John de Useflet, Robert Cortewys. At Athelingflet. (*Ibid.*, No. 38).

50. Tuesday after St. Mathew the apostle [Sept. 28], 1344. Grant and confirmation by Adam Nisant of Athelingflete, to William Gouk of the same and Isabel, his wife, and the heirs of the body of the said William of 3 strips of land lying in the territory of Athelingflete, of which 2 lie in the east field which is called le Thwerlandes, one lying between the land of Robert Uttyng and the land of John Barowe, and the other between the land once of William de Hustwayt, and the land of Robert Uttyng, and the third strip lies in the west field which is called Penteland, between the land formerly of Thomas de Egmanton and the land of John de Slengesby; to hold freely and in peace, of the grantor and his heirs, paying yearly at the feast of St. John the Baptist, a rose, if demanded, for all services. Warranty. Sealing clause. Witnesses: Dom. John Celar, chaplain, Nicholas de Hustewayt, John de Slengesby, Thomas Russell, Robert Cortewis. At Athelingflete. (*Ibid.*, No. 39).

[1] Round seal of white wax, blurred

[2] A small lozenge shaped hole has been cut in the middle of the document, possibly for filing purposes. On the back of the writ are various notes, and accounts, difficult to decipher.

51. Wednesday, St. Peter in cathedra [Feb. 22], 1345[-6]. Grant by Alan de Waterton, to William Gouk of Athelingflet and Isabel, his wife, and their heirs, of all his part of a messuage in Athelingflete, lying in breadth and length on each side of the messuages of the said William, which messuage the grantor had of the gift and feoffment of John Pytefote; to hold the said messuage and buildings thereon, of the chief lord of the fee. Warranty. Sealing clause.[1] Witnesses: Dom. John de Celar, Nicholas de Hustewayt, John de Slengesby, Thomas Russell, Robert Cortewys. At Athelingflete. (*Ibid.*, No. 40).

52. Friday after St. Matthew the apostle [Sept. 28], 1347. Quitclaim by John de Watreton of Athelingflete, chaplain, of all right in a certain messuage, 4 strips, a rood of land and a rood of moor lying in the vill, territory and moor of Athelingflete, to William Gouk of Athelingflete and his heirs, as is more fully contained in John's charter to him. Sealing clause. Witnesses: Nicholas de Hustwayt, Dom. John de Celar, chaplain, John de Slengesby, Robert Cortewis. At Athelingflete. (*Ibid.*, No. 41).

53. Thursday, St. Gregory the Pope, 23 Edward III [March 12, 1348-9]. Quitclaim by Robert son of John Cortewys of Athelyngflet. Recites that whereas John Cortewys, father of the said Robert, had by his charter enfeoffed Alan de Waterton of a strip of land with appurtenances in Athelyngflet called Fourstanges, lying between the land of Robert Daysing on the east and the land of Stephen Celar on the west; to hold to him freely and in peace, paying yearly for the next following 30 years, a peppercorn at Christmas for all services and after that period, 10*li.* of silver in equal portions at Whitsuntide and Martinmas, now Robert Cortewys quitclaims all right in the said rent of 10*li.* Warranty. Sealing clause.[2] Witnesses: Nicholas Hustewayt of Athelingflet, William Gouk, Thomas del Clif, John del Celer, chaplain, John de Slyngesby, James Dayuyll, Robert del Celar. At Athelingflet. (*Ibid.*, No. 42).

54. Dec. 4, 33 Edward III [1359]. Release and quitclaim by John son of William de Watertun and Simon de Craven, servant of Elizabeth de Waterton, to John Cuke of Estoft of all actions, transgressions, quarrels and demands, as well real, as personal. At Burton super Trent.[3] (*Ibid.*, No. 43).

55. St. Michael the Archangel [Sept. 29], 13[60]. Lease by Dom. John de Thorn', perpetual vicar of the parish church of Athelingflet, to Dom. Henry de Barton, chaplain, of his vicarage of

[1] Seal of red wax, diam 1 in ; in the centre of a six pointed device, a bird, on the points of the device 6 rings, the whole surrounded by a band of scroll work.

[2] Seal of white wax, undeciphered

[3] Fragment of small seal of black wax; a shield of arms, not deciphered.

Athelingflet, with all its rights and appurtenances, from Michaelmas 1360 to Michaelmas 1361, except the vicarage house (*mansio vicarie*), turbary on the moor of Athelingflet, a bovate of land and 2 acres of meadow pertaining to the said vicarage, paying yearly to the lessor during the said year 13 marks, 6*s*. 8*d*. in two portions, namely, 9 marks, 6*s*. 8*d*. at Michaelmas 1360 and 4 marks at Easter 1361, without further delay. Dom. Henry shall not interfere with the offerings made to the Cross or to other images or altars in the said church, nor with money offered to the box of the Cross (*trunco crucis*) or elsewhere. He shall keep (*reservabit*) the chrism cloths, according to the Synodal Constitution of the Church of York, for the use and repair (*ad usum et correctionem*) of the church vestments, and he shall not take tithes still owing for the preceding year, but the said John shall have them, as is just. Dom. Henry shall find all the lights in the church which the vicar is supposed to provide, and a chaplain suitable to serve the said church and the parishioners of the same. He shall also pay all manner of taxes, archidiaconal payments, synodal dues, Peter's pence and all other burdens incumbent on the vicarage of the said church, except 6*s*. 8*d*. tax to the king (*de taxa domini Rege*) for the previous year, which John shall pay. He shall find bread and wine up to next Easter, and John shall not be responsible for any further burdens, but he may serve the church in the office of a priest until Easter next and beyond to the Michaelmas following, if he has not embarked upon his journey to the Roman Curia. John shall have power to re-enter the vicarage if any money payments are in arrears. Both parties have sworn on the Gospels to observe the agreement and each is bound to the other in 10*li*. Dom. John has agreed on oath not to change his vicarage during this period. Alternate seals[1] together with the seal of Sir Robert de Eyuill, lord of Athelingflet who was called in as a witness. At Athelingflet. (*Ibid.*, No. 44).

56. Tuesday before St. Barnabas the apostle [June 8], 1361. Grant by Elizabeth de Eyuill of Athelingflet to Sir Robert de Eyuill her brother, of a strip of land lying in the Crofts of Athelingflet between the land of Robert Gouke on both sides; to hold to Robert, his heirs and assigns, of the chief lords of the fee. Warranty. Sealing clause.[2] Witnesses: Nicholas de Usflet of Athelingflet, John Russell of the same, Thomas Graunt of the same. At Athelingflet. (*Ibid.*, No. 45).

57. St. Martin in the Winter, 40 Edward III [Nov. 11, 1366]. Lease by Sir Robert de Eyuill, clerk, lord of Athelingflet, to William de Brigsley and Joan, his wife and their first-born, of that messuage with appurtenances which John son of Gilian once held in Kagath-

[1] Tongues for two seals, of which one, of green wax, much rubbed, remains.

[2] Seal of dark green wax, diam. 1 in.; a shield of arms, party per pale, dexter undeciphered, sinister, a fess between 4 mullets.

lande, also a garden lying between the said messuage on the north and the messuage of William de Waterton on the south; to hold for the term of their lives, paying yearly to Robert, his heirs and assigns, 6*s*. 8*d*. in equal portions at Whitsuntide and Martinmas, and doing suit of court at Athelingflet when the court is held there, namely after Easter and Michaelmas. After the death of Sir Robert they are to pay 4*s*. yearly at the two terms. If the rent should be in arrears either partly or wholly for 40 days after any term Sir Robert and his heirs have power to enter the messuage and garden, and William, Joan and their first-born to be responsible for repairs to the said messuage. Warranty. Sealing clause. Witnesses: Robert Gowk, Nicholas de Usflet, John Russell, Thomas Cortwys. At Athilingflet. (*Ibid*., No. 46).

58. Saturday after St. Martin in the Winter, 40 Edward III [Nov. 14, 1366]. Grant by Sir Robert de Eyuill, lord of Athelingflet, to Robert Gouk of the same, his heirs and assigns, of a strip of land lying in front of the garden of the said Robert Gouk in Athelingflet, between the land of the said Robert on both sides; to hold of the grantor and his heirs, by the due and accustomed services. Warranty. Sealing clause. Witnesses: Robert de Haldanby, Nicholas de Usflet, John Russell, Thomas Graunt. At Athelingflet. (*Ibid*., No. 47).

59. Tuesday after the Ascension [May 16], 1374. Grant and confirmation by William de Brigsley and Joan, his wife, to Robert Gouk of Athelingflet and his assigns, of a garden which they had of the gift of Robert de Eyuill, clerk, for the term of their lives; to hold of the chief lords of the fee. Witnesses: Alured, vicar of Athelingflet, John Mew, Thomas Graunt. At Athelingflet. (*Ibid*., No. 48).

60. Wednesday, St. Wilfrid the bishop, 3 Richard II [Feb. 15, 1379-80]. Grant by Alured, vicar of the church of Athelingflet to Robert Gouk of Athelingflet, his heirs and assigns, of a messuage and half a bovate of land and 2 strips of meadow in Lefour Stanges and a strip of meadow lying near Nudyck in the fields of Athelingflet, with appurtenances, all of which Alured had of the gift and feoffment of Thomas de Egmanton of Folquardby; to hold of the chief lords of the fee in perpetuity. Sealing clause.[1] Witnesses: Nicholas de Usflet of Athelingflet, Hugh de Horsington of the same, John Mew of the same. At Athelingflet. (*Ibid*., No. 50).

61. Sunday the vigil of St. Bartholomew the apostle [Aug. 23], 1383. Grant by Alured de Barton, vicar of the church of Athelingflet, to Thomas de Kydall of Southferiby, his heirs and assigns, of a moiety of the manor house of Athelingflet with the ditches and other appurtenances, namely, that moiety which Sir Thomas de Kydall, knt., father of the said Thomas, bought of the grantor the bounds of

[1] Seal of white wax, diam. 1 in , the letter I and sprigs of foliage

which extend between the portions of Sir Richard Basset, knt., and John de Disworth and Katherine, his wife, of the said manor on the north, and the land of Dame Agnes de Bliton and the land of the said Thomas de Kydall on the south, and which abuts on the east on the messuage once belonging to Gocelin Dayuill and the messuage of Matilda Dayuill, and on the west on the land of the said Thomas de Kydall; which moiety the grantor had with the other moiety, of the gift and feoffment of Sir Robert de Eyuill, clerk and lord of Athelingflet; to hold of the chief lords of the fee. Sealing clause. Witnesses: Thomas de Egmanton of Folquardby, Nicholas de Usflet, John Russell, Hugh de Horsington of Athelyngflet. At Athelyngflet. (*Ibid.*, No. 51).

62. Sunday the vigil of St. Bartholomew the apostle [Aug. 23], 1383. Surrender by Alured de Barton, vicar of the church of Athelingflet to Thomas de Kydall of Southferiby, his heirs and assigns, for ever, of all the estate which he has or could have in the fourth part of 20 acres of meadow and land called Watertonhyng and in the fourth part of 5 roods of moor in the moors of Athelingflet and in the rent and service of John Durand and Thomas de Neuton for a messuage near the messuage of Nicholas de Usflet, and in the rent and service of Ralph Attehall, and of their heirs, in Athelingflet; also in the rent and service of John de Duffeld, senior, of Folquardby, and in the rent and service of Thomas de Wolriby and in an acre of land in Folquardby which once belonged to Margaret *in ye lane*, together with the reversion of all the lands and tenements which the said John Durand, Thomas de Neuton, John de Duffeld and Thomas de Wolriby hold of the grantor in Athelingflet and Folquardby for the term of their lives, to the said Thomas after their deaths; to hold to Thomas, of the chief lords of the fee in perpetuity. Sealing clause. At Athelingflet. (*Ibid.*, No. 52).

63. Monday, St. Bartholomew [Aug. 24], 1383. Grant by Thomas de Kydall of Southferiby to Robert Gouk of Athelingflet, John, his son, and the heirs and assigns of the said Robert, of the moiety of the manor house of Athelingflet which lies between the portions of Sir Richard Basset, knt., John de Disworth and Katerine, his wife, on the north and the land of Dame Agenes de Bliton and the grantor's land on the south, and which abuts on the east on the messuage once belonging to Gocelin Dayuill and the messuage of Matilda Dayuill, and on the grantor's land on the west, with free entry and exit; he also grants the fourth part of 20 acres of meadow and land called Waterhyng and one and a quarter roods of moor with a piece of ground (*fundo*), in length from the Intackdyc as far as the moor of Athelingflet extends towards the west, with the rents and services [*as described in the preceding deed*]; to hold of the chief lords of the fee. Warranty. Sealing clause. Witnesses: Thomas de Eqmanton, William de Estoft of Folquardby, Nicholas de Usflet,

John Russell, Hugh de Horsington of Athelingflet. At Athelingflet. (*Ibid.*, No. 53).

64. Monday after the Conception of the B.V.M. [Dec. 12], 1384. In the name of the Father and Son and Holy Ghost, Amen.[1] Robert Gouk of Athelingflet, of whole mind, makes his testament in this form. *In primis*, he leaves his soul to Almighty God, the B.V.M. and all saints and his body to be buried in the church of All Saints, Athelingflet, and his best beast as his mortuary. Item: to the fabric of the church of Athelingflet, 40*d.* Item: he wishes that 5 candles shall burn about his body on the day of his burial. Item: to John Bone: 6*d.* Item: to Alice Hunt, 6*d.* Item: to John de Gerlthorp, 6*d.*; and to his wife, 6*d.* Item: to Alice Prest, 6*d.* Item: to Margery Aysynt, 6*d.* Item: to Alice Theyller, 6*d.* Item: to Isabel Tedwall, 6*d.* Item: to William Cowar, 6*d.* Item: to John Kaa, 6*d.* [Item: to the wife of John Buck, 6*d.*][2] Item: to William Hogun [of Useflet],[3] 6*d.* Item: to . . . Item: to Sir Simon Prik, 6*s.* 8*d.* Item: to Sir John de Gerlthorp, 2*s.* Item: to Dom. Henry the chaplain, 12*d.* Item: to John Melde, 6*d.* Item: to Robert Kem [?], 3*d.* Item: to Thomas Sothern, 3*d.* Item: to the Preaching Friars of Pontefract (*Pont'*), 2*s.* Item: to the Carmelite Friars of York, 2*s.* Item: to the Friars Minor of Beuerley, 2*s.* Item: to the Augustinian Friars of Hull, 2*s.* Item: to John Godall, one of his vestments. Item: to John Gouk . . . vestment. The residue of all his chattels (*utensiliorum*) not bequeathed he leaves to [Katherine de Kircby][3] Richard Dayuill of Gerlthorp, Hugh de Horsington and Isabel, his sister, his executors. Sealing clause.[4] Witnesses: Nicholas de Usseflet of Athelingflet, Thomas Clark of the same, John son of Philip of the same, Ralph Utting of the same. At Athelingflet. Item: he leaves to the archbishop for the proving of his will, 9*d.* and no more. Item: he leaves to William Rocelyn a *bassinet* with its gear (*auentayll*) and a hauberk (*hauberione*).

Probate attached, dated Dec. 21, 1385; administration granted to the executors named in the will. Sealed with the seal of the Dean of Pontefract, sequestrator in that district. At Wakefeld. (*Ibid.*, No. 54).

65. Monday after St. Andrew the apostle, 9 Richard II [Dec. 4, 1385]. Grant and confirmation by Robert Gouk of Athelingflet to John de Kircby of Cotenays, Robert de Haldanby, Richard de Eyuill of Gerlthorp and Hugh de Horsyngton of Athelingflet and their assigns, of all the lands and tenements, rents and services, with all manner of reversions which should come to the grantor and his

[1] The document is indistinctly written throughout.

[2] This crossed out.

[3] Inserted above the line.

[4] Seal of dark green wax, vesica shaped, 1 in. × ¾ in.; an eagle regardant; legend undeciphered.

heirs in the vills and territories of Athelingflet, Folquardby, Estoft, Usseflet, Wyttegift and Redenes, with appurtenances; to hold of the chief lords of the fee in perpetuity. Warranty. Sealing clause. Witnesses: John de Hustewayt of Athelingflet, Nicholas de Usseflet of the same, John Mew of the same, Thomas the clerk of the same. At Athelingflet. (*Ibid.*, No. 55).

66. Tuesday after St. Luke the evangelist, 10 Richard II [Oct. 23, 1386]. Grant by Thomas de Kidall of Southferiby, knt., to John de Kirkeby of Cottenesse and Robert de Selby, chaplain, their heirs and assigns, of all the lands and tenements, meadows, feedings, pastures, reliefs, escheats, wards, fisheries, tolls, rents, reversions and moor, with a piece of ground (*cum fundo*), and with all other profits and appurtenances belonging to the said lands and tenements in the vills and territories of Athelingflette and Folquardby which the grantor had after the death of Sir Robert de Eyuill, his uncle; to hold of the chief lords of the fee in perpetuity. Warranty. Sealing clause. Witnesses: Nicholas de Usseflette of Athelingflette, Hugh de Horsyngton, Thomas the clerk of the same, John Mew of the same, Thomas Graunt of the same. At Athelingflette. (*Ibid.*, No. 56).

67. St. Peter ad vincula, 13 Richard II [Aug. 1, 1389]. Grant by John de Kyrkeby of Cottenesse, Robert de Haldanby, Richard de Eyuill of Gerlthorp and Hugh de Horsyngton of Athelyngflett to John Gouk and his heirs, of all the lands and tenements, rents and services with the reversions which they had of the gift of Robert Gouk, father of the said John, in the vills and territories of Athelyngflett, Folqarby and Usseflett, with appurtenances except a messuage, half a bovate of land and 3 acres of meadow which formerly belonged to Richard Ougrym in Adlyngflett, and a messuage lying between that of Nicholas de Usseflett on the west and the messuage which once belonged to Robert Gouk on the east; to hold of the chief lords of the fee. Sealing clause.[1] Witnesses: Richard Bassett, Thomas de Reidenesse, knts., John Hustewayt, Nicholas Usseflett, William Esthalay. At Athelyngflett. (*Ibid.*, No. 57).

68. Sunday after St. John the Baptist, 20 Richard II [June 25, 1396]. Exchange whereby Thomas de Egmanton grants to John Gouke of Athelyngflete all his part of a certain hedge in the vill of Athelyngflete in a place called le Pergarth, with the soil (*solo*) of the same, and with a certain parcel of land of the grantor's, adjacent to the said hedge on the north side of it, being in width 2 feet and extending in length from the ditch of the place called le Pergarth on the west as far as the grantor's entry to le Pergarth near the eastern

[1] Seals; originally two small seals of red wax on each of two tongues, now one on each, the first of which bears the letter W, the second a man's head facing to the dexter.

end of a grange belonging to the grantor near le Motkik; also the ash trees (*fraxinis*) growing on the said soil, according to the bounds agreed by Thomas and John. He grants all the above in exchange for a part of the said grange with the soil, namely 25 feet in length and 40 feet in width at the southern end of the grange, as more fully appears in the charter made between them; to hold the said part of the hedge [*etc.*], of the chief lords of the fee. Warranty. Alternate seals.[1] Witnesses: Robert de Haldanby, John Hustwayt, Nicholas Usseflete, Richard Dayuill, Hugh Horsyngton. At Athelyngflete. (*Ibid.*, No. 58).

69. Easterday, 20 Richard II [April 22, 1397]. Grant by John Gouk of Athelyngflet to John Melde, chaplain, and Hugh de Horsyngton, their heirs and assigns, of all the lands and tenements, rents and services, meadows, moors and pastures with appurtenances in the vill and territory of Athelyngflet, which Robert Gouk, the grantor's father, and the grantor had of the gift and feoffment of Thomas de Kydall of Southferiby; to hold of the chief lords of the fee, in perpetuity. Warranty. Sealing clause.[2] Witnesses: Thomas de Egmanton, William de Lodyngton, Richard de Eyuill, John Hustewayt, Nicholas de Usflet. At Athelyngflet. (*Ibid.*, No. 59).

Allerthwaite.[3]

70. Sunday on which is sung 'Quasi modo geniti' [March 30], 1315. Release and quitclaim by Brother Richard de Halgton, prior of Bretton, and the monks and convent of the same, to Robert Russell of Tykhill, of all right in the manor of Allerthwait and also in 5 marks annually which they had hitherto sought before the justices of the bench against the same Robert by reason of the lord John de Nouo Mercato. For this quitclaim the said Robert granted to the prior and his successors 1*d.* rent in Hoton Robert and the advowson of the church of the same vill. Sealing clause. Witnesses: Sirs Thomas de Schefeld, John de Doncastre, knts., Walter de Hers, John Huringell of Hoton Peynell, William de Notton, Richard de Louersale. At the monastery of Bretton. (*Serlby Hall Muniments*, No. 1).

71. July 4, 10 Henry VI [1432]. Grant by John Raynebargh to John Skyrys of Allyrtwhayt, of 20*d.* of free rent which the said John Skyrys owes yearly to the grantor for divers lands in Gobkarre and Cobrode; to hold to John Skyrys, his heirs and assigns in perpetuity. Quitclaim of the same. Warranty. Sealing clause.

[1] Seal of reddish-brown wax, diam. $\frac{7}{8}$ in.; a phoenix rising from flames which issue from a pot or vessel, which is flanked on each side by the letter F.

[2] Small oval seal of white wax; the Virgin and Child; legend undeciphered.

[3] In Nether Hoyland, parish of Wath-upon-Dearne.

Witnesses: John Tylney, Reyner Tylney, John Coly, vicar of Wath, Robert Lygh', John Strete. At Holand. (*Ibid.*, No. 2).

72. May 4, 16 Henry VI [1438]. Notification by John Wyndyll that as a certain annual rent of 2*s.* 3½*d.* from certain of his lands called Adamrode, otherwise Bromrode is claimed by John Skyres as an appurtenance of his manor of Allerthwayt, and by virtue of which there are also arrears of the said rent from the day of the death of John Wyndyll, the grantor's father until the making of these presents; now John Wyndyll agrees to hold himself and his heirs bound for the future to the said John Skyres and his heirs in the said annual rent, to be payed from his lands in equal portions at Martinmas and Whitsuntide; and should the rent be in arrears power to John Skyres to distrain until satisfaction is obtained. Quitclaim of all actions, real and personal against John Skyres. Sealing clause in the presence of William Roydys and William Halle at the house of the said John Skyres. Witnesses: John Tylney, William Roydys, William Halle. At Holand. (*Ibid.*, No. 3).

Appleton-le-Street.

73. It is here recorded[1] that Thomas de Bolton claims the reversion of the manors of Yarpesthorpe and Apilton in Rydall[2], which Robert de Bolton holds for the term of his life, and which was granted to the said [*sic*] Thomas de Metham and his heirs by a fine[3] levied in the king's court bearing the date, the quindene of Trinity, the 43rd year of the king [June 18, 1369], but which Thomas de Bolton claims by force of a certain well-attested (*certenis connaunce*) indenture bearing the date of the 26th of January next before, and which indenture neither law nor conscience can set aside, because the fine was levied after the date of this said indenture; but notwithstanding such agreement (*parlaunce*) it is agreed (*il yanoit*) between them that Thomas de Metham will grant the reversion of the said manors after the death of Robert de Bolton, to Thomas de Bolton, to hold to him and his lawfully begotten heirs, and in default of such issue, remainder to Isabel, daughter of the said Thomas, and her lawfully begotten heirs, and should Isabel die without heirs, remainder to William de Bolton brother of Thomas, and his lawfully begotten heirs, saving the reversion in default of such issue as above written, namely, to Sir Thomas de Metham and his heirs, for all time, as promised by the assurance of John Fitz-William esq.; and Isabel and William are deceased without issue, and so the said Sir Thomas, in reverence to God and for the salving of his conscience, is ready to grant the reversion to the said Thomas de Bolton and his lawfully begotten heirs as above written (*Y.A.S.*, Md. 40, No. 19).

[1] In French.
[2] Easthorpe and Appleton-le-Street.
[3] For this fine see *Yorks. Fines*, 1347-1377, p 140.

Ardsley.

74. Jan. 24, 12 Henry IV [1410-11]. Grant by Beatrice Crappar of Erdeslaw, to Robert Crappar, her son, of a tenement with buildings thereon in Thynglaw, a hamlet (*hamlecto*) of Erdeslaw, with all the lands which belonged to her in the same hamlet; she also grants a messuage and buildings called Welleyherd and a croft called Nikcroft in Erdeslaw, also 3 butts of land above Caulwelcroft, with half a strip called le Hedland there towards the north, and 2 strips above Pasmaracre with a strip at Northend', also 3 closes there called Symhallroyde, Robcroft and Geffraycroft with le Mathouereng; she also grants 2 strips above Westharfurlang' there containing 3 roods of land; also a rood lying above Wetemerssh towards the west, and an acre and a rood above le Northsyde of Tilwelletoftes with an acre above Tillwelhill, and with a rood of land above le Longsuyp, also a quarter of a close called Longcarr' with a rood called Gossacre, and a quarter of a meadow named Ricardengge; to hold to Robert and his lawfully begotten heirs of the chief lords of the fee, and in default of issue remainder to, 1) John Crapper, his brother, 2) Joan del Gren, his sister, 3) reversion to the grantor and her right heirs. Warranty. Sealing clause. Witnesses: John Manyngham of Erdeslaw, Richard Manyngham, Thomas Willeson, John Robynson, William del Holins. At Erdeslawe. (*J. B. Payne*, No. 1).

Balne.

75. Grant by John Leysing of Pouelingtona to William his son, his heirs or assigns, for homage and service, of all the eastern moiety of all the land and wood in a croft in Balna, which he had held of Sir Thomas de Pouclingtona, one end abutting on the common marsh-land (*kar*) and the other extending to the land of the abbot of Seleby and that of the abbot of Roche (*Rupe*); to hold of the grantor and his heirs, with free entry and exit, rendering yearly 12*d.* at the four terms of the year fixed (*statutos*) in the soke of Snahit[1] for all service. Witnesses: John de Hecke, Henry de Goldale, Hugh his brother, John son of Adam de Wytelay, Adam de Arnethorpe, Hugh son of Ralph, John son of Nicholas, William de Trunflet, Richard Beuerege, Lucas son of Alexander. (*E. G. Millar, esq.*)

76. Grant[2] by Henry son of Thomas the carpenter of Norhbalne to Henry son of Robert de Pokenhal', his heirs or assigns, for a sum of money given beforehand as a fine (*in gersuma*), of a plot of wood and dike (*fossati*) in Norhbalne with its appurtenances, lying

[1] Snaith.

[2] By another charter in the same collection the grantee granted the same premises, for a sum of money, to Alexander son of Thomas de Crideling, and Agnes his wife, and the heirs or assigns of Alexander; the tenement of Agnes del Dike being described as that of the said Alexander and Agnes. Witnesses: Nicholas Denyas, William de Dyk, Matthew Mollyng, Thomas Quintrel, Peter son of John de Balne, broken seal of white wax

between the tenement of Agnes del Dike and that of Roger Douning, abutting on the land of Nicholas Denias and the toft of Giles and the grantor's own toft towards the north; to hold of the lord of the fee and his heirs, with all easements; together with the timber growing on the plot and with the road at the end towards the south. Witnesses, Nicholas Denias, Alexander de Balne, Thomas Quinterel, Robert Dilkoc, John son of Beatrice, William the blacksmith (*marescallo*).[1] (*Ibid.*).

77. Monday after All Saints [Nov. 6], 1340. Grant by John le Warner of Snayth to John de Metham, his heirs and assigns, of 2*s.* 8*d.* rent with appurtenances in Balne from a messuage and toft which Alan de Hyghgate was holding in Balne between Nouty . . .[2] on the west and the land of Peter de Balne on the east, one end abutting on *le Hyghgate* of Balne towards the north and the other on Hubert croft towards the south. Witnesses: Robert son of Alexander de Balne, Henry atte Lanende, John son of Beatrice, John T[em]pleman, Robert Dounyng. Balne.[3] (*Y.A.S.*, Md. 141, No. 1).

78. Monday before All Saints [Oct. 26], 1349. Grant by John son of William de Dyke of Balne to John de Metham of the same, his heirs or assigns, of a messuage with appurtenances in Balne, as it lay between the toft of John Alicok on the east and that of the grantee on the west, abutting on the land formerly belonging to Nicholas Denyas towards the south and on the common road of the vill towards the north; and half a butt of land lying between the land of Thomas Ricard on either side; with all easements. Witnesses: William de Burgon of Balne, Henry del Grene, Thomas de Birne, Alexander Ricard, John Templeman, all of the same. Balne.[4] (*Y.A.S.*, Md. 135, No. 1).

Barnsley.

79. St. Gregory the Pope [March 12], 1393-4. Indenture whereby Henry,[5] prior of the House of St. John the apostle and evangelist of Pontefract and the convent of the same, grant to Richard Keuerisforth of Barneslay, his heirs and assigns, a messuage and 1½ acres of land in Barneslay with appurtenances; and the messuage lies between the messuage of John Annotson on the south and the messuage once belonging to John de Cregileston on the north, and the 1½ acres both lie in the north field of Berneslay

[1] Seal: green wax, printed oval, 1⅜ × ⅞ in ; blurred, ✠ S: HENR' F' TOM'
[2] Torn.
[3] Seal: yellow wax, round, ¾ in.; the lamb and flag, the legend is possibly ECCE AGNVS D.
[4] Seal: red wax, round, ⅝ in ; a bull's head cabossed, [?] PRIVE SV.
[5] No prior of the name of Henry is given in the list in *Monastic Notes*, p.166.

between the land of Richard de Keuerisforth on the south and the land of Thomas de Dodeworth on the north; to hold to Richard, his heirs and assigns for the term of 200 years, freely and in peace with all liberties and easements within and without the vill of Barneslay, and paying yearly to the grantors and their successors, 12*d.* of silver at Whitsuntide and Martinmas in equal portions, and performing to them and their successors suit of court at their great courts held at Berneslay and suit at the mill, for all other services and demands. Warranty. Alternate seals.[1] Witnesses: William Dodeworth, John Annotson, Richard Nellson, John Daywyll, William de Clayton. At the House of St. John. (*Y.A.S.*, Md. 129, No. 1).

80. St. Luke the evangelist, 20 Henry VI [Oct. 18, 1441]. Grant by Thomas Cartwright of Barneslay in co. York, to Richard West of the same, of an acre of land lying scattered in the fields of Barneslay, of which half an acre lies in the west field of Barneslay below Bernescliff near Dullyerd between the land of Blessed Mary on the north and the land of John Kersford once belonging to Thomas Jacson, on the south; and the other half acre lies in the field called Milnefield above le Breribittes in two parts, of which two *bittes* lie adjoining between the land of John Boswell on the east and the land of Thomas Phelipp on the west, and the other *bitt* lies in the same furlong next to the lord's land on the west, which is held by John Jonetson; to hold to Richard, his heirs and assigns, of the chief lords of the fee. Warranty. Sealing clause.[2] Witnesses: John Jonet, Robert Britoner, Robert Galbere, Richard Wolthwayt, Robert Gravere. At Barneslay. (*Ibid.*, No. 2).

81. May 12, 38 Henry VI [1460]. Indenture whereby Richard son of John de Keresford of Barnesley, Thomas Halle of Pontefract and Richard Symmes of Barnesley, senior, grant to Richard Wylde of Monkebretton all the lands, tenements, meadows, woods and pastures with appurtenances which they recently had of the gift and grant of Nicholas, prior of the House of St. John of Pontefract and the convent of the same, in Barnesley and Doddeworth, in exchange for a messuage with buildings thereon and a croft adjacent and with all the lands, tenements, meadows, woods and pastures and appurtenances which the said Richard had by hereditary right after the death of William Wylde, his father, in Monkebretton; to hold to Richard, his heirs and assigns, of the prior and convent, by the due and accustomed services. Warranty. Grant and confirmation by Richard Wylde to Mag. Thomas Mannyng, secretary (*secretario*) of the king, Henry Sotehyll, Richard Keresford and Richard Symmes, senior, their heirs and assigns, of a messuage with buildings thereon and an adjacent toft, which he had by

[1] Seal: red wax, diam. 1 in.; a shield of arms; a cross, a label of four points; S. DE RICARDI . . .

[2] Seal of red wax; diam. 1 in.; broken; . . ILL'TH.

hereditary right after the death of his father, in Monkebretton, in exchange for all the lands which the said Richard son of John, Thomas Halle and Richard Symmes had of the gift and feoffment of Nicholas, the prior and the convent aforesaid. Warranty. Sealing clause.[1] Witnesses: William Skergyll, William Oxpryng, John Keresfrod, John Tynker, Richard Pogson. At Barnseley and Monkebretton. (*Ibid.* ,No. 3).

82. April 1, 7 Edward IV [1467]. Grant by Robert Haryngton, knt., Thomas Wortley, Thomas Metheley, esqs., Thomas Wyppe, chaplain, to Robert Morley chaplain, of all their lands and tenements in the vill and confines of Bernesley and Oldton de Bernesley; to hold to Robert, of the chief lords of the fee. Appointment of William Symmys and John Lyndley to deliver seisin. Warranty. Sealing clause.[2] Witnesses: Robert son of John Kereforth of Bernesley, Thomas Tregott of Kyrkeby, Robert Tregott of the same, Henry Bryg of Brereley, John Wylkoc of Holand. At Hymmesworth. (*Serlby Hall Muniments*, No. 4).

83. Nov. 6, 12 Edward IV [1472]. Release and quitclaim by Richard Keresford and Richard Symmys of Bernesley to Richard Wylde of the same, of all right which they have in a messuage with lands and tenements in Bernesley and Doddeworth called Pogmore, also in a close of land and meadow called Wheteclose and in 2 acres of land lying together adjacent to the said close on the east and an acre of land lying in the same fields in a place called Hollerodys and in an acre of land in Swythenhyll next to the land of John Kereforth on the north. Warranty. Sealing clause.[3] Witnesses: William Tayllour of Bernesley, John Pogson of the same, Richard Tynker of the same, Richard Marchall of the same, John Tynker. At Bernesley. (*Y.A.S.*, Md. 129, Mo. 4).

Baxby.

84. Agreement between Stephen de Berningham and Juliana, his wife, of the one part and Alan, son of John de Estlaton and his heirs, of the other, that indentures shall be drawn up relating to 2 carucates of land and appurtenances in Baxeby, at the next coming of the king's chief justices or of the justices in eyre to the county of York, and by the wish of the said Alan, the grantors agree for themselves and their heirs that if at the said time they should refuse (*contempserimus*) to make the indentures agreed upon, they will pay to Alan 20 marks within 15 days following their refusal, in respect of expenses, and they agree that they shall not be allowed

[1] Tongues for three seals, on 1 and 3 small seals of red wax; (1) a bird; (3) a merchant's mark and a spray of leaves.

[2] Tongues for 4 seals; blobs of red wax on the first three.

[3] Tongues for two seals; on the second a seal of red wax; a small animal; legend undeciphered.

to make a will or to dispose of any of their goods, moveable or fixed until Alan or his heirs are fully paid the 20 marks, and this without any fraud or delay; wherefor Stephen and Juliana swear on the gospels and take a corporal oath on the sacraments (*affidauimus et tactis sacrosanctis et corporale prostitimus sacromentum*) that they will pay the said 20 marks and they bring as guarantors of their good faith Eudo de Hertheford, Michael de Thorp', John le Norrays, Brian Pigoth, Henry de Midelton, junior, Thomas de Hiclig', Walter de Kneton, William de Martham, who bind themselves with the grantors in this sum and who also add their seals to the document[1]. Witnesses: Sir Gwyschard de Chaerud, steward of Richemund, Sir William de Buscy, Sir Richard Rybos', Richard de Muleton, bailiff of Richemund[2], Harschulf de Cleseby, Robert de Wykliue, Adam de Puntayse, Nicholas de Stapelton, Henry de Westlaton, Thomas son of Michael, Roger de Aske. (*Y.A.S.*, Md. 161, No. 2).

85. Grant by Thomas the clerk, son of William de Baxeby to John his son, of the land and tenements which he had of the gift of Robert Baxeby, also the charter which he had from Robert; to hold to John, his heirs and assigns, of the lord of Baxeby, freely, quietly, hereditarily and in peace, with all appurtenances, commons and easements within and without the vill of Baxeby; and the said John shall have in the meadows of Baxeby, 3 cows with their calves, 20 sheep and their lambs, one horse and a foal, and in the woods 10 pigs without pannage; paying yearly to the lord of Baxeby, half a pound of cummin at Easter and performing 4 perches of *loning'*[3] yearly for all customs, services and demands. The lord of Baxeby warrants the said meadows and tenements against all men, as laid down in the said charter of Robert, once lord of Baxeby. Sealing clause.[4] Witnesses: Dom. Richard, prior of Newburgh, Dom. Geoffrey, dean of Bulmer, Sir William de Buscy, William Griuel, forester of Gautrix, John de Hustwayt, clerk *de forest*, John Freinam of Thurkilby, William son of Helen de Hulueton', John son of Alan of the same, Ralph, his brother, Thomas the forester, Geoffrey the smith, Robert de Baxeby, reeve, Richard de Ponteburgh, clerk. (*Ibid.*, No. 3).

Berwick (Skipton).

86. Quitclaim by Peter de Haltstede to Gerard de Haltstede, his brother, clerk, of all right and claim which he has in the vill and territory of Beriwick in Crauen, namely: that land which he had by

[1] Tongues for 10 seals.

[2] Richard de Multon appears in a charter dated 1258 (*E Y.C*, *Vol.* V. p. 76).

[3] An open uncultivated piece of ground, *O.E.D* which suggests bringing in to cultivation 4 perches of lond yearly to improve the holding.

[4] Remains of a vesica shaped seal of dark green wax; device undeciphered; . . . ffiBI CL'I . . .

inheritance and feoffment after the death of his brother, Richard de Haltstede; to hold to Gerard, his heirs and assigns, freely [*etc.*], as contained in the charter which the said Richard, the grantor's brother . . . by the feoffment of Sir Walter Gramaire, knt. He renounces all claim for himself and his heirs. Sealing clause. Witnesses: William de Herlintone, William Mauleverer of Caltone, Richard de Kytheley, William de Alwoldeley, Thomas de Scocthorp, John de Fernhell, Peter the carpenter, Richard de Fauelthorp, Richard the clerk of Scipton, Dom Hamo, then chaplain of Heselwode. (*Cartwright Memorial Hall, Bradford*).

87. Quitclaim by Gerard de Haltstede, clerk, his heirs and assigns to Sir John le Vauasour, knt., and his heirs and assigns, of all right which he has in the whole or part of the land called Berwik in Crauene, with all appurtenances, in the same way as the grantor's brother Richard de Haltstede once freely held of Sir William de Gramar, knt., as in the charter of feoffment which Sir William . . . to said Richard. The said Sir John le Vauasour, his heirs and assigns are to have and to hold against all contradictions, and to give to the grantor 15 silver marks. Sealing clause. Witnesses: William de Chatherton, Roger Tempeste, Richard de Halton, William Maulverer, Thomas de Autreve, Robert de Halton. John de Fernhelle, Robert de Stiveton, Everard de Gordelby, William son of Robert, Geoffrey de Monte alto, Robert le Vauasour, Peter the carpenter (*carpentario*), Thomas Sakespeye. (*Ibid.*).

Bilton (Ainsty).

88. Grant and confirmation by Roger de Mubray of that gift in wood and plain and all easements which Bertram Hagat, his man, granted to the nuns of Sinningtuaith. He further grants and confirms that land with all easements and appurtenances which Geoffrey Hagat, son of Bertram gave to them because they received his sister; namely half a carucate in Biletun, a carucate and a half in Torp, a carucate in Witintun and half a carucate in Elnewic. If the said Geoffrey wishes to add to this grant, the grantor will support the grant. This grant is made in perpetual alms, quit of all services and customs pertaining to the land. Witnesses: Robert de Daivile, Ralph de Beuvair, Hubert son of Richard, Ralph de Novile. Robert de Beuscap, Hugh de Flamevile. (*Ibid.*).

Bolton-upon-Dearne.

89. Sunday after St. Martin, 29 Edward III [Nov. 15, 1355]. Grant by John son of Richard de Wombewell of Boulton on Dyrn' to John Cissor of the vill of Boulton, of half an acre of land lying in the west field in the place called Cartholme between the lands of Henry Lannell' on the west and the land of Robert Andrewe on the east and abutting at one end on les Hades and at the other on the

water of Dyrn'; to hold with all appurtenances and easements to John, his heirs and assigns, of the chief lords of the fee. Warranty. Sealing clause[1]. Witnesses: John Malet, Robert Andrewe, John F . . .[2] Carter and John the mason, all of the said vill of Boulton. (*Newburgh Priory Muniments*, No. 1/16).

Brackenthwaite (Pannal).

90. Quitclaim by Hugh son of William de Lelay and Christiana, his wife, to Robert son of Huckeman de Plumton of all their demands which they have against him, and at Brankineswait, namely the mowing service (*s. faucarum mecionem*)[3], saving the forinsec service. Sealing clause.[4] Witnesses: Nigel de Plumton, Mauger Vavasore, Alan son of Elias, Richard de .oolesburo, Matthew de Bram, Robert de Lelay, Alexander de Wicton, Robert son of Henry, Gilbert le Lardiner, Richard son of Alexander de Scotton, William de Stiueton, Henry de Screuin. (*Y.A.S.*, Md. 59/18, No. 1).

Bradfield.

91. Grant by John de Wyteley, son of Ralph de Smalefeld, to John his son, his heirs and assigns, of all the land which he had of Ralph de Holmes just as it is enclosed and lies in length and breadth between the rocky (*petrosam*) path and the path which leads to the church of Bradefeld, in return for a sum of money given to the grantor for a fine (*agressumam*) for entry; to hold of the grantor in fee and hereditarily, freely with all liberties and easements and paying yearly 12*d*. in equal portions at the Assumption of the B.V.M. and Martinmas for all secular services, exactions and demands. Warranty. Sealing clause. Witnesses: Elias de Mydehop', Geoffrey de Mora, Henry de Ferinley, Henry sub Egge, Henry de Spina, Thomas Brun, Thomas de Bosco, Roger de Mora, Hugh de Herteclif. (*Y.A.S.*, Md. 244, No. 1).

92. Grant by Thomas de Furniuall, lord of Hallumschir' to Robert the clerk of Bradefeld, of all that land which Robert's father held in Westmanshalgh; to hold of the grantor and his heirs, with all liberties and easements, with free entry and exit and all other appurtenances, paying yearly to the grantor, his heirs and assigns 1*d*. at the Nativity for all secular services and demands. Warranty. Sealing clause. Witnesses: Thomas de Mountenay, Thomas de Furneus, Robert de Waddislay, Thomas le Rous, William de Darnall,

[1] Seal of dark brown wax; diam. 1 in.; in a cusped border a shield of arms; 3 maces a border engrailed. SIGILLV IOHIS DE DULTONE.

[2] Document stained.

[3] The term is obscure, but mowing service seems the most probable rendering.

[4] Tongues for two seals, but both missing.

Henry de Brikferth, Robert de Esgathorp, John del Chapell, John de Morton, Richard Moriz of Wyrall, Robert the clerk of Sheffeld. (*Ibid.*, No. 2).

93. Grant by Thomas son of Thomas de Furniuall, to William son of John de Whyteles, his heirs and assigns, excepting religious and Jews, of a messuage with appurtenances, called le Hallefeld in Thornsette in the soke of Bradfelde, just as it lies in length and breadth without curtailment; to hold of the grantor and his heirs freely, peacefully and hereditarily, with all liberties and easements and rights of pasture in Hawkesworthe for his own beasts for their food, saving only to the grantor the products and profits of the waste; paying yearly to the grantor and his heirs, 3*s.* 6*d.* at the Assumption of the B.V.M. and Martinmas in equal portions, for all services, customs and secular demands, suits of courts and mills and all other services. Warranty. For this grant William gave a sum of money to Thomas. Sealing clause. Witnesses: Sir Robert de Mountney, Sir Ralph de Grelsall of Midehopp, Ralph de Acton, Robert de Chapell, John Wyteles, Henry de Spina, Geoffrey de Mora, Adam de Brickeshart, Adam de Blunt, William de Wicston, clerk. (*Ibid.*, No. 3).

94. St. Agatha the Virgin [Feb. 5], 1404[-5]. Quitclaim by Alice de Lode of Thrynschoo[1], once of Bradefeld, to John de Hawkesworth of Bradefeld, his heirs and assigns, of all right in a certain piece of land with a garden and a toft containing half an acre, with buildings thereon, between the rectory of Bradefeld on the west and the path which leads from the vill of Bradefeld as far as Roderham on the east. Warranty. Sealing clause. Witnesses: William Rayner, Robert Dykenson, Richard Tagg, William Wilkocson, John de Birlay. At Thrynschoo. (*Ibid.*, No. 4).

95. June 8, 5 Henry VII [1490]. Grant by John Morwode of Bradfeld to John Rewell of the same, and William Hudson of Rotheram, of all his lands and tenements with appurtenances, also all his goods and chattels, fixed and moveable, alive and dead, also all his debts wherever they may be found; to hold to the said John and William of the chief lords of the fee. Warranty. Sealing clause. Witnesses: William Obson, John Waynwryght and Richard Lokyslay. At Bradfeld. (*Ibid.*, No. 5).

96. Aug. 1, 5 Henry VII [1490]. Grant by John Morewode del Okes, to Thurstan Smyth, chaplain, of a parcel of land with appurtenances which lies between the water of Sten on the north and Bradfeld on the south, and abuts on a certain path leading through the middle of Chandrellclogh on the east; to hold to Thurstan and his heirs, of the chief lords of the fee, paying yearly

[1] Thurnscoe.

to the grantor, his heirs and assigns, 2*d.* in equal portions at Whitsuntide and Martinmas. Warranty. Sealing clause. Witnesses: John Shagh, William Sclatter, John Rivill. At Bradfeld. (*Ibid.*, No. 6).

Bramley.

97. Grant by Adam de Raineuill' to Matilda daughter of Richard de Ledes, for her homage and service, of a bovate of land with appurtenances in the vill of Bramleia, namely that which the grantor lent (*accomodaui*) to Beatrice, his niece, also a toft and a croft in the same vill next to the toft of the aforesaid bovate of land towards the south, also an assart which Warinus holds of the grantor in the territory of the same vill; to hold to Matilda and her heirs, of the grantor and his heirs, in fee hereditarily, in wood and plain, ways and paths, waters and pastures, with all other liberties and easements, paying yearly to the grantor a pound of cumin at the Nativity for all services and performing the forinsec services pertaining to a bovate of land where 6½ carucates make a knight's fee. For this grant Matilda gave 10*s*. Warranty. Sealing clause. Witnesses: Eydonus de Lungeuilers, Thomas his brother, William de Stapelton, Adam de Beston, Peter de Alta ripa, Robert de Raineuill', Henry Schotico, Simon de Ferselaia, Samson de Farnelaia, William Bec, Geoffrey de Raneuill', Norays the clerk, Simon the free tenant, Peter de Hal, Robert his son, Henry the baker. (*Newburgh Priory Muniments* [unnumbered]).

Brampton (Wath).

98. Grant by Roger de Svineheued to Thomas de Balne, of that bovate of land and appurtenances in Bramtun which Roger, son of Kaskin once held, and 4 acres of land in the addition (*in aumento*) to his demesne land in the fields of Mentun; namely, half an acre next to the ditch adjoining the land of Henry Palefrid, an acre and a half between the crossroads [?] (*cruces*) and the toft of Bramtun, half an acre near the well in the meadows and an acre and a half at the head of Mesebusc, as free marriage portion with Matilda, his daughter; to hold to Thomas and his heirs by Matilda, of the grantor in fee and hereditarily, performing the forinsec service pertaining to one bovate and 4 acres of land where 30 and a half carucates make a knight's fee. Warranty. Sealing clause. Witnesses: Adam de Nouo marcato, Henry his brother, Thomas de Reineuilla, Robert de Lasayceas, Ralph *le franceis*, Ralph de Waht, Lotte de Wath, Alexander de Adewic, Peter de Hudlestun. (*Y.A.S.*, Md. 244, No. 7).

99. Grant and quitclaim by John Thomas of Balne to William son of Reyner Malet of Boulton, his heirs and assigns, all right in a bovate and four acres of land with appurtenances which Roger de Swyneheued gave as a marriage portion with Matilda, his daughter,

to Thomas, the grantor's father, in the fields of Brampton; to hold of the grantor and his heirs freely and in peace, except for the forinsec service which pertains to a bovate of land in the same fee, where 30 carucates and a half make a knight's fee. Warranty. For this quitclaim William gave the grantor 15*s*. Sealing clause. Witnesses: Sir Reyner Fleming', Roger de Werth, Roger de Swineheued, John son of William de Boulton, Thomas Malet, Thomas Puleyn, William de Swinton, John del Skire, Nicholas the clerk. (*Ibid.*, No. 8).

Brandsby.

100. Wednesday after the Purification of the B.V.M. [Feb. 3], 1345[-6]. Indenture whereby John Chaumont and Henry de Bollyng grant to Thomas de Coluille, knt., all the manor of Euerslay near Brandesby, with all the services of free tenants and villeins and with the reversion of the third part of the said manor which Robert de Eure and Margaret, his wife, mother of the said Thomas, hold in the name of dower of the same Margaret, with all other appurtenances of the same manor, with the exception of 8 tofts, 6½ bovates and 25 acres of land, 8 acres of meadow and an annual rent of 17*s*. 2*d*. and the common pasture with appurtenances which Thomas son of Thomas de Coluille, and Ellen, his wife, hold to them and their lawfully begotten heirs, in the same manor, to hold to Sir Thomas for the term of his life, performing the due and accustomed services, and after his death remainder to Thomas, son of the said Thomas and Ellen, his wife, and their lawfully begotten heirs; and in default of issue to the right heirs of Sir Thomas de Coluille in perpetuity. John and Henry will and grant that Sir Thomas shall not be annoyed or disturbed by any action for waste, or by any other fines by reason of waste in respect of the said manor, or any part thereof, or in any tenement in Cokewald which he holds for a term of years by the demise of the said John and Henry. Alternate seals.[2] Witnesses: William de Malbys and William Darell' knts., Marmaduke Darell, John de Baxby. At Euerslay. (*Newburgh Priory Muniments*, No. 8/25).

Brierley (Felkirk).

101. Thursday after the Epiphany (*Thyfhayne*), 15 Edward III [Jan. 10, 1341-2]. Grant[3] by Hugh de Brerelay to William Scot and Alice his wife and their heirs, of pasture for all manner of their beasts everywhere within the bounds of the vill of Brerelay in the woods, wastes, moors, plains, common pastures at all seasons of the year, and in other places at open time and time of fallow, with free

[1] Seal: green wax, broken, ...S BALNE.

[2] Two seals of red wax, 1) diam. 1 in , broken; a shield of arms couchee; a chevron between 3 lozenges, . . . CHAU . . . 2) diam. 1 in ; in a decorated border a shield of arms; an escutchon ermine within an orle of 8 martlets, SIGI . . VM HENRICI DE BOLLING

[3] In French

entry and exit, chase and rechase, without having regard as to whether the beasts were couchant and levant; also undertaking to make an estate to them of a plot containing one and a half acres to be chosen by them in the woods or wastes of Brerelay, in which they could build cattle-sheds; also grant of free fishery in the ponds of the manor of Brerelay, housebot and haybot in the wood of Conynghagh at their manor of Halghton, timber in the same wood for repairs and other necessaries in their manor of Halghton; also undertaking, on behalf of the grantor and Thomas his brother, to use their best powers with dame Maud, dame de Holand, and Sir Alan her son and their counsel to effect a purchase as speedily as possible to the use of William and Alice and their heirs, of the tenements belonging to Maud and Alan in Halghton, with reversions and services of the tenants and with the wood of Westhagh, rendering yearly the true value. Undertaking by Hugh to secure Thomas's pledge for this in the presence of William and his wife or Sir Adam de Evirringham. Bond (against all men, saving the King and Sir Adam) by Hugh to dwell with William and Alice and their heirs for all his life, without taking anything from them, and to maintain their estate, fame and rights both as regards their wood and lordship of Erdislay as elsewhere; and promise on behalf of himself, his brothers and friends to be loyal and of good faith towards them; and if he should lease the manor of Brerelay they should have the preference. Permission to William to remove his chattels, timber, corn and hay and other things in the manor of Brerelay, namely all things attached to the soil, Hugh and his men to safeguard them in the meantime and also to safeguard William's corn sown on the land until harvest as agreed verbally. Undertaking to rectify or assure the estate of William and Alice or their heirs in the right of patronage (*vowerie*) of the priory of Bretton, and to do everything possible to effect this; also to pay to William all his costs for the repair of houses and for ploughing and manuring; and to perform all the conditions contained in indentures made between them. Witnesses, Sir John de Eland, Sir Nicholas de Wortelay, Sir Adam de Evirrinham, knts., Sir Richard de Rodirham, parson of Penyston, Thomas de Staynton, Thomas de Gresacres, Robert son of Thomas de Staynton. Oath to keep the terms of the agreement made on the missal in the chapel of Halghton. At Halghton. (*E. G. Millar, esq.*).

Brinsworth (Rotherham).

102. Grant by William Pigot of Brinysford to God, Blessed Mary and St. John the Baptist and the brethren serving there, for the health of his soul and for the souls of his father, mother, his ancestors and predecessors, in pure and perpetual alms, of $2\frac{1}{2}$ acres of land in the fields of Brinysford which lie scattered between the

[2] Seal: dark brown wax, round, *c.* 1 in; a shield of arms, a lozenge charged with a bend on a long cross crossed; [SI]GILL' HVGON[IS] . . . . left side chipped away.

land which once belonged to Richard son of Haldan, and the land of Roger son of Raynild; of which 2 strips lie in the west part of the said vill, 2 other strips lie in Crumlandis, 2 strips in Birtheriding, 2 on the west side of Hesilwelle, and a further 2 lie on the west moor abutting above Mockilclif on the northern side; to hold freely and quietly, in fee and hereditarily, with all liberties and easements, to the grantees and their successors in perpetuity. Warranty against all men and all manner of services, demands and suits of court. Sealing clause. Witnesses: Gilbert son of Roger, Thomas son of Euginie [?], John Marior of Brinysford, Robert de Herthil in Catteclue, Nicholas his brother, Richard son of Hugh de Brinysford. (*Serlby Hall Muniments*, No. 4a).

Great Broughton (N.R.).

103. April 24, 2 Henry VI [1424]. Release by William Osanson of Baddyrsby in Cleveland to John Lokewod of Little Broghton, of all right in a bovate of land with appurtenances in the vill and territory of Great Broghton, which the said John had of his gift and feoffment. Great Broghton. (*Y.A.S.*, Md. 135, No. 5).

Buckton.

104. Saturday after St. Edmund, 35 Henry son of John [Nov. 19, 1250]. Grant and quitclaim by William de Buketon to Simon de Hall, his heirs and assigns, of all right in Hecingtun, Bartun and Figeltun and in half a carucate of land in Buketun, concerning which Laurence son of Thomas de Buketun was impleaded and called upon the said Simon de Halle as warranty; he also grants and quitclaims a bovate and a half of land in Kirkeby in Kesteuen which the grantor had claimed in the court of Gilbert by a writ of right, with the exception of 2½ bovates of land and the capital messuage with the tofts in the same messuage, already made or being made, which Geoffrey the grantor's brother holds of him in the same vill in Kirkeby Enkesseuen, and for the quitclaim of Buketon and Beintun and for the homage and service of William son of Robert Vessiby of Buketun from the whole of his tenement which he held of the said Simon in the vill of Buketun. Warranty. Sealing clause. Witnesses: Sir Robert the constable, Sir Peter de Perci, Sir John de Ringtun, Sir Hugh de Cappolla, Sir Henry de Daiuille, Sir Walter de Grendalle, Sir Nicholas his brother, Sir William de Ergom, Mauger his brother, Alan de Bouington, William de Rudestan, John de Suwardby. At York during the itinerary of Silvester, bishop of Carlisle and Sir Roger de Thurkelby. (*Y.A.S.*, Md., 161, No. 4).

105. Grant by William, son and heir of Sir William de Buketon' to Arnold, son of Sir Walter de Buketon', of 2 bovates of land with appurtenances in the field of Buketon', which lies between the lands of the said Arnold and the lands of John son of Laurence,

throughout the length of the whole field, namely those lands which Arnold rented prior to the grantor; to hold to Arnold and his heirs and assigns, of the chief lords of the fee, freely and in peace, paying to the grantor or his heirs a rose at St. John the Baptist for all services suits and customs. Warranty. Sealing clause. Witnesses: Sirs William de Sancto Quintino, William de Flaynburg', constable, John de Heslarton, Robert de Bouington, knts., Robert de Wyerne, William Bard, Azon de Flixton. (*Ibid.*, No. 5).

106. St. Alban. June, 15 Edward I [June 22, 1287]. Grant by Arnold, son and heir of Sir Walter de Buketon to Sir Ralph son of William, as his sister Matilda's dowry, all his manor of Buketon with all his land in the same vill, also all his land in Bempton with appurtenances, and with the villeins, their issue and chattels and with all his rents from the said vills for the term of her life and after Matilda's death, reversion to the grantor. Warranty. Sealing clause. Witnesses: Sir Marmaduke de Thweng, Sir Robert de Buketon, William de Ergham, William de Sywardby, Robert de Bouyngton, William Bard. At the house (*hostium*) of the church of Butterwik in Crandale. (*Ibid.*, No. 6).

107. Indenture whereby Walter, son and heir of Arnold de Buketon grants and demises to William de Bucketon, his uncle, and Isabel his wife or to which ever of them is the survivor, 2 bovates of land in the territory of Bucketon with appurtenances, which is called Magelotland, in exchange for 2 bovates of land which he had of the grant of William and Isabel; to hold to the grantees for the lifetime of the survivor, paying yearly to the grantor, his heirs and assigns, 10*s*. of silver at Martinmas and Whitsuntide in equal portions. Warranty. Sealing clause. Witnesses: Sir William de Ergham, Robert de Sywardby, knts., John de Bouington, William son of William de Bucketon, Robert de Esington. (*Ibid.*, No. 7).

108. March 23, 1350-1. Grant by William Derman of Hundemanby to Walter son of Arnold de Bukton, of 2 tofts in Bukton which the grantor inherited after the death of Emma, his mother; which tofts Richard Derman of Bukton once held of the gift and feoffment of Walter de Bukton, grandfather of the said Walter; to hold to Walter, his heirs and assigns, of the chief lords of the fee, freely [*etc.*]. Warranty. Sealing clause. Witnesses: Walter de Staxton, Fulk Conestable, Gilbert de Acon, John de Sutton, Richard Bardolf, John Horegh, William Bell, vicar of Muston. At Bukton. (*Ibid.*, No. 8).

Burland.

109. Jan 2, 12 Henry VI [1433-4]. Grant by John Mustard of Thorp and John Thorp of Thorp to William Moston of Cayuill

and Richard Burton and Thomas Clayton, clerk, of all the lands and tenements with appurtenances in Birland, which they recently had of the gift and feoffment of Stephen Rok' of Birland; to hold to William, Richard and Thomas and the heirs and assigns of William, in perpetuity. Sealing clause[1]. Witnesses: William de Thorp, Thomas Stevenson, John Gybson. (*Serlby Hall Muniments*, No. 5)

Burton Agnes.

110. The morning after the Nativity [Dec. 26], 1358. Indenture[2] between Marmaduke de Grendal of the one part and Mag. John de Someruille of the other, in the presence of William de Aton and other lawful men, witnessing that Sir Marmaduke and Mag. John have agreed concerning a place called Grendalker in Burton Annays to that which Mag. John decrees (*a ceo que Mestre J. dist*), and also concerning a bond (*escript*) of 40*li*. made by Sir Marmaduke to John in this form, namely, that John shall bring an assize of novel disseisin at the first session against Marmaduke in respect of the said place in Burton Annays called Grendalker, and shall appoint (*mys*) certain men at the said assize who shall not be party to any indentures between Marmaduke and John, and who at the expense of the said Marmaduke and John shall be at York to tell the truth at the said assize, without being bribed by either Marmaduke or John to say otherwise than the truth of the matter; and if they say that the said place called Grendalker is in Burton Annays and not in Grauncemore or in Thirnom'[3] then the said John shall recover Grendalker for himself and his heirs in Someruille with whom the right shall then remain; and being thus said, Sir Marmaduke shall pay to Mag. John 40*s*. which is owing to John for expenses paid by him or his for the last plea for the bond of 40*li*. undertaken in respect of the said agreement, and John shall hand over to Sir Marmaduke the bond of 40*li*. to be his for ever; but if the assize states that Grendalker is in Grauncemore or Thirnom' then Marmaduke shall hold it well and peaceably to him and his heirs for ever, without contradiction from Mag. John or anyone belonging to him, and John shall receive nothing by his plea for the said agreement, and shall bear all the expenses which the said Sir Marmaduke incurred in the former plea concerning the bond of 40*li*. or by him or his in defence of the said plea, also the expenses incurred at the said assize; and Mag. John shall deliver the bond of 40*li*. to Sir Marmaduke into his keeping for ever. Both parties swear to keep faithfully to this agreement. Alternate seals. The year, day and place above written. (*Y.A.S.*, Md. 59/24, No. 1).

[1] Two seals of red wax; (1) the letter T; (2) conventional four-leaved device.

[2] In French.

[3] Gransmoor, Thornholme.

Carlton (Snaith).

111. Grant by Adam Smyle of Carleton to Thomas de Snayth, clerk, his heirs or assigns, for 8*s*. given beforehand, of a rood (*perticatam*) of land lying in an assart called Gedpolsick in length and breadth by the land of the grantee; with all easements, rendering yearly to the lord of the fee 1*d*. at the terms fixed in the soke of Drax, for all services, suits of courts, aids and demands. Witnesses: Peter at the hall, Richard the clerk of Snayth, Richard de Hauburg, Henry the clerk of Cuwic, Thomas of the chapel. (*E. G. Millar, esq.*).

112. Whit Tuesday [May 29], 1341. Grant[2] by Agnes daughter of William son of John Euot of Carleton by Snayth, in her virginity, to Alan del Hile of Cotes, his heirs and assigns, of a moiety of an acre of meadow with appurtenances lying in *le Newhenges* of Carleton between the meadow of Beatrice de Rouclif on the east and that of Richard del Hile on the west, and abutting on that of John son of Robert towards the south and on that of William de Letherton towards the north; with all easements. Witnesses: Roger son of Thomas de Carleton, John del Nesse, John le Smyth, Thomas Pykard, John Pykard. At Carleton.[3] (*Y.A.S.*, Md. 141, No. 2).

113. Dec. 11, 21 Edward III[4] [1347]. Although Roger son of Roger de Burton in Kendale, knt., had demised to John de Neuton of Snayth all his lands and tenements and possessions, and the rents and services of all his tenants and their heirs, with appurtenances in Carleton by Snayth, for a term of thirteen years, and was bound to him in 200*li*., half at the ensuing feast of the Nativity of St. John the Baptist, and the other half at the following Christmas by a statute merchant[5] dated at York in the same month[6], John granted that if he held the premises for the said term the bond should be of no effect. Alternate seals[7]. At York. (*Y.A.S.*, Md. 135, No. 2).

114. May 31, 15 Henry VI [1437]. Grant by Hawot Saundy of Cotes in the parish of Snaith, widow, and Richard Herdying, son of Thomas Herdying of Carleton in the said parish, deceased,

[1] Seal: white wax, pointed oval; a floral device; broken.

[2] Also, Trinity Sunday [June 3], 1341, release of all right by the same to the same therein (*Ibid.*, No. 2A); same witnesses, Thomas Pykard omitted; same place and seal.

[3] Seal: yellow wax, round, ¾ in.; head of a bearded man to the dexter; legend not deciphered.

[4] Et regni sui Franc' octauo.

[5] Statuti pro mercatoribus apud Actonburnell editi. This was the Statute of Merchants, 1283.

[6] The day of the month is torn away.

[7] Seal on a tongue of the parchment; red wax, much chipped; a shield of arms couché beneath a helm, charges on a fess not deciphered, the field behind the shield sown with small crosses.

to Cecily Porter of Carleton, widow, of 4 acres of land with appurtenances in the lordship of Carleton, which lie in a certain assart called Heecoumerbutt' above Wysemanland to the north above the highway called . . . morland towards the south; to hold to Cecily, her heirs and assigns, of the chief lords of the fee, freely and peacefully in perpetuity. Sealing clause. Witnesses: Robert Walcotes, Richard Porter, John Knaresburgh, John Clerke, Thomas Ruseholm' and others of Carleton. At Carleton. (*Y.A.S.*, Md. 161, No. 9).

Castleford.

115. St. Martin, 1 Henry V [Nov. 11], 1413. Indenture whereby John de Castleford of Hoghton' grants and leases to Thomas Lacy for a sum of money received, 3 acres of meadow with appurtenances in *le mere* near Castleford called le Brode Enge; to hold to Thomas, his heirs and assigns, from the feast of St. Michael next following for the full term of 4 years. Warranty. Alternate seals. (*Y.A.S.*, Md. 161, No. 10).

Cavil.

116. Grant by William de Kayuilla to Roger, his son and heir, for his homage and service, of all that toft which belonged to Ralph Brian in the vill of Kayuilla, and 2 acres of land, of which one lies in Aldwrth between the land of William son of Suayn and the land of Ralph de Klif, and the other lies in Sighuse in Appeltreske and in Westheng, and also a perch of land which lies in Rauenshirst, which Juliana, wife of Ralph Brian held; to hold to Roger, his heirs and assigns, of the grantor and his heirs in fee and hereditarily with all appurtenances, paying yearly to the grantor 2*s*. at the four terms customary in Houedenscyra, and 1*d*. at Martinmas for pannage if the grantee should have pigs to fatten in *ye more* of the lord bishop, for all other services, customs, aids and demands. Warranty. Witnesses: Thomas son of Romphari [*sic*], William de Birland, William de Lintona, Robert son of Thomas, Adam de Belasis, Peter son of Romphari, Rayner de Crigeltona, Thomas de Thorp[1]. (*Serlby Hall Muniments*, No. 6).

117. Grant by John de Keyull, knt., to Robert Wryde, his heirs and assigns, of a toft and land once held by Ralph Fadersaule; to hold to Robert, of the grantor, in fee and hereditarily, with all liberties and easements in perpetuity, paying yearly to the grantor and his heirs, half a mark of silver in equal portions at the four terms customary in Houedenschyr for all secular services and demands. Warranty. Sealing clause[2]. Witnesses: Robert Beaumunt, Adam son of Roger, Nicholas Westiby, Adam Westiby, John

[1] Vesica shaped seal of bright green wax; 1½ × 13/8 in.; a bird; SIGILL.WIE FIL THOME DE KEVIL.

[2] Seal of white wax, vesica shaped, very blurred.

son of Thomas, John Dauid, Roger the forester, Laurence de Bellerby, Adam son of William de Birland. (*Ibid.*, No. 7).

118. Monday before SS. Simon and Jude [Oct. 22], 1324. Grant by William de Moreby living in Kayuill' to Roger, son of Sir Peter Dayuill', knt., of a messuage with appurtenances in Kayuill' lying between the messuage of John Cowyng on one side and the messuage which belonged to William son of Adam de Kayuill'; he also grants an acre of land in the same vill which came to him by inheritance from Joan, his wife; to hold to Roger, his heirs and assigns, for the lifetime of the grantor, paying yearly to the chief lords of the fee the due and accustomed services during William's lifetime. Warranty. Sealing clause. Witnesses: John, lord of Kayuill, Nicholas de Portyngton, William atte Liddeyate, Richard de Thorp, John le Long, William de Waynflet, clerk. At Kayuill'. (*Ibid.*, No. 8).

Dorso: Cayuill, Morbyplace.

119. St. Gregory [March 12], 1331[-2]. Indenture whereby John, son and heir of Sir John de Kayuill', knt., grants to Alice, daughter of John de Kylpin of Kayuill' and John, her son, a toft with appurtenances in Kayuill, lying between the toft once of Simon son of Eve and the toft of William le Porter in breadth, and the common way as far as Loftdyk in length; also 5 strips of land in the territory of Kayuill, of which 2 strips lie in le Croftes between the land of John, son of Wydo, on both sides, and one strip is called Knokedland; to hold to Alice and John for the term of their lives, of the grantor and his heirs, freely and in peace with all appurtenances, paying yearly to the grantor 6*d*. at the four terms usual in Houedenschyr, in equal portions. Warranty. Should the grantees sell, demise, give or alienate the lands to the prejudice of the grantor or his heirs, he may enter and retain the lands without contradiction. Alternate seals. Witnesses: Sir Roger de Eyuill, knt., Nicholas de Portyngton, Thomas de Ousthorp, Thomas de Caue of Hythe, William Belassisse, John Oty of Grenaykr, John de Waldby. At Kayuill. (*Ibid.*, No. 9).

120. . . .[1] after Martinmas [Nov.], 138[7], 11 Richard [II]. Grant by Thomas Boisuill and Katherine, his wife, to Thomas de Metham, John Boisuill, John Scot, Robert Boisuill, Thomas de Elleston, chaplain, their heirs and assigns . . . of all the lands and tenements, rents and services belonging to the grantors in the vills of Kayuill . . . Wakholm, Birsay[2], Thorp, Houeden, Belby, with wards, reliefs, escheats and all other appurtenances; to hold to the grantees, of the chief lords of the fee. Warranty. Sealing clause[3].

[1] Document stained.

[2] Waxholme, Borsea.

[3] Two similar seals of brown wax; a shield of arms; 5 fusils conjoined in fess, a crescent; SIGILL . . . ROBERTI DE BOS . . . LLE

Witnesses: . . . Birland, Cuthbert de . . . William the smith of . . . William de Thorp. At Cayuill. (*Ibid.*, No. 10).

121. Monday, St. Andrew, 7 Henry IV [Nov. 30, 1405]. Grant by Thomas Bosuill, knt., and Katherine, his wife, to Robert Johnson of Cayuill' of a piece of land in Cayuill containing 14 feet in breadth next to the tenement of the said Robert; to hold to Robert and his lawfully begotten heirs, paying yearly to the grantors and their heirs and assigns 5*d*. at Michaelmas. Warranty. Sealing clause[1]. Witnesses: Peter Delahay, Thomas de Portyngton, John de Langton, William Waldby, Robert Cyssyll. At Kayuill. (*Ibid.*, No. 11).

122. Aug. 1, 16 Henry VI [1438]. Unto all maner of men to Whame this writing sal come to be sene or herde, Thomas of Santon, Esquier, heele in God euerlasting. In als mykell as hit is holden medefull to Witnesse to expresly knowelege the treuth and to lette oppresse the menes of untreuth on to whilk men oft tymes are monet and stired thurgh couetise and other vices abhominable, therfore be hit had in mynd un to your vniuersite that Piers of Santon, Esquier, my fader whas heir that I am, considering the birth and possibilite of enheritance of Anton Boseuille, son and heir apparant of Sir Thomas Boseuill of Cayuill, knyght, thurghe by the advis of his kyn and frendes mariede Elizabeth, his doghter and my full Sister un to the same Anton in the lyfe of the said Sir Thomas, unto his gretter and more charge and cost, for the said mariage so to be hadde by cause that the said Anton was the enheriter unto Dame Katharine, his moder, doughter and heir of John Cayuill Esquier, and wyfe un to the said Sir Thomas, and the same Sir Thomas was than son and heir un to Robert Boseuill of Neuhall, Esquier and Johan his wyfe, the whilk Johan was full Suster unto Sir Thomas, some tyme lord Furnyuall, the whilk Sir Thomas, lord Furnyuall was full uncle un to the said Sir Thomas Boseuill, also godefader. And for many wilde condicons that the said Sir Thomas Boseuill uset in his childehode after the nurtur, condicon and cherisshing of the said uncle and godefader, the same Sir Thomas Boseuill was mykell the better all his lyfe had in mynd for neuewe and godeson unto the said lord, and so neyset that tyme and oponly kende unto his grete wurshepe forthering and encresse, so that for default of issue of my lady Furynuall that last dyed, whas soul God asseild, the heirs of the said Anton and Elizabeth bodies issauntz are next of blode with other unto the said lord Furnyuall, and so likly possible to enherite with other his landes. In Wytnes whereof un to this my Writing I have sette my seall.[2] (*Ibid.*, No. 12).

[1] Two similar seals of red wax as to the preceding deed.

[2] Blob of red wax, with a twisted plait of straw; undeciphered.

123. St. Wilfrid, 33 Henry VI [Oct. 12, 1454]. Indenture[1] between William Moston, esq., and Thomas Monkton, whereby William 'has letten to ferme in the name of his feofees' to Thomas, his messuage, tofts, crofts and land, meadows and tenements in the manor of Cayuill, also 2 crofts in Duncots, lately held by Thomas Hankyn of Kilpin and others, excepting a cottage and the land held by Hoge Hilton and a little toft newly closed . . . in the same manor; to hold to Thomas from Michaelmas, 33 Henry VI for the term of 6 years, paying yearly to the grantor 20*li.* at the four terms customary in Houedenshir; Thomas is to maintain the said lands and to leave them in good order at the end of the term 'in closur and tilthe in all wyse as the war at his entre and no wers'. He also sells to Thomas divers 'graynes herberd in the lathes of the said manor and other catell and godes of husbandrye and household' to the value of 53*li.* 6*s.* 2*d.*; if Thomas should die within the 6 years and any rent be owing, power to William to enter and seize goods to the value of the rent owing. Alternate seals[1]. (*Ibid.*, No. 13).

124. Dec. 1, Edward IV, 1461. Settlement stating that William Moston, nephew of Thomas Longley, late Bishop of Durham, having married Joan, niece of Thomas Samcton and daughter of Antony Bosuill, who in her own right possessed lands to the yearly value of 40 marks in Birsayholme, Neswyk, and Dreuton in the East Riding; and that the said William and Joan granted on Oct. 20, 14 Henry VI [1435] to Henry Brounflete, knt., Henry Longley, Thomas Santon, Robert Sheffeld, William Swillington, Thomas Moston, senior, esqs., and Thomas Clayton, clerk, for the whole of their lives, their manor of Cayuille with all lands and appurtenances in Houeden, Thorp, Belby, Duncot, Kilpyn, Balcholme, Nuland, Benetland, Dyke, Birsay, Dreuton, Suthcaue and Nessewyke, paying to the grantors a rose yearly and to the said Joan 40*li.* yearly; which lands after the death of the said Joan, William Moston on Oct. 6, 37 Henry VI [1458] released to the aforesaid grantees; now, the said William Moston desires that he may be suffered to take all the profits and issues of the said lands and all other lands which ever belonged to him in Yorkshire, for the term of his life, but that the grantees shall continue in possession of the lands; also that after his death his eldest daughter and the heirs of her body may occupy his manor in Cayuill and the lands belonging thereto, also his part of Birland adjoining, with remainder to, 1) Margaret, his second daughter and her heirs, 2) Joan, his third daughter, 3) with all his other lands to Thomas Moston, his nephew; his second daughter shall be suffered also to have all his lands in Leek and Brawath with a quit rent yearly of 40*s.* from his lands in Duncote, with remainder to, 1) his eldest daughter, 2) his third daughter; his third daughter to have a yearly rent of 12 marks from his lands in Houeden, Thorp, Belby, Kilpin, Duncote, Nuland, Dyke, Benetland,

[1] Seal of red wax, broken; Agnus Dei; legend undeciphered.

Byrsay and Neswyk, also lands in Wiliam's possession in Melborne and Lathome; William Monkton, his son in law to collect and receive the said rents, keeping any surplus for himself. If his daughter be not thereby pleased and content, all the lands of the said William to remain after his death to his feofees for the support and payment of all costs arising therefrom. Sealing clause[1]. Witnesses: Edward Saltmersh, William de Cros, William of Lincoln. At Cayuill. (*Ibid.*, No. 15).

125. July 10, 16 Henry VII [1501]. Grant by Robert Monkton, esq., to John Monkton, senior, his brother, of an annual rent of 26*s*. 8*d*. from 24 acres of land in a certain enclosed close called Estfeld, with appurtenances in Cauell, which rent the same John Monkton had of the gift of Ellen Monkton, their mother; to hold to John for the term of his life; and should it be in arrears wholly or in part, power to the grantee to enter the 24 acres and distrain until satisfaction is obtained. Warranty. Sealing clause. At Cavell. (*Ibid.*, No. 14).

Cawton.

126. Grant and confirmation by Thurstan son of Bernard de Caluetona to Osmund Croere[1] and his heirs, of all his land adjoining the vill of Caluetona towards the west, in the southern part of the road the width of 4 perches of land and in length from the way which leads to Gillinge as far as the cultivated land of the said Osmund Croere; he also grants his two doles beyond the ditch at Grimeston and his wandale at Gillinge below the cliff (*kliuo*); also his wandale at St. Wilfrid's fountain; to hold of the grantor and his heirs for his homage and service, in fee and hereditarily freely and in peace, paying yearly to the grantor and his heirs a pound of cummin at Christmas for all services and secular demands. Witnesses: William de Stainegrif, Richard de Wiuilla, Reginald de Capetoft, Ralph de Surdeual, Robert de Buleford, Alan de la Mare, Robert de Chambord, William his son, Patrick de Ridal', Robert *de vado*, Ralph his brother, Arnold Percehaie, Richard Croere, Ralph B'ard. (*N. G. Hyde*, No. 1).

127. Grant by Osmund Cruer to John Cruer, his brother, of a messuage with 3 crofts and 2 bovates of arable land and meadow in the vill and territory of Calueton; to hold to John, of the chief lords of the fee for the term of his life, paying yearly to the Templars 12*d*. at Martinmas; after his death reversion to the grantor and his heirs in perpetuity. Sealing clause[2]. Witnesses: William Etton, Thomas de Pykryng, Simon de Stanegryff, Adam de Laystrope, John de Newton, Robert Stutewelle, William Asseleysse, John Serpynewelle. (*Ibid.*, No. 2).

[1] Osmund Croere appears as a witness to a grant which can be dated 1170-1176. *E.Y.C.*, ii, 73. For the full text of this charter with a collotype illustration see *E.Y.C.* ix, No. 77.

[2] Fragment of seal of red wax.

128. Grant by John Cruer to John Porte and Agnes, his wife, the grantor's sister, of 2 messuages and 2 bovates of land with appurtenances in the vill and territory of Calueton, in free marriage; which 2 messuages a 2 bovates lie between [the land] of Peter de Calueton, chaplain on the east and the tenement of the said [sic] Richard Croer' on the west which is held of the Templars; to hold to John and Agnes, their heirs and assigns, freely and in peace with all liberties and easements, of the grantor and his heirs, paying yearly 12*d.* at Martinmas. Warranty. Sealing clause. Witnesses: John Blakyng, John Fyrthby, Nicolory [sic] Clayworth, Richard Stybyng, John Besyngby, John Boysse. (*Ibid.*, No. 3).

129. Grant by Robert Cruer son of Osmund Cruer to Dom John Lythome, rector of Gilleyng, to Dom Peter de Calueton', chaplain, of 2 messuages and a croft adjoining and 5½ bovates of land with appurtenances in the vill and territory of Calueton, of which one messuage and 2 bovates is held of the Templars between the land of John Pertt on the east and the land of the grantor on the west and is inhabited by John Gudefellowe, and the other messuage and 3½ bovates is between the land of John Absolon on the east and the land of the grantor on the west and is inhabited by Richard Blakynger; to hold of the chief lords of the fee freely and in peace, in perpetuity. Warranty. Sealing clause. Witnesses: Thomas de Etton, Adam de Grynstone, John de Colton, William Warde, William Besyngby, John Rabotte. (*Ibid.*, No. 4)

130. Release and quitclaim by Robert son of Peter Ascelis of Calueton' in Ridal' to Stephen de Calueton' in Ridal' and Emma, his wife, of all right in a toft and a croft with appurtenances in Calueton' which lies between the land of Staci de Pert on one side and the land of William Cruer on the other; to hold to Stephen and Emma, their heirs and assigns, of the Templars of Jerusalem freely quietly and hereditarily in perpetuity, paying yearly to them 12*d.* in full at Martinmas for all secular services, exactions and demands. Sealing clause. Witnesses: Dom. Peter, chaplain of Calueton, William Cruer of the same, Absolon de Habtona, Absolon in le Wra, Richard de Blakedale, William son of Luke, Thomas de Etton. (*Ibid.*, No. 5).

131. Grant by John son and heir of William Cruer of Calueton to Robert son of Walter of York, of a toft (*thofftum*) with a croft in the vill of Calueton which lies between the land of Peter the chaplain and of Sir William de Lasceles; to hold with all liberties and easements to Robert, his heirs and assigns, paying yearly 1*d.* at the Nativity for all services. Warranty. Sealing clause. Witnesses: Sir William de Lasceles, knt., Walter, rector of the church of Gilling, Peter the chaplain, John de Cotingham, William de Gilling, John Le Wassre. (*Ibid.*, No. 6).

132. Sunday after St. John of Beverley [May 9], 1305. Grant[1] by William de Cotingham to Robert de Salton and Juliana, his wife, the grantor's daughter, of a toft and a croft with 8½ acres of land with appurtenances in the vill and territory of Calueton, namely, that toft and croft and 3½ acres of land which the grantor had of the gift and feoffment of Stephen de Cotingham, his brother, and that 5 acres of land which he had of the gift of John, his father; to hold to Robert and Juliana and their lawfully begotten heirs, freely and in peace, without reservation, with all liberties and easements, of the chief lords of the fee. Warranty. Sealing clause[2]. Witnesses: Sirs John de Barton, Ivo de Etton, knts., John de Thorneton, Robert de Colton, Ralph de Kirketon, William de Besingby, Stephen de Teuerington. (*Ibid.*, No. 7).

133. Thursday before St. Luke, 16 Richard II [Oct. 18, 1392]. Indenture stating that since Richard Stibyng of Caulton in Rydale and Emma, his wife had granted to Richard their son, and Agnes, his wife, and their lawfully begotten heirs, a toft and a croft with appurtenances in the vill of Caulton in Rydale, as is more fully described in their charter, now, however, Richard, son of Richard, and Agnes, his wife wish and grant for themselves and their heirs that the said Richard and Emma shall have and hold the toft with all liberties and easements for the term of their lives or the lifetime of the survivor, performing all the required services and paying to Richard and Agnes a rose in the season of roses. Sealing clause[3]. Witnesses: John Asplion, William Asplion, John de Newton, William Stibyng, John de Fortheby, William Clerk, William Patrykson. At Caulton. (*Ibid.*, No. 9).

134. Dec. 30, 1 Henry V [1413]. Grant by Robert Perci of Helmesley to John Moge, chaplain, of all the lands and tenements, rents and services, with all appurtenances which he has in the vills and territories of Hellmesley, Slengesby, Colton', Caulton' and Bodillom[4]; to hold to John, his heirs and assigns of the chief lords of the fee. Warranty. Sealing clause.[5] Witnesses: William Rolleston, vicar of Helmesley, William Sproxton, John Pikeryng. At Helmesley[6]. (*Ibid.*, No. 10).

135. Sept. 6, 29 Henry VI [1450]. Demise[7] by Robert Thornton to Christopher Crewer of all the lands and tenements

[1] Same day and date, a precisely similar indenture but with the insertion of a clause allowing for the reversion of the lands to the grantor, in default of lawful issue, and the addition of Roger Rabot to the list of witnesses. (*Ibid.*, No. 8).

[2] Seal, a blob of brown wax; the letter T below a crown.

[3] Vesica shaped seal of brown wax, broken; a floral device; ... SIGILL'M DE . . . D'

[4] Beadlam.

[5] Seal of red wax, diam. 1 in.; in a cusped border a floreated cross; S' . . . DE LOCTON.

[6] Endorsed: 1) A feoffement made by Robert Percy the secund to John Moge, prest. 2) Robarte Pearcie dede to Mugge.

[7] Quitclaim of the same to the same, dated Sept. 9. (*Ibid.*, No. 12).

which recently belonged to Thomas Crewer, father of Christopher, in Cawton in Rydall'; to hold to Christopher, his heirs and assigns in perpetuity. Apointment by Robert of Thomas Persy as his attorney to enter the lands and take seisin thereof on his behalf, and subsequently to deliver seisin of the said lands to Christopher in accordance with the form of this charter. Sealing clause.[1] (*Ibid.*, No. 11).

Chevet.

136. Final concord, York, 36 Henry III [1252], between Richard Normaunt, and Elizabeth his wife . . .[2], prior of Pontefract, Walter de Chyvet, William de Heton, William Gulet, Adam de Hyndeleg, Henry the forester (*forestar'*), Robert de Wambewell, William de Wodethorpe, Thomas Tyrel, and Agnes his wife, Alice de Plegewyc, Avice de Wambewell, and William son of Henry Plegewiki, *quer*: and Thomas de Burg', Adam de Myrefeld, William son of John, Adam Spryngant, Hugh Berca, Geoffrey son of Sweyn, Simon son of Matilda, Adam Wybec, John son of Gade, Walter son of Henry, William son of Robert, Adam Gylet, Robert son of John, Richard Sybil . . . Matthew Stepocleg, Henry Tulbing, Alice who was the wife of William de Walton, John de Byngeleg, and Ellen his wife, Sybil de Walton, Alice who was the wife of Robert de Pavey, Robert de Byteleg, Adam de Wodehus, Philip . . . pan, Roger de Wodehuse, Henry his brother, Gilbert Prudfot, William Warin, William Swyngeden, *def.*

The first party complain that the second party were summoned to show by what right they demanded common pasture in the land of the complainants, since the complainants had no common pasture in the lands of the second party. The latter say that they have done service to the first party therefore they ought to have common in their land. It was decided in the same court that the second party should release and quitclaim for themselves and their heirs all right and claim which they had in any common pasture in the said pasture of Chyvet, except certain pasture marked out by meres and bounds, namely, from the ditch of Sandal to the new ditch on the hill called Chyvethyl, and from that ditch to a certain thornbush (*spina*) near the path which leads from Chyvet to Walton, and from that thornbush as far as the ditch of Walton towards the north; and that the second party and their heirs in future may have common pasture for all their livestock, in such a way that if the stock enters the pasture by escaping from the said bounds, they shall not be impounded, but returned without harm, but if they should enter under custody (*per wardam factam*), they shall be impounded

[1] Small blob of red wax; a star and a crescent.

[2] The name of the prior is obliterated. Dalmatius' term as prior ended in 1252. He was followed by Geoffrey, known to be prior in 1268. *Chartulary of St. John of Pontefract*, ii, p. 681.

and the damage they do shall be emended in accordance with the view of lawful men, without any contradiction.

And for this quitclaim, fine and grant, the second party have granted for themselves, their heirs and their villeins, of Walton, and their tenants, that they in future shall provide each year for the said first party, and their heirs, two men in the autumn to mow (*metendam*), and from each of their ploughs and those of their villeins, one ploughing service for each day within fifteen days of the Purification of the B.V.M., except from the demesne plough of Thomas de Burg, to the use of the same first party; and if it should happen that said second party are unable to provide the said men and ploughing services, it shall be allowed to the first party to distrain on all the second party's cattle in the said pasture, within the said bounds, until the second party find men and ploughing services. (*Cartwright Memorial Hall, Bradford*).

137. June 3, 1 Edward VI [1547]. Indenture by which Thomas Dawnay of Cowyke, esq., and Christopher Haldenby of Haldenby, at the request of dame Elizabeth Nevyll of Cheite, widow, and Henry Nevyll, her son and heir, enfeoffed the said Elizabeth in their four closes with appurtenances in Cheite, namely, a close called *le Crokes* of the yearly value of 33*s*. 4*d*., another called *litle newe close*, 12*s*., another called *le greate newe close*, 14*s*., and another called *le greate Norwoode*, 20*s*.; which four closes they lately had of the grant and feoffment of her and Henry her son; to hold for life without impeachment of waste, with remainder to Henry her son and Dorothy his wife, and Henry's heirs. At Cheite[1]. (*Sd.*) Thomas Dawnay.

Dorso: seisin delivered, same day, to Elizabeth and Henry in the presence of Gerard Haldenby of Cowik, gent., Robert Thornton of Cheite, clerk, Robert Sikes of the same, yeoman, Humphrey Holmes of the same, gent., John Jakson of Sokburn in the bishopric of Durham, yeoman, Robert Howit of Notton, husbandman, Richard Gill of the same, tanner, William Fyxby of the same, husbandman. (*Y.A.S.*, Md. 135, No. 6).

Cowick.

138. Grant and quitclaim by Peter son of Henry Perheuid of Couwicke to Henry son of Walter Hoter of Casttelforhd and Margaret his wife, their heirs or assigns, of a toft with buildings thereon in the vill of Couwicke, as it lies in breadth and length between the toft of William son of Hugh the cowherd (*vaccarii*) towards the east and that of Philip de Croftona towards the west, of which one end abuts on the toft of William son of Adam Perheuid towards the north and the other on the highroad towards the south; to hold of dame Alice de Lascy and her heirs, with all easements, rendering yearly to her the service due. Witnesses: William de Wentework',

[1] Two seals of red wax; (1) broken; (2) letter R.

Lawrence de Hecke, John son of Thomas the clerk (*clerici*) of Snayh', Hugh son of Alan of the same, Edmund son of William the tanner (*tanator'*), John Godard, John son of Robert de Mora. (*Y.A.S.*, Md. 141, No. 3).

139. Release by Peter son of Henry Perheuid of Couwicke to Henry son of Walter Hoter of Castelforh and Margaret his wife, theirs heirs or assigns, of all right in a toft with appurtenances in the vill of Couwicke as it lay in breadth and length between the toft of William son of Hugh the cowherd (*vaccarii*) towards the east and that of John son of Philip de Croftona towards the west; and in all rents and escheats belonging thereto in the soke of Snayht; to hold of the lord of the fee with all easements, rendering to the latter the service due. Witnesses: William son of Robert the merchant (*mercatoris*) of Couwicke, Hugh son of Alan de Snayh', John son of Alice de Couwicke, John Godard de Mora, John son of Robert of the same, William the forester. (*Ibid.*, No. 4).

140. Monday after St. George [April 26], 1316, 9 Edward II. Grant[1] by Thomas son of William the merchant of Couwyck to Adam son of Adam the tailor of Snaith and Agnes his wife, and their heirs or assigns, of two sections of land in the east field of Couwyck between the land of Jordan son of William on the east and that of Henry Crotebul on the west, containing in length from the broad way towards the south as far as the hedge of the meadow towards the north and in breadth four perches, together with the reversion of the dower of Eve widow of William de Couwyk; a section of land lying in the west field of Snaith between the land formerly belonging to William son of James and that formerly belonging to Henry Brown, containing in length from the land formerly belonging to Simon de Rupa as far as that belonging to Richard Maddi, with the reversion as before; also half a rood of meadow lying in the north meadows of Snaith in *le Yole* between the meadow of William in the lane (*in venela*) and that of John in the willows (*in salicibus*); another half rood of meadow lying in the said Yole between the meadow of Joan daughter of William de Couwyck and that of John son of Robert the merchant, abutting on the dyke (*dick*) towards the east at one end and on the meadow formerly belonging to Hugh Perheuid towards the west; also half a rood of meadow lying in the said meadow in *le Smalheng* between the meadow of William in the lane and that of John in the willows; another half rood of meadow

[1] Also another charter, same date and place, making the same grant with small differences; the two sections lay in the east field of Snayth; Jordan son of William is called Jordan Anin; an additional item, three parts of the moor with the soil in Enkelesmor'; the common belonged to a quarter of land; and the tenement which Adam le Boyher' had purchased was inhabited by Hobert de Wrangell; Witnesses, John de Snayth, William his brother, John Warner, Thomas le Talyur', John son of Thomas son of Nicholas, Edmund le Barker, Adam the clerk.

in the said meadow between the meadow of Joan daughter of William de Couwyck and that formerly belonging to John the merchant, abutting on the dyke and on the hedge of the field of Couwyk; also a swath (*swayam*) of meadow lying in the said meadow in *le Smalheng* between the meadow of Simon de Rupa and that of Henry de Couwyk, abutting on the dyke and on the hedge of the field of Couwyck; a swath of meadow lying in *le Fordol'* between the meadow formerly belonging to William de Monte and that of John in the willows, abutting on *le Yole* and on *le Heuedland*; a swath lying in the said meadow between the meadow of William in the lane and that of John in the willows, abutting on *le Yole* and on *le Heuedland*; namely, the three swaths which Eve de Couwyck was holding in the name of dower after the death of William de Couwyk, the grantor's father and her husband; also a yearly rent of 1*d*. at the feast of St. Laurence from the tenement which Roger le Hunter was holding in Goldale; and a yearly rent of 1*d*. at Christmas from the tenement which Adam le Boyher' had purchased of the grantor and was holding in the vill of Snaith; and all the common belonging to a quarter of a bovate of land of the fee of Sir John de Crippeling in Snaith and Couwyk, in fields, meadows, pastures, woods, waters, moors, ways, paths and all other places belonging thereto. Witnesses: John de Snaith, William his brother, John son of Thomas son of Nicholas, Edmund the tanner, John le Littester, John Godard, Adam the clerk. At Snaith.[1] (*E. G. Millar, esq.*).

141. Court[2] of Guy Dawnay esq. of "Gramerr Fee" held at Snaythe Jan. 8, 24 Henry VII [1508-9]. Thomas Thwathys came and took from the lord a toft in Cowyk by the tenement of John Buthe, with buildings thereon, two acres of arable land in the fields of Cowyk, 9 mowings (*falc'*) of meadow lying in *le Yoll dik*, an acre of marsh [?] (*mer'*) by Ladymer', and an acre of land and meadow in *le Southefeld* beyond Depesyk; to him and the heirs of his body, rendering yearly 7*s*. at the usual terms, and suit of court twice a year as other tenants did; fine on entry, 20*d*. (*Y.A.S.*, Md. 135, No. 16).

Dalton (Topcliffe).

142. Monday, Martinmas [Nov. 11], 1342. Indenture whereby Robert Newby grants to Thomas de Allerton living in Dalton' and Elizabeth, the grantor's daughter, his wife, a messuage. with a croft and half an acre of land called Bradelayhedelande with appurtenances which lies next to the said Thomas's [land] on the east, in the vill and territory of Dalton; to hold to Thomas and Elizabeth and the lawfully begotten heirs of Elizabeth, of the grantor and his heirs, freely and in peace, paying to him a rose in the season of roses if demanded. Warranty. Should Elizabeth die without

[1] Seal: white wax, pointed oval; a star; legend blurred.
[2] Contemporary copy.

lawfully begotten heirs, reversion to the grantor. Alternate seals. Witnesses: Marmaduke Darell, John de Multon, William Darell, Edward *ad fontem*, William de Crekhale. At Dalton. (*N. G. Hyde*, No. 13).

143. Quitclaim by Roger Agnel of Sowreby to Roger his brother, for his service, of all right in a bovate of land with appurtenances in the vill and territory of Dalton, which the latter had of the grant of Agnes his (the former's) mother and of William his (the former's) brother; to hold to him and his heirs or assigns; and confirmation of these two grants. Witnesses, John de Newby, William son of the clerk, Hugh Ke, Ranulf de Dalton, Robert son of Alan, Henry the carpenter, Robert son of Gerard. (*E. G. Millar, esq.*).

144. Wednesday the Decollation of St. John the Baptist, 43 Edward III [Aug. 29, 1369]. Grant by William son of William Darell of Dalton of Topclif to Simon, parson of the church of Wenselawe, John, parson of the church of Danby on Wisk, John de Fulford, chaplain, Henry de Bellerby, and John brother of the said Henry, of all his lands and tenements, rents and services of free men, with appurtenances in Dalton by Topclif. Witnesses: John de Thorpe, John son of Robert, William son of Robert Chapman, Robert de Skelton, Peter Chapman. Dalton. (*Ibid.*).

145. Thursday in Easter week, April 7, 13 Richard II [1390]. Grant by Robert de Plumpton of Landemote to Nicholas de Sheffeld, lord of Landemote, his heirs and assigns, of a messuage and three and a half acres of land, with meadow and all other appurtenances in the vill and territory of Dalton *in the dritte*[1]. Witnesses, William Darell of Seszay, Marmaduke Darell, George Darell, Peter de Multon, Robert Buscy, Roger de Kepewik of Silton, Stephen de Herlethorpe. Dalton[2]. (*Y.A.S.*, Md. 141, No. 5).

146. Nov. 14, 9 Henry IV [1407]. Appointed by Isabel daughter of John Forester of Dalton, of John Fery as his attorney to deliver seisin to Marmaduke Darell of all the lands and tenements belonging to Bullasgarth in the vill and territory of Dalton, in accordance with her charter[3]. (*Y.A.S.*, Md. 135, No. 3).

147. March 1, 13 Henry VII [1497-8]. Indenture tripartite by which Richard Grene, esq., and Thomas Alanson granted to

[1] The deed is endorsed in a mediaeval hand: Dalton in le Dryte. Although this form of Dalton in Topcliffe is not given in *Place-Names of N.R.* (Eng. Place-Name Soc.), p. 183, Norton le Clay, about 4 miles away, occurs as Norton in le Drit in 1301, the term being used to denote the swampy nature of the land.

[2] Seal: yellow wax; signet; letter W, and either a cross or another letter before it.

[3] Fragment of seal of red wax.

Master John Brame, clerk, vicar of the church of Topcliff, John Fox, chaplain, Robert Burnett, John Helmesley, Richard Bell, William Kaa, William Clerk, William Tirwhitt the elder, Richard Stevynson, William Tirwhitt the younger, and William Manefeld all the following messuages, lands and tenements, namely, a messuage, a toft, a croft, forty acres of land and one acre of meadow, with appurtenances in Catton Northeby, then in the tenure of William Fall; a toft, a croft and nine acres of land and meadow, with appurtenances in Dalton, in the tenure of Thomas Parker; a moiety of a messuage, toft and croft and ten acres of land and meadow, with appurtenances in Dalton, in the tenure of John Thornton; a messuage, a toft, a croft and twelve acres of land and meadow, with appurtenances in Dalton, in the tenure of Thomas Lauson; and a messuage, a toft, a croft and twelve acres of land and meadow, with appurtenances in Crakall, in the tenure of Henry Sale; to fulfil their will[1]. (*Ibid.*, No. 4).

Draughton.

148. Quitclaim by Robert son of Martin de Dracton to Sir Mauger Wauasor, knt., his heirs or assigns of all right and claim in the service and rent due from half a bovate of land in Dracton; to hold to Sir Mauger Wauasor and his heirs and assigns for a certain sum of money. Warranty. Sealing clause. Witnesses: Sir John Wauasor, knt., Sir Richard de . . . , Sir Ralph de Burgel, William de Thorner, then bailiff of Ottel', Geoffrey de Ottel', then dean of the same and Ripon, William de Ottel', clerk, Geoffrey Fauvel of the same, clerk. (*Cartwright Memorial Hall, Bradford*).

149. Quitclaim by William de Boceland, son of Simon de Bramton, to Sir Mauger Vauasor, his lord, of a bovate with appurtenances in the vill and territory of Dracton, which land he formerly held of Mauger and which he inherited from his mother; also all the land called Le Forland adjoining that bovate; to hold of the said Mauger and his heirs with all appurtenances freely and hereditarily. Warranty. Sealing clause[2]. Witnesses: Sir John Vauasor, Sir Godfrey de Alta ripa, Sir Henry son of Sir Richard de Percy, William Mauleverer, Peter de Dracton, Robert de Cave, William son of William de Denton, William son of Thomas de Dracton, Simon de Ottel', clerk. (*Ibid.*).

150. Quitclaim by Peter son of Richard de Dracton to his lord, Mauger [Vauasor] . . . of his land in Dracton with the whole of the moiety of land adjacent to that bovate . . . of a toft

[1] Two seals of red wax: (1) a man's head, with cap, placed upside down on the tag; (2) letters.

[2] Seal: on a tag pendant from centre of deed an oval seal, brown wax, chipped, $1\frac{1}{8} \times 1$ in., small device in centre; legend, WIL. : F : SIOIS DE. Endorsed: Draghton iuxta Addingham, in early hand.

and a croft with the buildings, in such a way that the toft and croft . . . . to the said Mauger Vauasor, his heirs and assigns, freely quit, with all the appurtenances liberties and easements . . . said Peter and his heirs the moiety of the bovate aforesaid, with the moiety . . . toft and croft to Sir Mauger Vauasor, his heirs or assigns. Warranty. Sealing clause. Witnesses: . . . Sir Godfrey de Alta ripa, William Mauleverer, William son of Thomas de . . . William son of William de Denton, Robert de Caue. (*Ibid.*).

Drax.

151. Thursday after St. Lucy the Virgin [Dec. 15], 1323. Release by John son of John Emelot of Rouclef to John son of Thomas the clerk (*clerici*) of Snayth and Margery his wife, his heirs and assigns, of all right by inheritance or otherwise in all the lands and tenements which they had of the gift and feoffment of John Emelot his father in the territory of Drax, in a place called Alda as they lay in different places. Witnesses, John Sewal', Thomas de Neuland, clerk, William Sybry, Thomas le Spenser of Rouclef, Henry his brother. Rouclef[1]. (*Y.A.S.*, Md. 141, No. 6).

Dungworth (Bradford).

152. Grant and quitclaim by Thomas Morwode to William son of William de Lefton, his heirs and assigns, of all right in that piece of land and meadow with appurtenances in Dungwrth, which is called Holynwelleker and which lies between le Brodehenge on the north and le Holinwelle on the south, and one end abuts towards le Haeclif on the east and the other towards the west, in return for a sum of money given to the grantor by William; to hold to William and his heirs and assigns freely and in peace, of the grantor without any further condition. Warranty. Sealing clause[2]. Witnesses: Richard Riuel, William de Lefton, senior, Adam de Wggil, Henry of the same, Andrew de Dungwrt, Henry de Lefton, William de Spina. (*Y.A.S.*, Md. 244, No. 9).

Easthorpe (E.R.).

153. Whitsunday [June 7], 1332. Indenture whereby Sir William de Playce demises and grants to farm to Peter son of William de Estorp, his windmill of Estorp; to hold to Peter for the term of 12 years next following with all profits pertaining to the said mill, paying yearly to the grantor and his heirs 20*s*. of silver in equal portions at Martinmas and Whitsuntide, the first payment to be made at Martinmas next; the said Sir William shall find those necessities which he customarily found and Peter all other necessities usually found by the miller, and at the wish of Sir William he shall

[1] Seal (detached): yellow-brown wax, pointed oval, $1\frac{1}{8} \times \frac{3}{16}$ in., a star; +S' IOH' FIL' IOH' GILB'.

[2] Seal: green egg-shaped; a spray of leaves; ✠ S' THOME DE MOR.

grind his corn and malt without multure when the latter's corn and malt is at the mill. Warranty. Alternate seals. Witnesses: Robert de Playce, Thomas son of Angot de Lebreston, Thomas Jouetson, William son of Henry de Esthorp. Note that the millstones and sails are valued at 6*s*., and that in all things Robert shall leave the mill in as good condition as when he received it. (*E. Stanley Jones*, No. 1).

154. Thursday before Easter [April 9], 1338. Indenture whereby Sir William de Playce grants and demises to William Michel a messuage, a bovate and a piece of meadow which is called le Croft in the vill and field of Esthorp, also his new right of turbary of Lebreston; namely that messuage called le Stacgarth and that bovate which lies towards the south in the culture of the grantor, with all appurtenances, for the term of 14 years until 14 crops have been taken; paying yearly for the messuage 2*s*., for the bovate 6*s*. 8*d*. and for the meadow 10*s*. and for the turbary 16*d*., to be paid in equal portions at Whitsuntide and Martinmas, the first payment for the meadow to be made at Whitsuntide next, for the messuage at Martinmas next and for the turbary at Whitsuntide 1339. Alternate seals. At Gristhorp. (*Ibid*., No. 2).

155. St. John ante portam Latinam [May 6], 1338. Indenture whereby Sir William de Playce demises and lets to farm to Robert son of William de Esthorp· and William son of the same Robert, a piece of meadow in the field of Esthorp which is called le Bosoine[1]; to hold to Robert and William until they have taken therefrom 14 crops, paying yearly to Sir William and his heirs 5*s*. in equal portions at Whitsuntide and Martinmas, the first payment to be made at Whitsuntide next and the first crop to be taken in the same year. Warranty. Alternate seals. At Esthorp. (*Ibid*., No. 3).

East Marton (W.R.).

156. Grant by Richard son of Elias de Estmartham to Robert iuxta Rumulum, clerk, of a strip of arable land in the territory of Estmartham, lying above le Haydole between the land of the said Robert on one side and the land of Geoffrey le Nordys on the other and abutting on the headland towards the west and above le Haygatesty towards the east; to hold to Robert, his heirs and assigns and their heirs, freely and in peace without reservation, in perpetuity, paying yearly to the grantor and his heirs a silver halfpenny at the Annunciation of the B.V.M. for all secular services; and for this grant and confirmation Robert gave to the grantor a sum of money for right of entry. Warranty. Sealing clause. Witnesses: Thomas Derley, Robert, his brother, William son of Ralph, Thomas *ad fontem*, William son of Eve, Nicholas Burdun, Robert Scathclok, clerk. (*N. G. Hyde*, No. 14).

[1] This word has been written over in darker ink.

Ellerker.

157. The Morrow of Easter, 26 Henry VI and 11 of the Translation[1] [Mar. 25, 1448]. Indenture[2] whereby Robert, bishop of Durham granted to his kinsman and servant Thomas Monkton, esq., and Ellen, his wife, his manor of Ellerkar, with all lands, tenements, rents and services in Ellerkar; to hold to Thomas and Ellen and their lawfully begotten heirs, of the grantor and his successors, paying yearly 11*li.* 8*s.* 10*d.* in equal portions at the four usual terms, for all secular services and demands; and if Thomas and Ellen enjoy full and peaceful seisin of the said lands for the term of 60 years and if they die without lawfully begotten heirs, power to the grantor to enter and retain the lands as in their former condition this indenture notwithstanding. Sealing clause[3]. Witnesses: Mag. Robert Beaumont, rector of Brantyngham, Alexander Lounde of Southcave, William Roos, John Belyngholme, Thomas Waldby esqs. At Houeden. (*Serlby Hall Muniments*, No. 16).

Elmire.

158. Nov. 12, 15 Henry VI [1436]. Appointment by Isabel late wife of Edmund Darell of Seszay, knt., of William Craweford, knt., and William Malbysh, *gentilman*, as joint attorneys to receive seisin and possession of the manors of Eldmere, Dalton and Thorkylby with their appurtenances and all other lands, tenements, rents and services with appurtenances in the vills of Crakhall, Middelton, Catton on Swale, Harlesay and Thorneton on the Moor, co. York, and all lands and tenements with appurtenances in the city and suburbs of York, in accordance with a charter made to her by Henry Wyllisthorpe, clerk, William Darell of Mowegrene, Robert Crosse and William Barre, esqs. Also appointment of the same as joint attorneys to enter and take seisin of the manors of Terington, Lyuerton and Danby, co. York, with all profits, and of all other lands and tenements in the vill and territory of Sybsay with appurtenances in co. Lincoln, which had descended to her by hereditary right after the death of George de Etton her father and [blank] her mother[4]. (*Y.A.S.*, Md. 141, No. 7).

Eske.

195. Oct. 5, 38 Henry VI [1459]. Grant by Walter Grymeston of Eske to John Portyngton of Portyngton, *Thomas Portyngton, clerk, provost of the church of Hemyngburgh* [all crossed out], Thomas Grymeston senior and William Grymeston esq., of his capital

[1] Robert Neville was translated from Salisbury in 1437.

[2] Appointment by the same of Thomas Maudrs and Thomas Walkerr as his attorneys to deliver seisin of the same. Same date. Signet of Robert Neville; red wax; a saltire charged with a gimmel-ring; on a label, *en grace affie*.

[3] Fragment of an armorial seal.

[4] Seal: red wax; small signet.

messuage with the close adjacent, 2 bovates of land and a toft with a croft containing half an acre of land, 10 rods of fishing in Oxmerdike and one dole (*dale*) of meadow containing 10 roods, half the grantor's fishing in Oxmerdike and Leuenmere and 3 acres of meadow lying on the west side of Oxfrith, in the fields and vill of Eske, which lands and fishing he had of the gift and feoffment of Richard Newton; to hold to John, *Thomas* [crossed out], Thomas and William, their heirs and assigns, of the chief lords of the fee. Sealing clause[1]. Witnesses: John Melton, Thomas Metham, knts., Richard Portyngton, Thomas Garton, esqs. At Eske. The grantor grants all the above lands to Thomas Donyngton with the above feoffment that he may deliver seisin. (*Y.A.S.*, Md. 161, No. 11).

Eversley.

160. Grant by John son of William Oliver of Euerslay, to Thomas, called de Barton, of a toft and a croft, a bovate and 4 acres of land in the vill and territory of Euerslay, without reservation, namely that toft, croft, bovate and 4 acres which William and Richard the grantor's brothers once held of the demise of William their father and of his grant for the term of 20 years; to hold freely and in peace with all liberties and easements within and without the vill of Euerslay, namely in meadows, pastures, grazings, commons, woods, paths, ways, moors, marshes, waters and turbaries, paying yearly to the grantor and his heirs and assigns a rose during the octave of the Nativity of St. John the Baptist for all secular services, suits of court and demands. Warranty. Sealing clause. Witnesses: Sir Ivo de Etton, Sir Paul de Lilling, Sir William Burdon, knts., Roger Maunsel of Heton, Thomas Maunsel of the same, Richard son of Richard de Euerslay, William de Wyncestr' of the same, Robert de Foxoles, William Maunsel of Thormodby. (*Newburgh Priory Muniments*, No. 8/26).

161. June 10, 12 Henry VII [1497]. Grant by William Leefe to Thomas Cheuyncesown, chaplain and Richard Cheuyncesown, his brother, of a cottage with a croft and a bovate and 4 acres of land in the territory of Euerslay, also all the lands and tenements, rents and services and reversions, and with all other appurtenances which the grantor has in the vill and territory of Euerslay; to hold to Thomas and Richard, their heirs and assigns, of the chief lords of the fee. Warranty. Appointment of William Toy and Thomas Ebson as his attorneys to deliver full and peaceful seisin. Sealing clause.[2] (*Ibid.*, No. 8/27).

162. Jan. 10, 3 Henry VIII [1512]. Indenture whereby John Coluile, otherwise Euerslay, esq., grants and sells to Thomas Cheuyson, chaplain, all his new wood or orchard with all other

[1] Seal of red wax; a man's head.
[2] Seal of red wax; in a shield shaped border, the letter W.

growths, profits, commodities and pasture within the following boundaries, namely, from the cartroad near Wildonfold in le Peill' bank on the north descending and extending to Brandsbybek on the east and so continuing by Dailehed towards the way which leads from the vill of Stersby towards the vill of Euerslay, and from the said stream called Brandsbybek on the east to the shoulder (*supercelum*) of the hill on the west towards Coppichow; to hold to Thomas, his heirs and assigns, to take, retain, cut down, mow or enclose at his wish, and he may freely, whensoever it pleases him sell or carry away what he wishes within the period of, and up to the end of 7 years, with free entry and exit for himself and his men through all the said part of Euerslay; if at the end of the said time he shall pay a certain sum of money to the grantor, and do so for the future then the said John grants, that as often as he wills, the said Thomas, after John has at his own cost and expense made cuttings, mowings and enclosures, necessary for the cutting and enclosing of the pasture and other profits within the aforesaid boundaries for the term of 9 years, may appropriate, hold and occupy the same for his carthorses and other animals, but without harm or waste to the said orchard. Warranty. Sealing clause. Per me Thomam Cheuyson, Capell' (*Ibid.*, No. 8/28).

Farnley (Leeds).

163. Quindene of St. John the Baptist, 52 Henry son of John [July 8, 1268]. Final concord[1] made in the King's court at York before Peter de Brus, Gilbert de Preston, John le Bretun, Walter de Helvin and John de Oketon, justices, between Simon abbot of Kirkestall, *querent.* and Geoffrey de Nevile and Margaret, his wife, *deforc.* concerning 46*s.* 2*d.* being arrears of a yearly rent of 43*s.* 8*d.* which they owe to him.

Geoffrey and Margaret agree for themselves and the heirs of Margaret that they will pay to the said abbot and his successors to the church of Kirkestall, 43*s.* 8*d.* at Farneley by the hand of their sergeant (*servientis*), in equal portions at Martinmas and Whitsuntide; in return the Abbot granted to them a piece of land in Bramleye lying on the north side of their park of Farneleye containing in length 136 perches and extending from the bridge of Farneleye as far as Suomrodesyaghe and from Suomrodesyaghe to Haksike, with permission to enclose the same within their park for ever, paying to the Abbot and his successors a clove gilly flower yearly at the Nativity. Warranty. The Abbot remitted the arrears. (*G. T. Schofield*, No. 25).

164. Release and quitclaim by Thomas son of Sampson de Farnelay to Geoffrey de Nevill' and Margaret, his wife, of 15

[1] A copy of the original document, probably made early in the 17th century: and see *Yorks. Fines*, 1246-72, p. 163, where the spellings are Suainrodesyagh and Hoksik and the justice is Heliun.

acres of arrable land and meadow in the territory of the vill of Farnelay, namely, 9 acres in a culture called Osebarnerode with meadow; 2½ acres in a culture called Le Parchenges, with meadow; 2½ acres in a culture called Nortlay with meadow; one acre with meadow in a culture called Le Wellehenges; to hold to Geoffrey and Margaret, their heirs and assigns, in fee and hereditarily with all liberties and easements within and without the vill of Farnelay. Warranty. For this quitclaim Geoffrey has acquitted the grantor from the Jewry (*Judaismo*) at York. Sealing clause. Witnesses: Sirs Richard de Thornhill', Hugh de Swynlington', knts., John de Alta ripa, Ralph de Hethyrn, John le Norman, Robert de Wyrkelay, Richard de Hyperhum.[1] (*Ibid.*, No. 21).

165. Grant by Thomas Sampson of Farnelay to Sir Geoffrey de Nevile, his heirs and assigns, of 20 acres of land in the territory of Farnelay, of which 9 acres lie in a place called Osebarnerode and 5 acres lie in Nortlay, and 3 acres in the west field in Le Longefurlanges and 3 acres in the same field at Stykdoles; to hold to the said Sir Geoffrey, his heirs and assigns, in fee and hereditarily with all liberties and easements within the bounds of Farnelay. Warranty. Sealing clause.[2] Witnesses: Sir Richard de Thornhill', Richard de Hyperhum, John le Norman', Robert de Wyrkelay, William Gentill', John son of the parson of Farnelay. (*Ibid.*, No. 2).

166. Grant by William de Longeuilerys son of Sir John de Longeuilerys, to John de Farneley, his heirs and assigns, of all that land which the grantor bought from Richard Turypn, in the east field of Farneley, namely that land called Mickelgrene; to hold, freely and in peace with all appurtenances within and without the vill of Farneley, namely in woods, meadows, pastures and arable lands; of the grantor and his heirs in perpetuity, paying 2*s.* yearly in equal portions at Whitsuntide and Martinmas, or for the maintenance of the offices in the chapel of Blessed Helen of Farnley, for all services and demands. Warranty. Sealing clause. Witnesses: Sirs Geoffrey de Nevile, Richard de Thornehyl, John de Heton, knts., Ralph Hedon, William de Northalle of Ledes, William Pittoner of Hedingley, Thomas Sampson. (*Ibid.*, No. 3).

167. Indenture witnessing an agreement between John son of Robert de Longeuilers the elder of the one part and John his brother, the younger of the other part; whereby John the elder grants to his brother half of all the land and tenement which their father Robert once held in the vill of Farnelay, with all appurtenances without reservation, namely, the southern half of a toft, croft and messuage, and the norther half (*medietatem . . . remociorem*) of of all the land in the fields; to hold to John the younger, his heirs

Dorso: [1] Acquietacio de Judaismo apud Eboracum scilicet usury ut opinor', in a later hand.
[2] Broken seal of light brown wax; a fleur-de-lis.

and assigns, of the chief lords of the fee, performing half the service due, provided the services are only 3*d.* of silver payable in equal portions at the Nativity and the nativity of St. John the Baptist; John the younger quitclaims the other half of the property to John the elder in perpetuity. Alternate seals. Witnesses: Sir Geoffrey de Nevile, Thomas son of Sampson de Farnelay, Robert de Wyrkelay, Richard de Alta ripa, John son of Marjory. (*Ibid.*, No. 17).

168. Thursday after St. Peter, in the Gules of August, 8 Edward III [Aug. 6, 1334] Release[1] and quitclaim by John de Nevill', lord of Horneby to Walter de Brampton of an annual rent of 10 horseshoes and 60 nails (*dys feres e sessaunt clows*) from the tenements which Walter holds of him in Farneley, saving to himself a yearly rent of 1*d.* during the lifetime of Walter. Sealing clause. Witnesses: Sir Ralph de Beeston, knt., Roger de Ledes, John de Manston, Thomas le Wayt, John de Sayuill'. At Farneley. (*Ibid.*, No. 15).

169. Whitsunday [May 19], 1336. Indenture[2] whereby Robert de Nevill' of Horneby leases to Robert son of Isabel de Farneley and to Isabel, his wife, a piece of enclosed land called le Hallerode in the demesne of Farneley, with all appurtenances; to hold to Robert and Isabel and their heirs from Whitsuntide in the year of Our Lord, 1336, for the full term of 12 years next following, paying yearly 4*d.* in equal portions at Whitsuntide and Martinmas, and doing suit of court at Farneley and at the mill there, and performing all other accustomed services. They are to maintain the land and surrender it in good condition. Warranty. Alternate seals. Witnesses: Thomas de Eure, John Abot, Adam son of Walter. (*Ibid.*, No. 16).

170. St. Martin [Nov. 11], 1336. Indenture[3] whereby Robert de Nevill' of Horneby leases to Thomas de Eure of Armeley and Matilda, his wife, a messuage and half a bovate of land in the vill of Armeley and a cottage and an acre of land in the demesnes of Farneley, with all appurtenances in Armeley and Farneley; to hold to Thomas and Matilda and their heirs from Martinmas, in the year of Our Lord, 1336, for the 12 years next following; paying to Robert, his heirs or assigns, 4*s.* 10*d.* yearly in equal portions at Whitsuntide and Martinmas and doing suit of court at Farneley and at the mill there, with all other accustomed services; they shall maintain the said messuage, and surrender it at the conclusion of the term in as good a condition as they received it, or better. Warranty. Alternate seals. Witnesses: Alan son of Reginald, William the cobbler (*le souter*), William the thatcher [?] (*le theker*). At Farneley. (*Ibid.* No, 7).

[1] In French.
[2] In French.
[3] In French.

171. Martinmas, 20 Edward III [Nov. 11, 1346]. Grant[1] by Robert de Nevill' of Horneby, knt., to Walter de Nevill', his uncle of all his cattle, corn and hay growing year by year at Horneby, Farneley and Kirkeby, and all his other moveables, and the farm (*ferme*)[2] of Ascheton and the watermill of Horneby, with all the profits of the said mill and the profits of his courts of Horneby and the grass of his park of Horneby and Farneley, for the sustenance and aid of Joan, his [*the grantor's*] wife and his children, at the will of the said uncle. Sealing clause. At London. He also grants to Walter, for the support of his wife all the profits arising from all his manors and lands in the counties of Lancaster, York and Lincoln, except his farms. (*Ibid.*, No. 23).

172. The day before St. Dunstan the archbishop, 36 Edward III [May 18, 1362]. Release and quitclaim by Robert de Nevill' of Horneby *chyualer*, to Robert de Nevill' his son of all right in the manor of Farneley and in all the lands and tenements, rents and services of freemen and villeins and their sequel and chattels and with all other appurtenances which Robert his son has on the day of the making of this deed in the vills of Farnelay, Okenshawe, Heton', Scoles, Collyng and Conynley. Warranty. Sealing clause.[3] Witnesses: Richard le Scrop, Michael de la Pole, Godfrey Foluaumbe, Robert de Swylyngton, Edmund de la Pole, knts., William de Hertford, Thomas Dautre, Dadam [*sic*] de Hopton, Robert Passelewe. At Farnelye.[4] (*Ibid.*, No. 20).

173. Jan. 8, 11 Henry VI [1432-3]. Bond by William de Haryngton of Horneby to John de Langton, knt., in 1000*li*. of English money to be paid to John or his attorney at Easter next following. Sealing clause.[5]

Condition: if William de Haryngton and Margaret his wife, after the castle of Horneby and all the manors, lands tenements, rent, services and advowsons of churches and chantries in the counties of Lancaster, York and Lincoln which Thomas, late duke of Exeter held by English law of the inheritance of the said Margaret and John, are out of the King's hands, shall, at John's reasonable request, make sufficient partition thereof between them and the said John, on the advice of their counsel, by an indenture, as follows:—John and his heirs shall have the manor of Appylby, co. Lincs. and the manor of Great Farneley, co. Yorks. and all the other manors [*etc.*], lately held by the said Duke in the counties of York and Lincoln;

[1] In French.

[2] Rent.

[3] Fragment of fine armorial seal of red wax; a shield of arms couchée beneath a helm and mantling; a cross.

[4] Dorso: Irr' in dorso claus' concellar' Regis infrascripti mense maii anno infrascripto'; in a contemporary hand.

[5] On a tongue cut from the bottom of the deed, a fragment of red wax; undeciphered.

also a certain annual rent of 12*li.* from the lands held by the Duke in Ayntre and Mellyng in co. Lancaster, payable in equal portions at Whitsuntide and Martinmas, with power to enter and distrain, if the said rent is in arrears; also the advowson of the priory of Thorneholme in Lincolnshire; William and Margaret and the heirs of Margaret shall have the castle and manor of Horneby and all other lands and advowsons lately held by the Duke, and they shall pay to John the aforesaid rent of 12*li.*, then the bond shall be null and void. (*Ibid.*, No. 4).

174. March 27, 11 Henry VI [1433]. Grant by John Longton, knt., to Robert Haryngton, Robert Ughtrede, knts., William Scargyll, Richard Ask, John Nevyle, esqs., John Wodham, chaplain, their heirs and assigns, of all the manors, lands, tenements, rents and services which he has in Great Farneley, Little Farneley, Collyng', Conynglay, Clakheton, Scoles, Okenshawe, Gargrave, Poterton, Grymston, Kyrkeby and Northmylford, with all appurtenances in co. York, in perpetuity; to hold to the grantees, their heirs and assigns, of the chief lords of the fee. Warranty. Sealing clause. Witnesses: Robert Waterton, Robert Hoperton, William Ryther, knts., Thomas Clarell', Thomas Wombewell, esqs. (*Ibid.*, No. 6).

175. April 3, 11 Henry VI [1433]. Indenture between William de Harynton' of Horneby, knt., and Margaret his wife, kinswoman and one of the heirs of Margaret who was the wife of Thomas, late duke of Exeter, namely, the sister of Thomas, father of the said Margaret who was the wife of the said late duke, of the one part, and John Langton, knt., kinsman and the other heir of Margaret who was the wife of the said duke, namely, son of Joan sister of the said Thomas father of Margaret who was the wife of the said late duke; of the second part; whereby the parties agree to make partition of the castle and manor of Horneby with its members and appurtenances in co. Lancs. and of the manors of Great and Little Farneley, Okenshawe, Clakeheton, Scoles, Collyng, Conyngley, Gargrave, Poterton, Grymston, Kyrkby super Wharfe, Northmilford and Hoton Longvillers with their appurtances in co. York, and the manor of Appilby with appurtenances in co. Lincoln, and all other manors, lands, tenements, rents and services which lately belonged to Robert Neville of Horneby, knt., of whom, Margaret wife of William de Haryngton, is daughter and one heir, and John de Langton is kinsman and the other heir; with the exception of the manor of Brerelay and the advowsons of Monkbritton and the churches of Badesworth, Kyrkheton, and Hoghland in co. York and all the other lands [*etc.*], which belonged to Margaret wife of the said late duke: the partition to be made in the following manner, namely that William and Margaret shall have to them and the heirs of Margaret in perpetuity, the castle and manor of Horneby and

all other lands [*etc.*], which belonged to Robert and Margaret in co. Lancs., paying yearly to John de Langton his heirs and assigns for and in all the lands and tenements, rents and services in Ayntre and Mellyng[1] 12*li*. in equal portions at Whitsuntide and Martinmas, with power to John to enter and distrain on these premises should the rent be in arrears for over 40 days; and the said John de Langton shall have and hold to himself, his heirs and assigns the manors of Great and Little Farneley, Okenshawe, Clakeheton, Scoles, Collyng, Conyngley, Gargrave, Poterton, Grymston, Kyrkeby super Wharf, Northmilford, and Hoton Longvillers in co. York, and the manor of Appilby, co. Lincoln and the advowson of the priory of Thornholme, with the said annual rent of 12*li*., with all other lands [*etc.*], which once belonged to Robert and Margaret in the counties of York and Lincoln. Sealing clause.[2] (*Ibid.*, No. 9).

176. April 6, 11 Henry VI [1433]. Indenture whereby John Nevyll', esq., and John Wodham, chaplain grant to John Langton, knt., and Euphemia, his wife, all the manors, lands, tenements, rents and services with all appurtenances in Great Farnley, Collyng, Conyngley, Clakheton', Scoles, Okenshawe, Gargrave, Poterton, Grymston, Kyrkeby and Northmilford in co. York, which they, with Robert Haryngton, Robert Ughtrede, knts., William Scargyll, Richard Ask and Roger Ask, esqs., recently had of the gift and feoffment of the said John Langton; to hold to John and Euphemia and their lawfully begotten heirs, of the chief lords of the fee, and in default of issue remainder to Joan, who was the wife of John Langton, mother of the said John Langton, knt. Alternate seals.[3] Witnesses: Robert Waterton, Robert Hepton, William Ryther, knts., Thomas Clarell', Thomas Wombewell'. (*Ibid.*, No. 12).

177. Saturday before the Epiphany, 27 Henry VI [Jan. 4, 1449-50]. Indenture whereby Thomas Meryng, esq., grants to John Langton, knt., all his dwellings called *lez Smythiez* in Tonge which were lately in the tenure of the same John, to hold and to occupy by John from the date of these presents until the feast of St. James the apostle [July 25] next following; paying to Thomas at the said feast, 6*s*. 8*d*. Sir John grants to Thomas or to his attorney, for his own use, licence to fetch and carry ironstones (*petras ferreas*) called *vreston'* to the said dwellings called *lez Smythiez*, beyond the soil of the said John in Farnley, namely from the said feast of St. James, for 6 years next following, paying to John 2*s*. for so long as Thomas carts the stone in this manner, on the far side of John's land. Finally John grants to Thomas all his share in a certain stream flowing between the lordship of Farnley and the lordship of Tonge during the said term, also that Thomas may build and

[1] Co. Lancs.
[2] Three small seals of red wax; (1) and (2) undeciphered, (3) a lion rampant.
[3] Two similar small seals of red wax; in a hexagon the letter I, flanked by sprigs of leaves.

make ponds (*stagn'*) on John's land to divert the course of the stream to the said dwellings called *lez Smithiez* as necessary for Thomas, paying yearly for this share and right, 2*s.* at Martinmas. Alternate seals. (*Ibid.*, No. 1).

178. March 8, 29 Henry VI [1450-1]. Appointment by John Langton, knt., of Robert Caldbeke, chaplain, and Thomas Nuby, *Gentilman*, as his attorneys to deliver seisin to John Langton, esq., his son and heir apparent, of all his woods and undergrowth called Farnley wodde, of or in the desmesne of Farnley, in accordance with his indenture to his son, dated March 8, 29 Henry VI. (*Ibid.*, No. 22).

179. June 6, 32 Henry VI [1454]. This present writyng beris wittenes that Sir John Langton knyght hafe latyn to ferme to John Langton his son and heir all his watyrr and smethystedys wyth all maner of turffe grast and easement belongyng to ye seid smythysteds of ye lordschip of Farneley, for ye terme of 9 yhers fully to be complet eftir dat of this present writyng, yhildyng yerfore yherely 3*s.* 4*d.* at the termes of martynmes and Whesonday be evyn porcions, also the seid Sir John hath latyn to ferme to ye seid John his son all his mynes of Iryn Ure wyth in the seid lordschip duryng ye forseid terme of 9 yher, yheldyng yerfore le dosan tale for evere dosan, and also the seid Sir John hafe graunt to ye seid John his son fre entre and isshwe wyth waynes, carts, horse and all othir maner of cariags that is nessesarie to ye seid John his son his debits, warkemen or assignes; and the seid Sir John for all maner of covenaunts abofe rehersyd sall waraunt and defend the seid John his son and his assignes agayns all maner of men. In wittenes wherof the seid Sir John hafe set to his seale. Writtyn at Farneley the vj day of June. In the yher of ye reigne of Kyng Henry sext eftir ye conquest of Ingeland xxxij te. (*Ibid.*,-No. 19).

180. July 5, 5 Edward IV [1465]. Indenture between John Langton, esq., and Robert Neville esq., whereby John Langton grants to Robert Neville a messuage and 2 bovates of land and meadow in Scoles in the vill of Clakheton in the tenure of John Smyth', senior; a messuage and 4 bovates of land and meadow in Scoles in the tenure of John Smyth', junior; a bovate of land and meadow in Clakheton held by William Broke; certain parcels of land and meadow called Bordeland in Clakheton and Scoles, namely, a close called le Halrode, a piece of land and meadow called les Flatz, a piece of meadow in le Chopeling, a piece of land called le Halgrene, 8 acres of land in Scoles called Midelholmes and a piece of land there called les Twentyrodes; the said John reserves to himself and his heirs 2 other parcels of Bordeland in Clakheton and Scoles, that is, a parcel of land lying in Hetonkarr and another parcel of meadow in le Newynge; saving also the small parcel of land adjoining le Halrode, as is said was once given by Langton's

ancestors to the use of the chaplains celebrating in the chapel of Clakheton; all of which are granted to Robert and his heirs in exchange for a messuage, croft and garden containing 21 acres of land and meadow in Farneley in the parish of Ledes, namely 11½ acres and a rood lying in le Chapelfeld, 5½ acres in le Morefeld, 3½ acres and a rood in le Westfeld; and for certain other closes in Farneley, namely, one called le Cliff, another called le Cliffynge, a third called Cecilrode, a fourth called Brakeleyjnge, and two others called Brakenlays; and for all the other tenements of Robert Neville in the tenure of John Caldbek in Farneley.

John Langton also grants free entry and exit to the said lands in Clakheton and Scoles and common of pasture, just as his ancestors and their tenants were wont to have. For these lands Robert Neville is to pay John 1*d.* at the Nativity for all exactions and demands; power to John to enter and distrain should the rent be in arrears. Alternate seals. Witnesses: John Hopton, Amer Burdhed, Richard Beaumont, esqs. (*Ibid.*, No. 29).

181. June 26, 21 Edward IV [1481]. Bond by James Haryngton, knt., to James Danby, knt., in the sum of 100*li.* sterling, to be paid to James Haryngton, his attorney, heirs or executors at the feast of St. Peter advincula next following. Sealing clause.[1]

Condicion of this obligacion is suche that if James Haryngton, knyght, stond abey and performn the ordynans and jugement of Thomas Mydilton, William Savile, John Dawnay, Thomas Langton, Gilberd Legh and Thomas Trigott, arbitors indefferently chosyn by the seid James Haryngton knyght, and the seid James Danby, knyght, of all maner of querels accions and debats and esspecalle of the right tityll and possession of the chauntre or chapelle of Farnlay and all therto belongyng now dependyng in vareance be twix the seid James Haryngton, knyght, on that one parte and James Danby, knyght, and Agnes, his wyfe, as in the right of the seid Agnes on the other parte, so that the seid ordynans and jugement of the seid arbitors be maid and gyfen in writyng indentid under the seales be for the fest of Saynt Michell the archaungell next after the date of this obligacion, and severally delyverd to the seid partes, and if the seid James Haryngton apon his parte wele and truly performn the seid ordynans and jugement that then this obligacion be woide, or els to stond in strengh and vertu. (*Ibid.*, No. 5).

182. July 12, 22 Edward IV [1482]. Grant by James Danby, knt., and Agnes, his wife, to John Kendall', Richard Danby, William Calverlay, junior, and Thomas Danby, all their manor of Farnlay, with all the lands and tenements, rents and services with appurtenances in Farnlay, Clakheton, Okynshagh, Scoles, Popelwell'

[1] Fragment of a seal of red wax on strip of parchment cut from the bottom of the deed.

and Wybsay, with all their other manors of Gargrave and Poterton with appurtenances in co. York; to hold to the grantees in perpetuity. Warranty. Appointment by James and Agnes of Henry Walker and Richard Uttyng as their attorneys to deliver seisin. Sealing clause.[1] (*Ibid.*, No. 13).

183. April 9, 8 Henry VII [1493]. Indenture whereby Sir James Danby, knt., grants to Ralph Evers, Geoffrey Frank, Thomas Langton, William Babthorp, Richard Danby, esqs., Thomas Danby and Brian Hardy clerk, all his lands, tenements, rents and services with appurtenances in Kirkby Massham, Swynton, Wardermarsk, Sutton, Ellyngton, Ellingstring, Heiley, Thornbargh, Firthby, Exilby, Scabbednewton, Little Lemyng, Scruton, Warlainthby, Thrintofte, Yafforth, Newbiging, two closes in Little Danby called Mashaw and Execlose, Overwhitwell and Nethrewhitwell in co. York, and also all his lands [*etc.*], in Great Langton, which lately belonged to Thomas Langton there; also all his lands [*etc.*] in Derlington, Little Staynton, Sudbury, Bicheburn, Mawemedowe, Brafferton, Shynkley, Olduressam in the bishopric of Durham; to hold all the aforesaid lands to the grantees, their heirs and assigns, in perpetuity. Warranty. Appointment of Christopher Aslakby, chaplain, John Gower, Christopher Doddisworth, Ralph Doddisworth, *gentilmen*, and William Metcalff of Thorp, *yoman* as attorneys to deliver seisin. Sealing clause. At Fernley. Witnesses: Thomas abbot of Cristel,[2] John Newil, knt., William Mirthfeld, William Calverley, Ralph Besedon, Henry Rokeby, esqs.[3] (*Ibid.*, No. 10).

184. Aug. 8, 22 Henry VII [1507]. Will in the form of an indenture of Dame Agnes widow of Sir James Danby, knt.

Whereas she has enfeoffed Sir Rauf Everes and others of all her manors and lands in Mowthrope, Lutton, Poterton and Gargrave, co. York, and of a close or pasture called the Hallfeld in the city of York, she now declares that, as the enfeoffment of certain lands[4] by her late husband for his sister Elizabeth Danby, 'and for the fyndyng of oure yonger childer and for the mariageis of our daghters,

[1] Fragments of 2 seals of red wax, on tongues cut from the bottom of the deed.

[2] Kirkstall.

[3] A deed annexed and of the same date, whereby, Sir James Danby sets out the uses to which the feoffees are to hold the lands, namely, that the profits are to be employed 'to the behaff of the mariage of my suster according to the will of my fathre and also for the mariage of myn owne daughters after the disceccion of me and my wife, and after the disces of me then by the discrecion of my wyfe, my son Cristofor and my said feffes'. If any of his daughters will not be guided by himself and his wife Agnes, they are not to benefit. After the provision of his daughters the feoffees shall make life-estates of lands, except the manor of Thorp which is his wife's jointure, to the value of 10 marks yearly to 'every and ych of my yonger sonnes'. The two deeds are joined by tongues for two seals, both of which are missing.

[4] See the preceding deed.

and for estate to be made for our yonger sonnes', does not provide speedily enough for the marriage of their daughters, her feoffees are to allow her son, Christopher, and her executors to take the issues and profits from the aforesaid lands to the more 'hasty speedyng' of the payment of the sums agreed by her husband for their said marriages; provided that Christopher and her executors pay 40*s*. each, yearly to their daughters Anne and Margaret until their marriage portions be paid; her son, Antony is also to have 3*li*. 6*s*. 8*d*. yearly after her death until the age of 22, or is advanced to some spiritual benefice of equivalent value, or to his 'fyndyng at the scoles or in oon universitie if he be so disposyd to go ther'. After the above payments have been secured and following her death, her younger sons are to receive 10 marks each to be taken from the issues of the said lands. Sealing clause.[1] (*Ibid.*, No. 11).

185. Oct. 16, 8 Henry VIII [1516]. Bill[2] witnessing that John Heron esq., treasurer of the King's chamber acknowledges that he has received to the use of the King from Christopher Danby, knt., by the hand of Roger Doddisworth, receiver of the manor of Ferneley, co. York, 100 marks in part payment of a greater sum of money due the preceding Michaelmas, by reason of a recovery of the manor of Ferneley, as appears in certain indentures between Thomas, Cardinal archbishop of York and John Heron of the one part and the said Sir Christopher of the other. Seal and sign manual of John Heron. (*Ibid.*, No. 26).

186. October 17, 12 Henry VIII [1520]. Indenture[3] between Dame Margerye Danby 'Wydow laite of Cristofre Danby Knyght' and Peter Merefelde, esq., touching 'theatre common' between the lordships of Ferneley and Tonge, whereby Peter grants to Dame Margery and her assigns the right, during her life, to sever and enclose to her own use the lordship of Ferneley from the lordship of Tonge, with hedges and ditches, and to keep and defend it from the lordship of Tonge, as agreed between her late husband and the said Peter. Similarly Dame Margery grants to Peter the right to enclose the lordship of Tonge.

Peter also grants that Dame Margery may when necessary make and bynde in uppon the grounde and soyll of the said Petre a damstede to the use of her Smythyes or oderwyse' and to take earth upon the ground of Peter to the use of the said dam. Dame Margery similarly grants to Peter the right to make a dam upon her ground. If either of the parties shall make such a dam a payment of 2*d*. yearly is to be made to the other at the Nativity of St. John the Baptist; and should either party buy ore, stone or other

[1] Large blob of red wax, blurred.

[2] On paper, possibly a draft or copy, as there is no indication of seal or signature.

[3] In English.

'caryagez' the other shall allow the said carriages free ingress and egress, keeping the highway. Both parties are bound to the maintenance of this indenture in the sum of £100. Alternate seals.[1] (*Ibid.*, No. 30).

187. May 20, 18 Henry VIII [1526]. Indenture between Christopher Danby, esq., son and heir of Sir Christopher Danby, knt., deceased, of the one party, and Peter Merfeld, esq., of the other party, being in the form of an award made by Sir Richard Tempest, Sir Robert Nevyll, knt., John Lacy and Rawf Hopton, esqs., as a result of 'divers variances, tresspasses, debats, chalenges, clames and demands' concerning the right title and possession of common pasture for themselves and their tenants in Fernelay and Tong, 'as well of the Est part of oon beke or brooke callyd Rynghaybeke as also of the West part of the same Rynghaybeke, which beke is a dyvysyon and lymet or bownd betwyx the lordships of Fernelay and Tong.'

The two parties bind themselves in the sum of £100 to abide by the award of the said arbitrators, namely, they shall be 'full luffers and frendes for every cause or matter . . . amongest them befor the daite of these presentes', and Christopher Danby, his heirs and assigns shall occupy the common pasture in Fernelay on the 'Estsyd' of Ringhaybeke for the term of 80 years next following without hindrance from Peter Merfeld, his heirs or assigns; and shall 'attach, beyld, make and festyn . . . the dame for to kepe the watter of the same beke conveniently necessarie to serve for his smythies', during the said term. He shall also keep in repair his part of the fence between the two lordships as did his father Sir Christopher, and as his mother, Dame Marjory does at the time of these presents.

For his part, Peter Merfeld and his heirs and assigns shall have the pasture on the west side of the beck for the term of 80 years, and he shall build and fasten 'dames for to kepe the watter of the same beke conveniently and necessarie for to serve his myls beyldyd and to be beyldyd ther' during the said term; he shall also maintain his part of the fence, as he does at the present time.

Christopher Danby promises, before the feast of St. John the Baptist next to release all his right in the title of the lordship of Tong. Sealed[2] with both the seals of the parties and the arbitrators. (*Ibid.*, No. 9).

188. Sept. 5, 5 and 6 Philip and Mary [1558]. Indenture whereby Christopher Danby of New Parke in Masshamshire, co. York, in consideration of the son's portion which Marmaduke, one of his younger sons claims from his goods and chattels after his death, grants to the said Marmaduke, for the term of his life, a

[1] Small blob of red wax on tongue cut from bottom of deed.

[2] Tongues for 5 seals only; on 1, 2, 3, 5 blobs of red wax.

tenement in Ferneley held by John Smythe, of a yearly value of 14*s*. 7*d*., another tenement held by Christopher Watson, value, 16*s*. 3*d*., another held by John Ferneley, value 20*s*., another in the tenure of Richard Pekersgill, value 20*s*., another held by William Hill, value 56*s*. 8*d*. which includes a water mill, another held by Robert Otes, value 21*s*. 10*d*., another held by John Casson, value 8*s*., making a yearly total of 7*li*. 17*s*. 4*d*., and also a annual rent of 42*s*. 8*d*. from a close in Ferneley called le New Close; all on condition that the said lands shall revert to the heirs of the grantor if Marmaduke should claim by action in any court a son's portion of his goods and chattels. Alternate seals.[1] (*Ibid*., No. 31).

189. Sept. 5, 5 and 6 Philip and Mary [1558]. Indenture whereby Christopher Danby of Newparke in Massamshire, co. York, in consideration of the son's portion which James, one of his younger sons claims from his goods and chattels after his death, grants to the said James a tenement in Ferneley of the yearly value of 29*s*. 5*d*., and now held by William Crake; another tenement there in the tenure of William Chapman, value, 48*s*. 6*d*.; another held by John Walker and worth 28*s*. 7*d*.; another held by William Wodds of the value of 21*s*.; another in the tenure of Henry Saxton, value, 19*s*. 9*d*.; another held by Christopher [*document stained*], worth 43*s*. 10*d*.; and another held by John Otes, value 9*s*., making a yearly total of 10*li*., all on condition that the heirs of the said Christopher may recover the same should James claim any son's portion after his death. Appointment of Ralph Beckwith and William Ediyngton as his attorneys. Alternate seals.[2] (*Ibid*., No. 24).

190. Sept. 27, 30 Elizabeth [1588]. Indenture[3] whereby Sir Thomas Danby of Farnley, knt., in consideration of a sum of money, has let to farm to Christopher Roodes of the same, husbandman, a tenement 'buylded' with all the closes, meadows, pastures, arable lands and commons, in Farneley, lately in the occupation of William Wynn, for the term of 21 years at 20*s*. a year. Christopher Roodes is to maintain and keep the buildings in repair 'great tymber onely exceptyd' which is to be found by Sir Thomas and his heirs; also to perform such services as rendered by Sir Thomas's other tenants in Farneley, and be 'chargyd withall for any such lyke rent or farmynge there' during the said term. Warranty.[4] (*Ibid*., No. 18).

191. March 10, 39 Elizabeth [1597-8]. Replication[5] of Christopher Wythes maintaining the sufficiency of the statements made in his previous Bill, and that the defendant, John Wood's

[1] Seal missing, signed Xp̄ofer Danby K.

[2] Seal missing, signed, Xp̄ofer Danby K.

[3] In English.

[4] Tongue for seal below the mark of Christopher Roode. Dorso: 'Scalyd' in the presence of Thomas Colyer, William Walker and James Sykes.

[5] In English: paper copy in an 18th c. hand.

answer is insufficient, more especially as he, the complainant does not aver that he could have presented anything at the 'Weapontack' Court nor show that any offence 'inquirable' in that court was committed at Farneley; he maintains that the defendant wrongfully distrained the ox mentioned in the said Bill, in Moor Close, that the ox was the property of the complainant and not of Stephen Wythes, nor is it material that Stephen Wise [*sic*] was constable of the town of Farneley; the constable of Farneley and 4 of the inhabitants have been used from time without mind to appear at the sheriffs' tourn held yearly at Morley to present a new constable for Her Majesty's service, but there has been from time out of mind a court leet held twice yearly at Farneley, namely, within one month after Easter and one month after Michaelmas, to which all offences committed within the manor, have been presented and the amercements levied, and that no presentments were made to any court at Morley.[1] (*Ibid.*, No. 27).

192. June 16, 1629. Deed[2] whereby Hector Danbye of Earnwood Lodge in the parish of Kynlett, co. Salop, gent., in consideration of the sum of £10 paid to him, assigns to Ralph [*sic*] Richards of Oxford, gent., an annuity of £4 granted to the said Hector for the term of his life by Sir Christopher Danby, knt., deceased, issuing out of Farnley Park, which grant bears the date August 28, 4 and 5 Philip and Mary [1557]. The annuity to be paid to Raph in equally portions at Martinmas and Whitsuntide during the rest of Hector Danby's life.[3] (*Ibid.*, No. 28).

193. Sept. 29, 1649. Indenture[4] whereby Sir Thomas Danby of Farnley, knt., sells to John Labley and Richard Labley of Pudsey, clothiers, for the sum of £25 13s., all that parcel of land lately enclosed from the commons of Farnley called Pine Welliehill, which abuts on the land of Sir Thomas on the east, on the way between Farnley and Tonge on the south, Farnley beck on the west and the lands of William Walker on the north, and which is in Farnley and in the occupation of the said John and Richard Labley. Warranty.[5] (*Ibid.*, No. 14).

[1] Dorso; Since this cause there is a Grant from K. James 1st to establish the Rights of holding Court leet in Farneley to my Great Grandfather Christofer Danby, the Coppy of which my son has in his Custody, 10 July, 1715. Patent 18 James, pt. 14, No. 13.

[2] In English.

[3] Dorso: Sealed and delivered in the presence of Will: Richards, William Danbye, William Walker. In a later hand, 'Mr. Hector Danby of Earnwood Lodge in Kinlitt Parish in ye County of Salop, ye Assign of his Annuity of 4*li*. a year out of Farneley Parke by which it hereby appears he held this Annuity 71 years.

[4] In English.

[5] Two blobs of red wax, adjoining the marks of John and Richard Labley. Dorso: 'Sealled, signed and delivered in the presence of Christopher Hofton, John Barker, Thomas Walker Kytchin.

Farnley (Otley).

194. Annunciation of the B.V.M., 24 Edward son of Henry [March 25, 1296]. Grant by Thomas son of Alan de la More of Ferneley and Agnes, his wife, to Constance de Essold and Beatrice, her daughter, of a messuage and 40 acres of land and 4 acres of meadow and 2 acres of wood with appurtenances in the vill of Ferneley, in a place called Elstanbothem, which Adam de Elstanbothem once held; to hold to Constance and Beatrice, their heirs and assigns, freely [*etc.*] paying yearly to William Faukes of Newall, the chief lord of the fee, 4*s.* for all secular services, exactions and demands. Warranty. Sealing clause[1]. Witnesses: Walter de Middelton, William son of Henry de Ferneley, Robert Gayfayr, Robert de Fosse, William Malebranche, Thomas de Northwode, William Faukes of Newall, William de Otteley, clerk. At Ferneley. (*Farnley Hall Muniments*, No. 80).

195. Grant by Jordon son of Robert de Farnelay to Alice, daughter of William son of Beatrice de Farnelay, and her lawfully begotten heirs, of all the land and buildings thereon which he bought from Peter son of Walter, the priest (*sacerdotis*) of Farnelay, with the meadow which William *le pinder* once held, lying in the vill and territory of Farneley; to hold to Alice, freely with all liberties and easements within and without the vill, paying yearly to the lord of the fee or his attorney 2*s.* 3*d.* in equal portions at Martinmas and Whitsuntide. Warranty. Reversion to the grantor in default of issue. Sealing clause.[2] Witnesses: Fulk de Lindeley, Henry de Scoteni, William son of Henry de Farnelay, Henry son of Ralph of the same, Thomas de . . .[3] ede, Adam de Elstanboem, Walter the clerk of Ottelay. (*Ibid.*, No. 81).

196. Grant by Alan de Farnely to William de Lindelaya and his heirs, in return for 4*s.* of silver, payed to him by William, of 3 perches of land and appurtenances in the territory of Farneley, which lie adjacent to the land of Thomas son of Orp' on the east and abut above Fricfal; to hold to William and his heirs, paying to the grantor a silver halfpenny at Whitsuntide for all secular services. Warranty. Witnesses: Hugh de Lelay, William Vauasore, William de Castel', Henry de Weschoic, Thomas Hurscheci, Roger de Hunby. (*Ibid.*, No. 82).

197. Grant, sale and quitclaim by John de Rude to William de Lindelay of 4 acres of land with appurtenances in the territory of Farnelay, namely, 2 acres and a half in Rude adjoining the land which belonged to Hugh the dispenser (*dispensatori*) on the west,

[1] Tongues for two seals, on the second a small oval seal of white wax; the Agnus Dei.

[2] Seal of white wax; a star-shaped device; . . . ORD . . . ROBE

[3] Document torn.

and 1½ acres in Calfal near the road; to hold to William, his heirs, freely and in peace, with all liberties and easements, paying to the grantor and his heirs 2*d.* yearly in equal portions at Whitsuntide and Martinmas, for all services. For this grant William gave 2*s.* of silver. Warranty. Sealing clause.[1] Witnesses: Nicholas Ward, William Vauasore, Hugh son of Hugh de Lelay, William de Castel', Henry de Weschoc, Alan de Farnel', Thomas of the same, Robert le Scot, Thomas Hurchesci. (*Ibid.*, No. 83).

198. Grant by Richer son of Adam de Wassand and Margaret, his wife, daughter of Richard de Monte alto, to Fulk de Wakefeud, butler of the lord archbishop of York, of all the land which belonged to . . .[2] son of Ingrith de Farnelay, and half of all the lordship with the land and the meadow of Fernelay, and all the land which Richard de Monte alto, ancestor of . . . Hallecroft near Neuhalle, also half an annual rent of 2 marks sterling received jointly from all the tenants of . . . of Fernelay at the two appointed terms, with half the homages, services, wards, reliefs and escheats of all the said tenants and with all other liberties and easements and increments pertaining to the lands, just as enjoyed by the grantors, without reservation; to hold to the said Fulk, his heirs and assigns freely and in peace, paying yearly to the grantors 1*d.* at the Nativity for all services. For this grant Fulk has given to the grantors 40*li.* sterling. Warranty. Sealing clause. Witnesses: Sir Robert de Ripers, steward of the lord [archbishop] of York, Sirs Mauger le Uauasur and Gilbert Berneuall', Sir Simon Ward and William, his brother, William de Plumton, Matthew de Bram, Thomas de Screwing, John de Caylly, Robert de Pouel, William de Beaugrant, William le Scot, Benedict de Rolleston, William Malleuerer, Walter de Hautlay, William de Middelton, William de Alwaldelay, Ralph de Arthington, Gilbert and Elias de . . . William de Lindel'. (*Ibid.*, No. 84).

199. Indenture whereby Walter de Scoteny and Alice, his wife, grant to Fulk de Farnley [*sic*], his heirs and assigns, in perpetuity, their mill of Farnley [*a word erased here*] with the site and with suit both from Farnley and Lindel', with all appurtenances, in return for 20*s.* in equal portions at Whitsuntide and Martinmas; they shall also receive from the tenants of the said Fulk yearly as rent due, 13*s.* 10*d.*, with an indenture of services, escheats, suit of court, homage, reliefs, wardships and all other necessities pertaining to the whole of all that half of the fee of Farnley which he bought from Nicholas de Wassand and Margaret, his wife; to hold to the said Fulk and his heirs, of the grantor and his heirs, quietly, freely and in perpetuity. The said Walter and Alice shall have of the demesne

[1] Oval seal of green wax, 1 x 1¼ in.; a star-shaped device; ✠ SIGILL' IOHIS DE RVDE

[2] Holes in document.

land of the said Fulk de Farnley, 9 acres and a rood of land for the remainder of the said rent of 6*s.* 2*d.*, namely, in the fields of Farnley 3 acres, in Hekelgarth 3 acres, in Forneby 3 acres, and the residue towards the water of the Werf; they shall also grind sufficient corn for the house of Farnley [*word erased*] at the said mill, empty vessels (*vacuo vase*), except for the corn of the said Fulk and his heirs. And Fulk shall pay yearly to the lord of Lindel' 12*d.* for the rent of the mill and pond, and he and his heirs may take from the woods of Farnley whatever is necessary for the maintenance and repair of the said mill and pond, without contradiction from the grantor and his heirs; he may also move the site of the mill to whatever place seems desirable to him, without contradiction or calumny from the grantor. They also grant to the said Fulk [*words erased*] in Hallecroft near Neuale with appurtenances for 4 acres of land in the fields of Farnley lying in Colebrandcrot and Leuetof. The grantors may distrain on the said tenants of Fulk if necessary. Warranty. Alternate seals. Witnesses: Richard de Luterington, Mauger Vauasor, William Ward, Ralph Maunsel, Michael de Hek, Oliver de Ottelay, William de Lindely, Thomas de Farnley, William de Middelton. (*Ibid.*, No. 85).

200. Grant and quitclaim by Matilda, widow of William de Scotteni in Farnelay, and Richard, son of the said William, to Fulk son of William de Lindelay, of all the land and tenements with meadows and with lordships, homages, rents, services, wards, reliefs, escheats, commons, profits, suits of courts, liberties and easements with all other appurtenances in woods and plains, which lands and tenements Fulk *le botiler* of Wakefeld bought from Sir Richard de Wassand and Margaret, his wife, and gave to William de Lindelay, Alice, his wife, and Fulk, their son, in the vill and territory of Farnelay; by this charter Matilda and Richard acknowledge Fulk's right to the lands and quitclaim the same without reservation. Warranty. Sealing clause. Witnesses: Sir Simon Ward, Sir Mauger le Wauasur, Sir Henry de Hertlington, Walter de Middelton, William son of Henry de Farnelay, William de Castelay, William Faukes, William, junior, de Castelay, Simon son of Jordon de Farnelay, Simon called Godbarn of the same, Paul del Grene, Henry son of John, William the clerk of Farnely. (*Ibid.*, No. 86).

201. Grant[1] by Thomas de Mulso and Maud, his wife, to Sir Ralph de Wyginton and Sir Geoffrey de Wyginton, his brother, of their manor of Farnley in Werfdale, with appurtenances and with all the lordship in lands, meadows, pastures, agistments, woods, moors, turberies, waters, fishings, wastes, great and small (*mygne and maerle*) also the reversion of a messuage and land and rent which Henry de Northwode holds of the grantors and with all other reversions which they have in the said vill, together with the homage,

[1] In French.

suit and services of Fulk de Lyndelay, William de Farnelaye, John Malebrank, Robert de Fosse, William le Cleerk, Simon Godebarn, Paul del Grene, Jordon son of Robert, William de la More and Agnes, his wife, Agnes wife of Geoffrey, John de Yukflet, Thomas de Northwode, Robert son of Hugh, Henry son of John, Henry Cournays, Henry de Northwode, John le Sauser, Robert Gaffair, John Colstan, Richard Ketel of Ottelay, Henry Bonefaunt, William son of Ellis, Isaac the shoemaker (*suour*), Ellis the tanner, Hugh le Kew, Thomas, Thomas le Couper, Robert the carpenter, Richard Pertrik, Adam le Scoler, William Faukes of Newal, William son of Paul, with the services of all other free tenants and bond tenants who hold of the grantors in Farnelaye, Newal and Snawdon;[1] to hold to the grantees, freely, quietly, of the chief lords of the fee. Warranty. Sealing clause. Witnesses: Sir Richard de Goldesbourgh, Sir Mauger le Vauasor, Sir Robert de Plumton, knts., Fulk de Lyndelay, William de Castelay, Walter de Burlay, William son of Henry de Farnelaye, William Faukes of Newal, Richard de Skytheby. (*Ibid.*, No. 87).

202. Grant by Simon de Snaudon' with the agreement of Simon, his son and heir, to William de Lindelaya, his heirs and assigns, of 4 acres of land with appurtenances in the territory of Farnelay, namely 2 acres in Alueridinges on the west which abut above the land of the said William, and one acre in . . .[2] adjoining the land of Thomas son of Thomas de Farnelay on the east, and half an acre which abuts on Brademire and Cringelmire with the adjacent meadows, and half an acre next to Mapellessic with the adjoining meadow; to hold to William, his heirs and assigns, in fee and hereditarily with all liberties and easements, paying yearly to the grantor and his heirs 1d. at the Nativity for the payment (*ad oblacionem*) for all secular services, exactions and demands. For this grant William gave a silver mark to the grantor in his great need. Warranty by the grantor on all his lands in Farnley. Witnesses: Sir William de Wichington', Hugh de Lelay, William Vauasore, Nicholas Ward, Richard de Muhaut, Paul, bailiff of Ottelay, Henry de Weschoc, William Castel, Robert Scotto, Alan de Farnely, Thomas of the same, Thomas Hurchesci, Stephen de Farnelay. (*Ibid.*, No. 88).

203. Grant by Juliana, daughter of William son of Paul de Ottelay, and Alice, her sister, to William Faukes, of an annual rent of 4*d*. from an acre of land called Simoncroft in the territory of Farnelay, with all payments received from the same tenement from Gilbert son of Paul de Fernelay, they also grant an annual rent of 7*d*. from an acre of land and meadow in a place called le Storthes in the field of Ottelay, from Matilda, daughter of Alan the

[1] Snowdon, parish of Weston.
[2] Document stained.

forester; also a rent of *2d.* with appurtenances from half an acre of meadow in Migelay from Isaac the cobbler (*sutoris*); to hold to William, his heirs and assigns, freely. Warranty. Sealing clause. Witnesses: Walter de Midelton, Henry Bonenfaunt of Ottelay, Paul Ketyl, Nicholas de Aberford, William son of Henry de Ferneley, Robert de Fosse, William Malebranche of Farnelay, Robert the clerk of Ottelay. (*Ibid.*, No. 89).

204. Tuesday before St. Michael the Archangel, 15 Edward III [Sept. 25, 1341]. Grant by Robert Brok to Thomas de Disseford, *trumpour*, Robert, his son, and the lawfully begotten heirs of the said Robert, of a messuage called Horrokstanes and all the land and meadow which Robert de Fosse once held in the vill of Farnelay; to hold freely and in peace, of the chief lords of the fee; should Robert die without lawful issue remainder to 1) Margaret, his sister and her lawfully begotten heirs, 2) Alice, his sister and her lawfully begotten heirs, 3) to Thomas de Disseford and his heirs in perpetuity. Sealing clause. Witnesses: William de Monte alto, James, his brother, John de Wyginton, Robert de Meyelay, Richard Faukes. At Farnelay. (*Ibid.*, No. 90).

205. Saturday, St. Wilfrid [Oct. 12], 1357. Quitclaim by John de Castelay to John de Wyginton, of all right in all the lands and tenements, demesne lordships, woods, mills, grazings, pastures, reversions and services in the vill and territory of Farneley, to hold with all appurtenances to John de Wyginton. Warranty. Sealing clause.[1] Witnesses: William de Lyndelay, William de Kirkeby, William le Uauasor, Thomas de Marton, Richard Faukes, William son of Paul, Adam del Brotes of the same. At Farnley. (*Ibid.*, No. 91).

206. Friday before the Nativity of Our Lady [Sept. 6], 1359. Grant[2] by John de Wyginton to Richard Bonenfant, chaplain, and Richard Barker of Ottelay, chaplain, of his manor of Farnelay in Wherfdale with seisin of all the lands, tenements, rents, services of free tenants, woods, pastures and all other appurtenances which the grantor has by purchase or hereditary right, and with all his lands [*etc.*], which he has in Newall, Asquith, Denton and Castelay; to hold to Richard and Richard, their heirs and assigns, freely and in peace, of the chief lords of the fee. Warranty. Sealing clause.[3] Witnesses: Thomas de Marton, Thomas de Bradelay, William de Kirkeby, Edmund de Wykelay, Richard Faukes, William del Grene of Farnelay, Simon, his brother. At Farnelay. (*Ibid.*, No. 92).

[1] There is no evidence that the document was sealed.

[2] In French.

[3] Seal of red wax, diam 1 in.; in a decorative border a shield of arms, a mascle; SIG . . . M IOHIS DE WYGINTON

Filey.

207. May 17, 12 Edward IV [1472]. Indenture whereby John Thomson son of Alice Lyncolum of Whitby grants to William Foster of Fyuelay, *yoman*, a messuage with an acre of land lying in le Bailycroft, which messuage extends between le Hewynlane on the east and the land of Brian Constabyll of Fyrsmarst on the west and the highway on the north as far as le Hewyngarth on the south; to hold the said messuage and acre with appurtenances, also a bovate of land lying in the field of Fyuelay between the land of John Sainctquinctyn on the east and the land of William Bekwit on the west, to the said William Foster, his heirs and assigns, from Whitsuntide, 12 Edward IV, for the term of 40 years next following, paying yearly to the grantor and his heirs 2*d*. at Martinmas and Whitsuntide in equal portions. William to maintain the lands during the term and yield them up in good repair. Warranty. Alternate seals. Witnesses: Dom. Robert Geffreson, chaplain, Dom. Christopher Tow, vicar of Muston, Thomas Humber, Robert Foston, Richard Kolyng. At Fyuelay. (*E. Stanley Jones*, No. 4).

208. April 10, 14 Edward IV [1474]. Grant by John Thomson, son of Alice Lincoln of Whitby to William Foster and Isabel, his wife, of a messuage in Fyuelay, a bovate and an acre of land [*as described in the preceding deed*]; to hold to William and Isabel, of the chief lords of the fee. Warranty. Sealing clause. Witnesses: Dom. Robert Gefrason, Dom. Thomas Snayth, chaplains, John Tarthom, William Mawe, Richard Kolynge. At Fyueley. (*Ibid*., No. 5).

Follifoot.

209. Grant by Hugh son of Apolitus to Robert son of Hukkeman de Plomton, for his homage and service, of 2 bovates of land with appurtenances in Folifait, namely, those which Philip de Buuinton holds of him; he also grants all that part of his meadow of Cracwad adjoining, of his fee of Folifait, and an acre of meadow which lies next to Prestheng to the north towards Crepel; he also grants in addition to the 2 bovates aforesaid, a toft with a croft which belonged to Hugh Lainde; to hold to Robert, his heirs of the grantor and his heirs in perpetuity in fee and hereditarily, freely and in peace, in woods, plains, meadows, pastures, ways, moors and marshes, with all liberties and easements pertaining to the 2 bovates, within the vill and without, paying yearly to the grantor 6*d*. at Michaelmas for all services, and performing the forinsec services pertaining to 2 bovates of land where 14 carucates make a knight's fee. Warranty. Sealing clause[1]. Witnesses: Nigel de Plumton[2].

[1] Seal of green wax; diam. 1¼ in.; an animal, blurred; ✠ SIGILL . . . GONIS FIL APOL . . .

[2] As Nigel de Plumpton was dead in 1213-14, the date of this deed would be late twelfth or early thirteenth century.

William de Stiueton, bailiff of the wapentake, Mauger Vauasore, Robert de Wiuelestorp, Richard de Godelsburg, Hugh de Lelay, Gilbert the larderer (*lardin'*), John de Plumtom, Robert de Linton, Thomas de Walton, Henry de Screuin, Robert de Munketon, Robert son of Swain, Robert son of Henry.[1] (*Y.A.S.*, Md. 59/18, No. 2).

Foulby.

210. Grant by Geoffrey Spauald to Robert his son, junior, of annual rent of 8*d.* received from Robert Robilard of Foleby in equal portions at Whitsuntide and Martinmas for a toft, croft and an acre of land in Foleby of the fee of Mauger Vauasur; to hold to Robert, his heirs or to whomsoever he may wish to sell, give or assign it. Warranty. Sealing clause. Witnesses: William de Thoneton, William Maydenfote, William the baker (*pistore*), William Stubber of Scarueston, Henry Palfryman, Ralph Snart, Alexander de Sartrino. (*Serlby Hall Muniments*, No. 17).

Ganton.

211. Penultimate day of July, 1367. Indenture. To all sons of Holy Mother Church to whom these present letters shall come, John, by divine permission, archbishop of York,[2] primate of England and legate of the Apostolic See, greeting. Since a dispute had arisen between the prior and convent of the priory of Bridlyngton of the order of St. Augustine, who hold the parish church of Galmeton, of the one part, and Dom. John de Oustwyk, perpetual vicar of Galmeton, of the other, the said parties submitted themselves to the decree of the archbishop, who having ascertained what the said prior and convent and the said vicar were accustomed to receive, ordained that the prior and convent should take as they had always done from that time when the memory of man knoweth not to the contrary, two parts of the tithes of corn, hay, lambs and wool and two parts of the mortuary fees of those living who belong to the said church; and the said John and his successors shall take as their right as they have hitherto, a third part of the tithes of corn, hay, lambs and wool and of the mortuary fees of the living of the whole parish, also the whole tithes of all crofts and all other rents and perquisites belonging to the said church and altarage; as to the charges to the said church, the prior and convent shall support and provide two parts of the extraordinary burdens and two parts of the repair of the chancel of the said church and of the books and ornaments; all the other ordinary burdens falling on the church and a third part of all extraordinary burdens and repair of the chancel, books and ornaments shall be suffered by the vicar; and because the said prior and convent have from ancient times exonerated the vicars of the church from the payment of thraves of the Blessed

[1] A number of Follifoot deeds also from this collection were printed in *Yorks. Deeds*, vols. 4 and 5.

[2] John Thoresby.

John of Beverley, the same vicars in recompense are held to pay a certain yearly pension of 4*s.* at the Nativity to the same religious or their official procurator at Galmeton in accordance with an agreement anciently made in this connection. The archbishop therefore ordains that the said prior and convent shall exonerate the said John de Oustwyk and his successors from the payment of the thraves for ever, and the vicar and his successors shall pay the annual pension of 4*s.*, and if the said pension should be in arrears in part or whole for 40 days the said vicar shall pay 40*d.* sterling for each occasion on which he fails to make payment, to the fabric of the cathedral church of St. Peter of York. In witness of which he has caused these present letters to be written by John de Scardeburgh, notary public, his scribe, and to be signed with John's sign and subscription, and to be strengthened by the attachment of his own seal.[1]

I, John de Scardeburgh,[2] clerk of the diocese of York, by apostolic authority notary public and scribe, in this matter, of the venerable father and lord John, by the grace of God, archbishop of York, primate of England and legate of the apostolic see, was present together with the venerable and discreet Masters John de Irford, chancellor of the said reverend father, Nicholas de Burton, canon of the chapel of the Blessed Mary and Holy Angels, York, John Beaupyne, notary public and others, at the submission of the said parties, and saw and heard all these matters performed and by the order of the archbishop have written them in this public form and signed them with name and sign as requested. (*H. Wrigley, Esq.*, No. 1).

212. March 10, 1386[-7], 10 Richard II. Release and quitclaim by Henry de Acclom, son of William de Acclom, William de Harum, Walter de Boynton, John de Wylton, clerks, John de Kendale, Thomas Caluehird, chaplains, Peter Cock and Robert Bacon to Mary, widow of William Percehay, knt., of all right in all that messuage and 3 bovates of land, 7½ acres of meadow with appurtenances which they lately had of the gift and feoffment of the said Mary, in the vill and territory of Galmeton in Hertfordlyth. Warranty. Sealing clause.[3] Witnesses: John de Aske, John de Lokton, Thomas Thurkill, Thomas Barry, John de Newland. At Galmeton. (*Ibid.*, No. 2).

213. Oct. 8, 16 Richard II [1392]. Indenture whereby Elizabeth, widow of Thomas Barry grants to Mag. Thomas Walworth, canon of the cathedral church of Blessed Peter of York,

[1] Fragment of the seal of John de Thoresby in dark green wax.

[2] An elaborate notarial mark.

[3] Tongues for five seals; (1) yellow wax, diam. ½ in.; beneath a crown and between two sprays of leaves, the letter I; (2) fragment of red wax; (3) very small seal, beneath a crown the letters IG; (4) red wax, the letter I; (5) pink wax, diam. ⅞ in., a floral device, legend undeciphered.

Robert de Acclom and Margaret, his wife, all her manors of Bossall, Galmeton, Stanton with all demesnes and appurtenances and all messuages, lands, tenements, meadows, mill ponds, with all reversions and with the services of free tenants, villeins and their sequel, and with the reversions of all her tenants in Bossal, Galmeton, Staxton, Barneby, Claxton, Willardby, Shirburn in Hauerfordlyth and a turbary in the marsh of Brumpton in Hauerfordlyth, and 3 acres of meadow in a place called Gormyre in Pikeryngl yth with appurtenances, all of which belonged to Robert de Bossall, her father. She further grants all those lands and tenements, rents and services with the reversions of free tenants, villeins and their sequel which formerly belonged to Thomas de Acclom, once her husband, and of which she and the said Thomas were jointly enfeoffed, in Galmeton. She also grants all those lands and tenements, rents and services in the vills of Foxholes, Neuton in Whitbystrand together with all her other lands and tenements in co. York and in Ryseby, co. Lincoln which she holds as dower after the death of the said Thomas Acclom; to hold to the grantees and the lawfully begotten heirs of Robert and Margaret for the term of the grantor's life, of the chief lords of the fee, and paying to her 40 marks sterling yearly at the four terms, namely, Palm Sunday, the Nativity of St. John the Baptist, Michaelmas and the Nativity, in equal portions; should the rent be in arrears wholly or in part for 40 days power to Elizabeth to distrain on all the said manors, messuages [*etc.*], until satisfaction is obtained; should the rent be in arrears for so long as 13 weeks power to enter and retain. Should Robert and Margaret die without lawful issue it shall be lawful for Elizabeth in her lifetime, and the heirs of Robert after her death, to enter and retain all the said lands in perpetuity, this present charter notwithstanding. Warranty. Alternate seals.[1] Witnesses: John de Ask, Thomas Thurkill, Adam de Bekwyth, John Lascy, Robert Bret, Peter de Appilton, clerk. At Galmeton.[2] (*Ibid.*, No. 3).

214. Easterday [April 7], 1409. Grant by Robert de Acclom of Gaunton to Thomas Haxsay, Robert Wolden, Richard Blackburn, John Munkgate and John de Langtoft, clerks, of all his goods and chattels, as well living as dead, of all kinds and wheresoever found, together with all and singular debts owed to him; in such a manner that the grantees, their executors and assigns, may give, bequeathe, sell or assign all the said goods, chattels and debts without impediment from the grantor. Sealing clause.[3] Witnesses: William Wandesford, Thomas Ward, William de Skelton. (*Ibid.*, No. 4).

[1] Fragment of an oval red seal, a stag leaping up to a tree; legend undeciphered.

[2] Endorsed in a later hand: Eliz. ye wyffe of Thomas Barry and sometyme wyffe to Thomas Acclum to Mr. Thomas Walworth cannon of York Robert Aclam and Margaret uxor eius.

[3] Seal of red wax, diam. ½ in.; two birds facing, a sprig of leaves between them; S. Roberti Acclom.

215. Aug. 14, 1409, 10 Henry IV. Quitclaim by Thomas Walleworth, canon of the cathedral church of Blessed Peter of York, to Thomas de Garton, Richard Blakburn, Nicholas Holme, John Munkgate, clerks, William Hemyngburgh, John de Garton, John Crome, chaplain, and John de Langtoft, chaplain, their heirs and assigns, of all right and claim which he has in the manors of Galneton in Hauerfordlyth, Neuton in Whitbystronde, Foxholes in the wapentake of Dykeryng and in Parva Ryseby in co. Lincoln, with all their demesnes and appurtenances, and in all the messuages, lands and tenements, with all services of free tenants, villeins and their offspring, and with all appurtenances in the said vills. He renounces all claim for himself and his heirs. Sealing clause.[1] Witnesses: Henry Wyman' mayor of York, John de Moreton, Robert Gaunt, sheriffs, John de Braythwayt, Robert de Talkan, Robert de Howom, Thomas de Horneby, Peter de Appilton, clerk, citizens of York. (*Ibid.*, No. 5).

216. Jan. 3, 35 Henry VI [1456-7]. Indenture by Guy Rouclif, William Houthorp, Richard Banks of Quixley and Peter Banks. Recites that whereas John Cuke, vicar of Gaunton and Thomas Cuke of Willardby demised and quitclaimed to the said Guy, William and Richard, Peter, and to Robert Willesthorp, son and heir of William Willesthorp, esq., and to George Willesthorp and John Coke of Brompton, now deceased, their manors of Gaunton, Foxholes and Stanton with appurtenances and all their lands and tenements in Willardby and Shirburn with 3 acres of meadow in le Gormyre with all appurtenances which they lately had of the gift and feoffment of the said Robert Willesthorp; to hold to the said Guy, William [*etc.*], for the term of their lives with remainder to the right heirs of Robert Willesthorp; now the said Guy, William, Richard and Peter release and quitclaim to the said Robert Willesthorp, his heirs and assigns, all right in the said premises. Sealing clause.[2] (*Ibid.*, No. 6).

Gilling (Ryedale).

217. 14 Kalends March [Feb. 16], 1320[-21]. Grant by Elizabeth, widow of John de Butterwik, for the health of the soul of the said John, to Peter Absolon of Calueton, of 3 acres of wood in the marsh of Gilling' called Gilling ker, which lie at the head of the cultivated land belonging to the said Peter and are called Sywardholme, towards the north, and which the grantor knew to have been wrongly acquired by a plea of novel disseisin brought against Peter by Thomas de Butterwik, and for which reason a

[1] Broken seal of red wax, diam. 1 in., within a cusped border a shield of arms, pendant from two branches; a bend raguly between two objects not deciphered; . . . WALLWOR . . .

[2] Tongues for four seals, on the fourth a fragment of red wax bearing a crowned head.

feoffment was made to him by the said John concerning all their lands and tenements in Gilling for the term of the life of the said Thomas, which lands and tenements the said Thomas after the death of John gave up, freely and of his own will to the grantor, without reservation; to hold the said 3 acres to Peter, his heirs and assigns, of the chief lords of the fee, as previously held by him. Sealing clause. Witnesses: William de Sproxton, William de Thorton, Ralph de Kyerketon, William Ward, William his son, John de Calueton. (*N. G. Hyde*, No. 15).

Glusburn.

218. To the Kynge our souerayn Lorde.

Full humbely schewyth and besecheth your gracius heghnesse your pouer oratour and tenaunt Robert Bisschop of Selysden with your lordeschip of Skypton in Craven, that for so much as by your gracius comaundement and wryttyng direct unto your seruaunt Richard Midelton comaundyng him yat the trewe tytill of the liuelod of your said suppleaunt in Glusburn wyth in your saide lordeschip of Skypton sulde be understoud ther be twyx Thomas Hakysworth esquier and your saide pouer suppleaunt, and it is that the contre ther fynd the ryght in me your saide suppleaunte, qwherfore it woll pleise you of your moste aboundaunt grace to directt your gracius letter unto your saide seruaunt Richard Midelton, as he knawth the trewyth in the said metter, to put me in pesabill possescion acordyng to my ryght and your concience. And as I sall euermore pray to God for the preservacion of youre most gracius wellfare. (*Farnley Hall Muniments*, No. 93).

Gowdall (Snaith).

219. Grant[1] by Richard son of James de Goldale to Geoffrey son of Lefwin de Rameslomt (*sic*) and his heirs, for his homage and service, of half a bovate of land with appurtenances in the vill of Goldall, which Jamel his father had held; and all the toft belonging thereto in the same vill, lying next the toft of John son of John towards the east; to hold of the grantor and his heirs, in wood, plain, moors, marshes, waters, meadows, pastures, feedings, turbaries, ways, [and] paths in the vill and without, all places, easements and liberties, with all the free customs of the vill of Goldall belonging; rendering yearly 1*d.* at the feast of St. John the Baptist for all service, excepting forinsec service. Witnesses: William de Pouilligtun, Alexander his brother, Hylard de Hecke, John his son, Reginald de Goldale, Henry and Hugh his sons, Adam de Witelai, Simon his son, Alexander de Rameslomt, Hugh de Monte, Thomas his son, Simon de Gardin[o], Hugh son of Ralph. (*E. G. Millar, Esq.*).

[1] Early thirteenth century.

220. Quitclaim by Adam Carnewat of Goudale to dame Joan de Heck, her heirs or assigns, of all right in a messuage and the land and meadow which Henry de Goudale had granted him by charter;[1] for this quitclaim she gave him a mark of silver. Witnesses: William de Poulingtona, Henry de Heck, John son of Hugh de Goudale, William son of the parson of the same,[2] John son of Nicholas de Poulingtona, Thomas (*Tohm'*) de Snayt, clerk[3]. (*Ibid.*).

221. Thursday after St. Andrew the Apostle [Dec. 2], 1395. Grant by John Daunay to Thomas son of William Laweson of Heck, his heirs and assigns, of a toft in Goldale called Naggetoft, as it lay between the tenement of Thomas Maunsell on the west and the common pasture on the east, and abutted on the tenement of John Nichol at the north and the common pasture at the south; with all appurtenances, rendering yearly to the grantor, his heirs or assigns, 1*d*. at Easter and doing yearly two suits at the next courts of the grantor and his heirs held at Heck after Easter and Michaelmas for all other services. The grantee put his seal to the part of the indenture remaining with the grantor.[4] Witnesses: Thomas de Goldale, Thomas Hobson, William Brown, William Huwet, Adam Vendiloc, Thomas de Rednesse. Goldal'. (*Y.A.S.*, Md. 141, No. 8).

Gristhorpe.

222. Grant by Roger de Morepathe and Agnes, his wife, to Ralph son of Ralph de Ledbristune and Alice, the grantors' daughter by marriage, and their heirs, of 2 bovates of land in Grisetorp, with all appurtenances within and without the vill, freely as held by the grantors, of the king; namely, that forinsec bovate (*bovatam forinsecam*), which John son of Wice held, also that bovate which Henry, brother of Girard held, with 2 tofts which lie between [the land?] of Roger Aundcum and William son of Gumar. Warranty. Witnesses: William de Kaitona,[5] William de Angoteby, Gervase de Prestona, Robert son of Simon, William his son, Robert de Kaitona, Oliver de Croum, William Fossard, Robert de Prestona, Thomas son of Oliver, Roger son of William Fossard, William son of Gervase.[6] (*E. Stanley Jones*, No. 6).

223. Wednesday after Low Sunday, 22 Edward [April 28, 1294]. Indenture of agreement between Robert de Playce and Matilda, widow of Roger de Morepathe, whereby Robert handed over and delivered to Matilda as her dower, all the lands and tenements

1 No place mentioned; but probably Gowdall.
2 'Willelmo filio persone de cadem.'
3 Fragment of seal of green wax.
4 Fragment remains.
5 William and Robert de Kaitona were both witnesses to a document which can be dated between 1185-1195. *E.Y.C.*, II, p. 153.
6 Large seal of white wax, rubbed and broken.

which once belonged to the said Roger, her husband, 3 messuages and 4 bovates of land with appurtenances in Grisethorp with a third part of the mill belonging to the said vill, also 2 bovates with appurtenances in Lebbriston and a third part of an annual rent of 2 marks in Haterbeg'; concerning which dower Matilda agrees to hold herself well content in the future. Alternate seals. Witnesses: Sir William de Aton', knt., Adam de Briddesale, Thomas de Playce, Robert de Wyerne, William de Dales, Simon de Kilwardby, Stephen de Flotemanby, Alan Fox. (*Ibid.*, No. 8).

224. Grant by Robert Tayt of Gristhorp to Robert son of Robert de Playce of Grysthorp of a toft and a croft in the vill of Grysthorp which contains 5 strips of land which lie between the toft of Robert de Playce, father of the said Robert, and the water, in exchange for a toft with a croft in the same vill, which contains 6 strips of land which lie between the toft of Henry Baty and the toft of Reginald Strande; to hold of the chief lords of the fee, with all commodities, rights, liberties and easements in perpetuity. Warranty. Sealing clause. Witnesses: Robert de Wyeryn, Simon de Kilwardeby, Stephen Colum, Ralph son of Alice, Roger de Cayton, Roger son of Gilbert, Thomas son of Augustine. (*Ibid.*, No. 9).

225. Indenture whereby Thomas de Playce grants to William his son and heir, all his lands and tenements in Gristhorp and Lebreston which he received by inheritance after the death of Robert de Playce, his uncle; to hold to William and his lawfully begotten heirs, of the chief lords of the fee, freely and in peace, and in default of issue, reversion to the grantor. Warranty. Alternate seals. Witnesses: John Bard, William his son, Simon de Kiluardby, John his son, Robert de Playce. (*Ibid.*, No. 10).

226. The Morrow of the Purification of the B.V.M., 8 Edward son of Edward [Feb. 3, 1314-15]. Indenture whereby Robert Tayte of Gristhorp' grants to Thomas de Playce of Neuton a bovate of land with appurtenances in Gristhorp', which lies between the land of William de Playce on both sides; to hold to Thomas, his heirs and assigns, of the chief lords of the fee, paying yearly to Robert, his heirs and assigns 20*s*. of silver in equal portions at Whitsuntide and Michaelmas; the first payment to be made at Whitsuntide next following the full term of 10 years, so that Thomas and his heirs shall take 10 crops before this first payment. Warranty. Alternate seals. Witnesses: William de Playce, John de Kiluardby, Robert de Playce, Thomas son of Augustine, Robert Hode. At Neuton. (*Ibid.*, No. 11).

227. The morrow of the Purification of the B.V.M., 8 Edward son of Edward [Feb. 3, 1314-15]. Appointment by Thomas de Playce of Robert de Playce or Adam de Duggleby to take seisin on his behalf of a bovate of land with appurtenances in Gristhorp which he bought from Robert Tayte. At Neuton. (*Ibid.*, No. 12).

228. Easterday [March 23], 1315-16. Agreement between William de Playce and Robert de Playce whereby William demises and grants to farm to the said Robert, all his manor of Gristhorp, with all appurtenances in lands, meadows, pastures, grazings and with his windmill and all other appurtenances except the turbary called Stengraft; to hold to Robert until the grantor wishes to demise it to another; Robert to pay to William 16 marks, 5*s*. 3*d*. in equal portions at Whitsuntide and Martinmas, the first payment to begin . . .[1] 1316, and to perform the due and accustomed services with the exception of suit of the wapentake court; and the said William shall find such timber for the manor and the mill as is necessary, and he also grants that Robert may dig in the turbary called Stengraft 40 cartloads each year while he holds the manor; and the said manor must be handed back in as good condition as when he received it. Alternate seals. (*Ibid*., No. 13).

229. St. George the Martyr, 20 Edward son of Edward [April 23, 1326[?]].[2] Indenture whereby Thomas Plaice, knt. grants to Thomas Faukes of Gristhorp and Matilda, his wife, for the term of their lives and for the lifetime of the survivor, a bovate of land in Gristhorpe which Agnes the mother of Thomas first held of the grantor in the field of the same vill; to hold with all appurtenances, liberties and easements, of the grantor and his heirs, paying yearly 10*s*. 4*d*. of silver at Whitsuntide and Martinmas in equal portions for all services, exactions and demands. Warranty. Alternate seals. Witnesses: William Barde, John de Kilwardeby, Robert Plaice, Robert son of Geoffrey, Stephen Colome. At Newton near Wintringham. (*Ibid*., No. 14).

230. St. Luke [Oct. 18], 1327. Grant by Robert de Playce of Lebreston to William de Playce of a toft with a croft in the vill of Gristhorp, which lie between the dovecot of the said William and the stream (*torrentem*), which toft and croft the grantor had of the gift and feoffment of Robert Tayt in exchange; to hold to William, his heirs and assigns, of the chief lords of the fee. Warranty. Sealing clause. At Grisethorp. Witnesses: William Bard of Osgodby, John de Kyluardby, Thomas son of Jouet de Gristhorp, Stephen Colum of Lebreston, Robert son of William de Gristhorp. (*Ibid*., No. 15).

231. St. Peter in cathedra [Feb. 22], 1332[-3]. Indenture whereby Sir William de Playce grants and demises to William son of Thomas son of Augustine de Lebreston a croft lying adjacent to the toft which Thomas son of Henry once held of the prior of Brydlington in Gristhorp, on the east of a culture which is called Pychowdayl, and one acre of land lying in the culture called Cophowdayl adjoining towards the south, in the territory of Gristhorp;

[1] Document torn away.
[2] 20 Edward II began in July, 1326, and ended January, 1327.

to hold to William for the term of his life, paying yearly to the said Sir William and his heirs 6*s*. 8½*d*. in equal portions at Whitsuntide and Martinmas, the first term of payment to begin at Whitsuntide, 1334; and for the croft he shall pay 3*s*. in the same manner. Warranty. Alternate seals. At Esthorp. Witnesses: Robert de Playce, Thomas son of Augustine, Thomas son of Juett de Esthorp. (*Ibid.*, No. 16).

232. Easterday [April 19], 1332. Indenture whereby Sir William de Playce grants and demises to Robert Faukes of Gristhorp a culture which is called Midydayl between the moor and the seashore and half an acre in the culture which Thomas Faukes holds in the same culture in the field of Gristhorp, and the park which is called Coningholm and 2 strips lying near the said park on the west; to hold to Robert for the term of his life, paying to the grantor and his heirs 8*s*. 9*d*., namely, 4*s*. 5*d*. at Martinmas and 4*s*. 4*d*. at Whitsuntide, the first payment to be made at Martinmas, 1333. Warranty. Alternate seals. At Gristhorp. Witnesses: Robert de Playce, Thomas Jouettson, Thomas Faukes of Gristhorp.[1] (*Ibid.*, No. 17).

233. St. George the martyr [April 23], 1338. Indenture whereby Sir William de Playce demises and grants to Robert Faukes of Gristhorp a bovate of land and part of Richardlandes, his meadow in the field of Gristhorp, which lies towards the south in his culture, with exception of the other two bovates; to hold the said land and meadow to Robert until he has taken 14 crops, paying yearly to Sir William and his heirs 6*s*. 8*d*. for all services, in equal portions at Whitsuntide and Martinmas, the first payment to be made at Whitsuntide 1339 and the first crop to be taken in the following year. Warranty. Alternate seals. At Gristhorpe. (*Ibid.*, No. 18).

234. Ascensionday [May 10], 1347. Indenture whereby Sir Thomas Playce, knt., demises and grants to farm to John Penbroke his windmill of Gristhorp; to hold to the said John for the term of 6 years next following, paying yearly to Sir Thomas and his heirs 6*s*. in equal portions at Whitsuntide and Martinmas, the first payment to be made at Martinmas next; John to find all necessities for the mill except large timbers. Warranty. Alternate seals.[2] At Grisethorp. Witnesses: Robert de Wyerne, Thomas de Kylwardby, Henry Malbys, Thomas Jouetson. (*Ibid.*, No. 19).

235. Whitsunday [May 20], 1347. Indenture whereby Sir Thomas de Playce, knt., grants to Thomas Canoun and Emma, his wife, a piece of meadow called le Bothum, in Gristhorp; to hold to Thomas and Emma for the term of their lives, paying yearly to the grantor 5*s*. in equal portions at Whitsuntide and Martinmas, the

[1] Dorso: Mem. that Robert Faukes paid 2*s*. 6*d*. at Whitsuntide, 1333.

[2] Seal of yellow wax; a shield of arms in a cusped border, blurred and undeciphered.

first payment to be made at Whitsuntide, 1352, and possession shall first be taken in the same year. Warranty. Alternate seals.[1] At Gristhorp. Witnesses: Robert de Wyern, Thomas de Kulwardby, Henry Malbys, Thomas Jouetson. (*Ibid.*, No. 20).

236. Easter [April 20], 1348. Indenture whereby Thomas Playce, knt., grants to Walter Mous of Muston and Agnes, his wife, a messuage and a croft with appurtenances in Gristhorp, which lie between the toft and croft which John the miller holds of the grantor, and the croft which Peter son of William holds of the same; to hold to Walter and Agnes for their lives, paying yearly to the grantor 6*s*. in equal portions at Whitsuntide and Martinmas, the first payment to be made at Whitsuntide, 1348; Walter and Agnes to maintain and return the messuage and croft in good condition. Warranty. Alternate seals[2]. At Gristhorp. Witnesses: [*as to preceding deed*]. (*Ibid.*, No. 21).

237. The Nativity [Dec. 25], 1370. Indenture of agreement between Sir William de Playce of the one part and Robert de Playce of the other, whereby the said William grants and lets to farm to the said Robert, all his manor of Gristhorp with appurtenances, and with all his lands and tenements in Leberston and Wilhardby, in mills, meadows, pastures, grazings and other appurtenances; to hold to Robert for the full term of 20 years from the day of the making of these presents, paying yearly to William, his heirs and assigns 20 marks in equal portions at Whitsuntide and Martinmas, and performing the due and accustomed services; and Robert shall give as fine to the Wapentake court yearly, 5*s*., and if more ought to be given then the said William undertakes to pay it for the fine; and Robert shall maintain the close, hall, 2 chambers, the kitchen, 2 granges, a dovecot, the gates of the lands and tenements, the mill, the chapel and the great building for the animals near the gate, in as good condition as when he received them, and return them in the same condition; and he may dig in the turbary called Stengraft in order to maintain his household, but without waste or destruction. Warranty. Alternate seals. At Neuton. (*Ibid.*, No. 22).

Guisborough.

238. May 26, 1408. Indenture reciting that whereas John de Helmeslay, prior of Gisburne, and the convent of the same, have by 3 indentures dated at Gisburne, May 20, 1408, granted to Robert Conyers, knt., Richard de Norton, John Conyers of Horneby, Gilbert Eluet, John Killyngale and Robert Dobley, their heirs and their tenants in Pynchonthorp', common pasture for their animals [*as described in No. 234, Y.D. IX*]; now the grantees agree for themselves and for their heirs that they will not take or hold by reason

[1] Seal as to preceding deed.
[2] Seal as to preceding deed.

of the said indentures, any other common pasture or perquisite (*avantagium*), unless granted to them by a further charter. Alternate seals[1]. Witnesses: [*as to No. 234, Y.D. IX*]. At Gisburne. (*R. W. Lee*).

Hawksworth.

239. [1279]. Demise by Simon Warde son of William Warde of Gyvendale to Sir Thomas de Huke, his heirs and assigns, of all his rents in Haukeswurthe, to be received at the same times as the grantor was accustomed to take them, namely, from Walter de Roudon' 6*s*. 1*d*., from Adam, son of William ½*d*., from Richard de Lakkok 5*s*. 1*d*., from Walter de Haukeswurthe 3*s*. 9*d*., from Ralph the carpenter 2*s*. 3*d*., from William son of Matilda, 7*s*. 7*d*., from John le Vauasur 15*d*., from Richard, son of Michael 7*s*. 5*d*., from William, son of Constance 8*s*. 11*d*., from Walter the clerk 6*s*. 7*d*., from Thomas de Mensington 5*s*. 4*d*., from William son of Hugh, for his father's land 9*d*., for the meadow called Caluecroft 5*d*., from the same William 6*s*. 4*d*., for Wuluerikeng 12*d*., for Michael de Godhouwe 8*s*. 10*d*., from Robert Ruff 7*s*. 5*d*., from Thomas Fraunceys 17*d*., from Simon de Hille 13½*d*., from William son of Matilda and Walter the clerk 5*s*. 4*d*., from the same Walter 2*s*. 8½*d*., from the land *ad murum* 18*d*., from John le Vauasur 8*d*.; all of which are payable in equal portions at Martinmas and Whitsuntide, the first payment being due at Martinmas, 1279, and to continue until Sir Thomas, his heirs, assigns or executors shall have received 20 marks, in which sum Simon was bound to him for certain dwellings which he had of Thomas in the city of York. Warranty. Sealing clause. Witnesses: Sir William de Sancto Quintino, Sir John de Melsa, Dom. Simon Warde, rector of the church of Gyselay, Mag. Thomas de Brumpton, Robert Vilayn, Walter de Hauuekeswurthe, Thomas de Ulschelf[2]. (*Farnley Hall Muniments*, No. 97).

240. St. Peter in cathedra, 9 Edward I [Feb. 22, 1280-1]. Indenture[3] whereby Walter son of Simon de Heukeswarthe grants and quitclaims to Walter son of Walter de Haukeswurthe and Beatrice, his wife, their heirs and assigns, all that tenement with appurtenances which once belonged to Simon his father, in Haukeswurthe, just as contained in the original charter which the said Walter son of Walter had of the gift and feoffment of the said Walter son of Simon, namely, both the plain which Simon once held

[1] Seal of brown wax, the seal of the Chapter; see C. T. Clay, *The Seals of the Religious Houses of Yorkshire*, in *Archaeologia*, 1928, p. 19.

[2] Dorso: Valor omnium terrarum et tenement' Simon Warde filii dom' Willi' Warde infra vill' de Haukiswrthe.

[3] Also a further quitclaim of the same to the same, witnessed by: Sir William de Lasceles, Sir Simon Warde, Sir Alexander de Ledes, Robert Vilayn, John de Marthelay, William de Midelton, William le Paytefin, William de la Sale of Ledes, Matthew de Mensington, William son of Michael of the same, Hugh de Berewyk, Thomas Fraunceys of Haukeswurthe, William son of William of the same, Hugh del Rodes. (*Ibid*., No. 100).

and the lordships and services of the vill of Haukeswurthe; to hold to Walter and Beatrice of the chief lords of the fee by the due and accustomed services. For this grant and quitclaim and also for the ratification of the first feoffment, Walter son of Walter grants to Walter son of Simon, a messuage and 6 acres of land with appurtenances in the vill of Haukeswurthe, namely, that toft and croft which Jordan de Horsford once held, and an acre of land lying near Hughthorp buttes towards the south above the wood, and half an acre lying at the top of Holenge and a rood lying at Copperode and 3 roods of land at Lidyeteflat towards the east, and an acre towards Daniacre and half an acre at Kirkegate, and a rood above Keryes, and 3 roods at Lyolfstighel, and 3 roods at Wulfrykeenge, and a rood at Spyrte; to hold to him and lawfully begotten heirs, of Walter son of Walter in perpetuity, paying yearly 12*d.* at Whitsuntide and Martinmas in equal portions, and the homage and forinsec service due from that land in the same fee, for all secular services and demands. Warranty. Should Walter son of Simon die without heirs, reversion to the heirs of Walter son of Walter. Alternate seals. This deed also ratifies the first feoffment. Witnesses: Sirs William de Lasceles, Simon Warde, Alexander de Ledes, knts., William de Stopham, Robert Vylayn, Robert de Arthington, William de Alwaldelay, Matthew de Brame, John Geremy, William de Midelton, Walter de Midelton, John de Marthelay, Alexander de Mensington, William son of Matilda de Haukeswurthe, Thomas de Ulschelf. (*Ibid.*, No. 99).

241. Indenture[1] whereby Hugh son of Alan de Heukeswrth grants and quitclaims to Sir William Warde all right in a rent of 15*d.* from 2 bovates of land with appurtenances which Matilda, daughter of Robert Rufi of Heukeswrth gave to Alan the grantor's father with all reliefs, wards, escheats; paying yearly to the grantor and his heirs 15*d.* in equal portions at Whitsuntide and Martinmas and performing the forinsec service which pertains to that tenement in the same fee; if the rent and forinsec service is not duly paid and performed, power to the grantor and his heirs to retain a similar sum from their own land and to distrain for the same without contradiction from William and his heirs. Sealing clause. All the charters which the grantor has relating to the said two bovates he hands over to Sir William. Witnesses: Dom. Simon Warde, rector of the church of Giselay, Dom. Walter, vicar of Ottelay, Walter de Heukeswrth, John Vauasore of the same, Hugh de Berwyc. (*Ibid.*, No. 96).

242. Nativity of St. John the Baptist [June 24], 1294. Release and quitclaim by Elizabeth, daughter of Hugh de Collum, deceased, to Richard de Collum, her brother and executor of the will

[1] Also counterpart, the words CARTA DUPLEX being written along the cut.

of Hugh Collum their father, of all actions arising from the will of the said Hugh, and of all petitions for the goods and chattels which once belonged to Hugh and Matilda, his wife, whatsoever their value, in return for 40*li*. of silver which Richard gave to the said Elizabeth for her dowry. Sealing clause[1]. Witnesses: John de Hayton, Adam de Thorp, Gilbert de Wilberfosse, Richard del Flet, Richard de Herlethorp, Jordan de Houeden. At Wilberfosse. (*Ibid*., No. 94).

243. St. Peter ad vincula [Aug. 1], 1294. Grant by Walter de Haukesword, for the whole of his life, to Walter his son, and Elizabeth his wife, of food and clothing and all other necessities in his manor of Heukesword, just as enjoyed by himself and his wife, without any impediment or contradiction, in return for 40*li*. of silver which Richard de Collum, brother of Elizabeth gave as her dowry at her marriage with his son Walter. Sealing clause[2]. Witnesses: Adam de Thorp, Gilbert de Wilberfosse, John Scot of Caluerley, Richard del Flete of Bubwyth, Robert Gillyng', Robert de Gildusdall, Jordan de Houeden. At York. (*Ibid*., No. 95).

244. Grant by Simon Warde, senior to Walter, son of Walter de Haukisuuorth, of 2 acres and a rood of land in the field of Haukisuuorth, namely, in Sunnirodis half an acre, at Layrelandis half an acre, at Braderane half an acre and at Grenehowe 3 roods; to hold to Walter and his lawfully begotten heirs, of the grantor and his heirs, freely with all liberties and easements, and performing for the grantor the forinsec service due to the king from the said lands. Warranty. Sealing clause. Witnesses: Sir William de Stoppeham, knt., Adam de Neyleforth, John Scot of Caluirley, Walter de Midilton, Robert de Carleton, Alexander de Mensington, William Lele. (*Ibid*., No. 98).

245. Saturday after St. Bartholomew, 41 Edward III [Aug. 28, 1367]. Grant[3] and confirmation by William de Marton and Nicholas de Driffeld to Walter son of Walter de Haukesworth and Isabel, his wife, and their lawfully begotten heirs, of all the lands, tenements, rents and services with mills and other appurtenances in Haukesworth, Loftosum in Spaldyngmore and Mensyngton near Burlay, also the great wood of Haukesworth; to hold freely and in peace, of the chief lords of the fees. Should either Walter or Isabel die without heirs remainder to the right heirs of Walter in perpetuity. Warranty. Sealing clause, and for further confirmation of this

[1] Seal of red wax, diam. $\frac{5}{8}$ in.; two crossed hands below a fleur-de-lis; legend undeciphered.

[2] Small seal of dark green wax; a kneeling figure; legend broken away.

[3] Aug. 28, 1367. Appointment of John de Mitton and Laurence de Grenacres to deliver seisin. Sealing clause. At Hawkesworth. Two small seals of brown wax, (1) a device of four leaves; S' D' MVOXPRIVE; (2) a hare; . . . TSO . . . (*Ibid*, No. 102)

charter it is sealed by William de Rilleston, Robert de Arthington, Thomas de Bradlay and Robert de Bradlay[1]. Witnesses: Robert Paslewe of Leeds, John son of John Vausur of Weston, William Gascoyne, William Fraunke and John de Carleton. (*Ibid.*, No. 101).

246. April 16, 8 Henry VIII [1517]. This indenture maide the xvjth day of Aprill the viijthe yere of the reigne of owre suffereyn lorde Kynge Henry the viijth wyttenesseth that Thomas Hawkesworth of Hawkesworth, squyere, haith solde and delyuered to William Forster and Agnes his wyff the wardship and custodie of the body of James Mitton' son and heire of Christopher Mitton' late of Hawkesworth, descessed, with the maredge profettes of all the landes and tenements of the seid James. To holde and to have the seid wardship, custodie, maredge, landes and tenementis to the seide William Forster and Agnes his wyff and to their assignes durynge the noneage of the same James for the somme of iiij markes xl*d.* to the seide Thomas Hawkesworth paid by the same William and Agnes, of the wyche iiij markes xl*d.* the same Thomas Hawkesworthe knowleges hym contented and payed, and the seide William and Agnes and theire assignes theroff to be acquytte. In wittenes wharoff haith put to theire seales. Yeven the day and yere aboveseid, theyse beiynge wuttenesse, John Steede, Thomas Dailzaye, John Pyccard and other. (*Ibid.*, No. 104).

Hawnby.

247. Thursday before the Nativity of the B.V.M. [Sept. 7], 1363, 37 Edward III. Grant and demise by Walter Malbys to John Fayrfax, rector of the church of Halmeby, of a waste place containing half an acre of land which lies between his rectory in the same vill on the south and a certain cottage which William Tylly holds on the north and which abuts on the highway of Hameby towards the east; he also grants to the said John half an acre of land lying in 4 strips adjoining the said rectory garden and which adjoins the said waste place towards the east and a certain culture called Howlandes on the west; to hold to John and his successors holding the said church from the day of the making of these presents for 200 years next following; paying to the grantor and his assigns 5*s.* of silver in equal portions at Whitsuntide and Martinmas. Warranty. Sealing clause. Witnesses: William Coluyll, William de Aklum, knts., William Fayrfax, Thomas de Etton, William de la Ryuere, Robert de Sproxton, William del Hall, Adam del Schaumbr'. At Walton. (*Newburgh Priory Muniments*, No. 8/30).

[1] 6 seals, (1) brown wax, diam. ½ in.; a shield of arms, blurred; (2) brown wax, diam. $\frac{6}{10}$ in.; as No. 1. above; (3) red wax, broken, fragment of a shield of arms; (4) brown wax, as No. 2. above; (5) red wax, diam. ¾ in.; in a geometric border a shield of arms, blurred; WILLELMI DE RILLES . . . (6) below a stag's head a shield of arms; on a bend 3 chaplets; legend undeciphered.

Hayton.

248. Sunday after the translation of St. Thomas the Martyr [July 13], 1343, 17 Edward III. Grant by Thomas son of Richard de Bossall of Hayton, to William de Holthorp of Friton, of a messuage and 2 bovates of land with appurtenances in Hayton, which messuage lies in length and breadth between the toft of Mabel de Grace on one side towards the east, and the toft of William Rate on the other towards the west; he also grants 20*s*. annual rent from a messuage and 4 bovates of land which William Ward of Hayton holds and from a messuage and 4 bovates which Mabel and John le Grace hold in the same vill; he further grants a bovate which John his brother had of the gift and feoffment of Richard de Bossall his father, in the same vill; also the reversion of a bovate which Nicholas, his brother holds for the term of his life, also 2*d*. annual rent from a toft in which the siad Nicholas dwells; also the reversion of 2 bovates of land which Margaret his mother holds as dower in the said vill: he also grants 2*d*. annual rent from a messuage which Richard his brother holds, and 1*d*. annual rent from a toft in which Richard dwells; he also grants his mill, pond, suit and lordship to whatsoever pertaining, in the said vill; to hold with all liberties and easements, reversions and rights, to William, his heirs and assigns, of the chief lords of the fee. Warranty. Sealing clause[1]. Witnesses: John de Cunnays, John Bell of Hayton, John de Ruddestan, Thomas Raustern, Simon de Cunnays, William de Wythwell, Gerard Saluayn of Brounby, John Fancourt of the same, Nicholas Brounby. At Hayton. (*Serlby Hall Muniments*, No. 18).

249. Sunday after the Invention of the Cross, 20 Edward III [May 7, 1346]. Appointment by William son of William de Holthorp of Friton, of John Bell of Hayton, junior, and Thomas Gurnays to take seisin of all the lands and tenements in Hayton which he has of the said William, his grandfather [*sic*]. Sealing clause. At Friton. (*Ibid*., No. 19).

250. Friday before Trinity Sunday, 36 Edward III [June 10, 1362]. Appointment by Dom. John Buk and Dom. James de Malton, chaplains, of William de Whyteby as their attorney to take seisin of all the lands and tenements which they have of the gift and feoffment of John de Holthorp and Isabel dau. of Robert de Malton, in Hayton. Sealing clause[2]. At Malton. (*Ibid*., No. 20).

251. Wednesday after Corpus Christi, 2 Richard II [June 15, 1379]. Appointment by John Hastygas, Robert Boulot, William Spenser, Alan de Kyrkebie, chaplain, and Peter de Seterington,

[1] Seal of pink wax; two heads facing below a quatrefoil; legend undeciphered.

[2] Seals of red wax, (1) an animal curled up; ✱GRO . . . OI; (2) Agnus Dei; ORA P . . .

chaplain, of Richard Athekyrcstil to deliver seisin to John de Holthorp of all the lands and tenements which they had of his gift in the vill and territory of Hayton. Sealing clause[1]. At Hayton, (*Ibid.*, No. 21).

252. Jan. 4, 21 Richard II [1397-8]. Release and quitclaim by Agnes, widow of John de Esyngwald to John, son and heir of John de Holthorp of Hayton, of all right in all the lands and tenements, rents and services with appurtenances in Hayton, which she and John de Esyngwald had of the gift and feoffment of John father of John de Holthorp. Warranty. Sealing clause[2]. Witnesses: Walter de B . . . John de Hayton, Robert Gunnays, William Hungate, Robert de Fenton, Robert de Rudstane, John Gerardson. At Hayton. (*Ibid.*, No. 22).

253. March 31, 1392, 15 Richard II. Indenture witnessing that whereas John de Holthorp of Hayton has by his charter granted to Beatrice de Roos and William de Roos, knt., their heirs and assigns, a certain annual rent of 100*s*. sterling in equal portions at Whitsuntide and Martinmas, from all the lands and tenements belonging to the grantor in the vills and territories of Hayton and Fryton, as is more fully contained in the said charter, now, the said Beatrice and William agree that if they may hold and peacefully enjoy without disturbance the manors of Northolm and Great Eddeston in Rydale with appurtenances, from the date of the making of these presents for the term of two years, according to the form of certain indentures granted to them by John de Holthorp, then the said writing concerning the annual rent of 100*s*. shall be null and void; but if Beatrice and William are evicted or not allowed to complete the said term in peace, then the said John or his heirs shall pay to them 40 marks sterling in equal portions at Martinmas and Easter next following their eviction. Alternate seals[3]. (*Ibid.*, No. 23).

254. May 8, 5 Henry IV [1404]. Quitclaim by Beatrice de Roos to Mag. Robert Marras, rector of the parish church of Gyselay, Dom. William Teryngton, sometime prior of Warter, Mag. Robert de Appilton, rector of the parish church of Stretton en le Clay and John de Holthorp son and heir of John de Holthorp of Hayton, of all right in a certain annual rent of 100*s*. sterling which the grantor held jointly with William de Roos, knt., of the grant of John de Holthorp of Hayton, from all the lands and tenements of the said John in the vills and territories of Hayton and Fryton, as is more fully described in their charter; she also quitclaims all actions real

[1] Two seals on one tongue; (1) small red shield of arms, undeciphered; 2) dark brown wax, broken.

[2] Small seal of red wax; the letter H.

[3] Seal of red wax; diam. 1 in.; a shield of arms, 3 water bougets; ✱ S' . . . . ROOS.

and personal against the said John. Sealing clause[1]. Witnesses: William Cherwyn, knt., William de Hundegate, Walter Rudstone, Robert Gunnays, Richard de Hayton. At Hayton. (*Ibid.*, No. 24).

255. Nativity of St. John the Baptist [June 24], 1430, 8 Henry VI. Indenture whereby William Holthorp, esq., grants to Thomas Craven of Selby, esq., and Elizabeth, his wife, their heirs and assigns, for the lifetime of the said Thomas and Elizabeth, all the lands and tenements, rents, services, meadows, pastures, woods and marshes, with all other appurtenances in the vill and territory of Hayton; to hold of the grantor and his heirs by the service of a rose at the Nativity of St. John the Baptist if demanded. Warranty. Sealing clause.[2] Witnesses: Robert Rudstane of Hayton, John Portyngton of Portyngton, John Hertlington, Peter de Cawod, John Submondo' esqs. At Hayton. (*Ibid.*, No. 25).

Heck (Snaith).

256. Easter [April 4], 1344. Demise by Ellen and Katherine daughters of William de Langtoft to Robert son of Richard de Goldale of two thirds of the manor of Hek which had fallen to them by hereditary right after the death of Katherine de Hek their grandmother, and which Robert had of the demise of the latter during her life by indentures made between them; to hold from Easter, 1344 until Michaelmas, 1345, rendering yearly 33*s*. 4*d*. at the Nativity of St. John the Baptist next following the former date, 33*s*. 4*d*. at the following Martinmas, and 33*s*. 4*d*. at the Nativity of St. John the Baptist in the second year; with power to distrain in the premises and in all the lands and tenements of Robert should the rent be in arrear at any term. For greater security they had found William de Langtoft their father as surety, who had affixed his seal with theirs. Alternate seals[3]. Witnesses: John de Snayth, Alexander de Crideling, William de Goldale, William de Couwik, William Dennyson of Hek. At Goldale. (*Y.A.S.*, Md. 141, No. 9).

257. All Souls day, 38 Edward III [Nov. 2, 1364]. Grant by Thomas Elys the younger to Thomas Elys his uncle, his heirs and assigns, of all his lands and tenements, woods, meadows, pastures, mills, rents and services of all his tenants, and all his demesne in the

[1] Seal of red wax, diam. 1½ in.; a shield of arms; a chevron [Stafford], impaled by, on the dexter, three water-bougets [Roos] and, on the sinister, three bars on a chief two palets, and an inescutcheon three bars ermine [Burley]; supporters two greyhounds, above the shield, an anchor, SIGILLUM . . . . . . CIS DE ROOS

Beatrice was the daughter of Ralph, Earl of Stafford. She was the widow of Thomas de Roos, who died in 1384,a nd then the wife of Sir Richard Burley, K.G. (J. W. Clay, *Extinct and Dormant Peerages of the Northern Counties*, p. 183).

[2] Tongues for 2 seals; on the second a blob of red wax, a fleur-de-lis.

[3] One tag to this part; seal missing.

vills of Hek, Goldale, Snath and Heuensale, with all appurtenances which had descended to him by hereditary right after the death of Joan his mother: rendering yearly 4*li.* 13*s.* 4*d.* of silver at Whitsuntide and Martinmas in equal portions, with power to re-enter if the rent were in default for forty days. Alternate seals[1]. Witnesses: Sir Thomas de Metham, knt., William de Wyntworth, John de Schirwode, John Wyte, Henry de Schirwode. At Hek. (*Ibid.*, No. 10).

258. April 30, 22 Richard II [1399]. Sale[2] by John Daunay to John de Lylburne of Esthadylsay of all his wood growing in Hekfalles which was formerly divided between three (*soers*)[?], between the following bounds, namely, between the bounds of Thomas at Freres towards the east and *le Southangle* and the edge of the wood towards the west and so forward as the site of the plot (*place*) of the said John Daunay extended, and between the old dike enclosing the tofts [of] *le Dufcotzerd* and the wood at the limits as bounded between them towards the south, and the moor towards the north and the west *angle*; to cut and remove it without disturbing the soil or undergrowth (*spryng*), otherwise than necessary, from the feast of St. Eigne [*sic*] next following until Michaelmas two years later; with free entry and exit by three roads to the moor towards the north where it should be best for carting by John de Lylburne and his assigns and least damage to John Daunay, his heirs or assigns; paying 14 marks before any work in the wood should be begun. The vendor to be responsible for enclosing the wood, except that the purchaser would repair any enclosures made by the vendor or his agents or any one else previously, which might be broken in the course of carrying. Warranty against any who had taken an estate or feoffment made by the vendor or Adam de Wentworth. If the vendor paid 5 marks 5*d.* at Snaith on the Sunday next after the following feast of Corpus Christi the bargain to be of no effect[3]. Alternate seals. At Hek. (*Ibid.*, No. 11).

259. Feb. 3, 2 Henry IV [1400-1]. Grant by John Daunay to Roger Smyth of Kelyngton, his heirs and assigns, of his windmill of Hek with its site and all appurtenances, situate in the field of Balnehek[4] on the end of a certain section of land lately belonging to John Robyn of Hek; rendering yearly 12*d.* at Easter and Michaelmas in equal portions; with power to distrain if the rent should be fifteen days in arrear, and to enter and retain the premises if the rent should

[1] Seal: yellow wax, round, $\frac{7}{8}$ in.; a shield of arms, apparently vair; legend not deciphered; blurred and chipped.

[2] In French.

[3] There are some further clauses which appear to be formal; the bottom part of the document is badly stained.

[4] The part of Heck which is nearest to Balne (*Y.A.J.*, X, 352)

be forty days in arrear. Alternate seals[1]. Witnesses: William de Burgoyne of Wentworth, Thomas Dilcok, William de Hek, William de Fenwyk, William Broune, bailiff. At Hek[2]. (*E. G. Millar, Esq.*)

Hemingbrough.

260. [1399]. Be it knawyn that we William Goldesburgh, William Hatylsey, Robert Race, Robert Hatilsey, William Thomason, John Drax, John Watkynson, William Riffan, John Naborne, John Clerke, and William Proudefotte tenauntz to ye prior off Durham within his lordeshep of Hemyngburgh witnessesse and Certifiez yt ye Custome with in ye seide lordeshep is and has beyn of tyme wherof no mynde rynnes that wher a man has issue diuerse doughters the Eldest doughter shall inherite and have after ye custome of ye seide manoir all his land with in the seide lordeshep holdyn be ye custome of ye seide manoir; And non of hirr sisters shall inherite nor have parte ther in; And this custome is att this daye and euer had beyn peaseable contenned with oute any interrupcion of any persones. And for a prese of the seide mater at the court of the prior of Durham and view of frankplege held at Hemyngburgh on Tuesday the morrow of St. Michael, 1 Henry IV [Sept. 30, 1399], Margaret Burne, sister and heir of John Burne sought admittance and did fealty for a messuage, a cottage and 27 acres of land with appurtenances in Hemyngburgh, was admitted and came and according to the custom of the manor and gave to the lord as a fine for entry, 20*s*. and did homage[3], And at ye entente of thys writynge at the custome off our inheritaunce and tenoir after ye forme of ye custome of ye manoir aforeseide as we and our neghbors will certefie and declare sufficiantly and for the trueth of our custome by this present writynge we certifie and declare; And to this writynge seuerally has sett our seals. And we, Robert Babthorp in ye paryshynge of Hemyngburgh, son and heir of Ralph Babthorpe, laate stewarde of the same lordeshep, Thomas Hagthorpe, the elder, of the same parysh, gentilman, William Lawson of the same parish, gentilman, Thomas Hagthorpe of the same parish, gentilman, and oder moo, knowynge that trueth of ye custome within the seide lordeshep of Hemyngburgh is and has beyn of tyme wherof no mynde rynnes as it is aboven expressed, whar fore we seuerally has sett to our seals. (*Farnley Hall Muniments*, No. 103).

Hemingfield.

261. Grant by Thomas, son of Jordan de Caldelaue to Nicholas de Skiris, for his homage and service, of all that land which Alice, the grantor's mother gave to him, namely, all the half of that land

[1] Huic presente carte indentate in capite. The indented cut is at the side and not, as usual, at the top of the charter.

[2] Seal: red wax, round, $\frac{11}{16}$ in.; bird above a nest; legend undeciphered.

[3] In Latin.

which she held in her widowhood in the field of Skiris, with all appurtenances just as the land lies in length and breadth, for 3 acres and 3 roods which lie towards the south (*apud ortum sol'*); to hold to Nicholas, his heirs and assigns, with all liberties and easements, of the grantor and his heirs, in fee and hereditarily, in fields, woods, pastures, waters, ways and services in the territory of Hymlingfeld; paying yearly to the grantor, 6*d*. in equal portions at Whitsuntide and the Assumption of the B.V.M. for all secular services. Warranty. And for this grant Nicholas paid to the grantor a silver mark. Witnesses: Reyner de Wambwelle, John Walegrim, Robert de Wodehuses, Robert de Crigliston, Roger de Rodis, William de Stouinisby, Robert de Wath, clerk, John Deynel, Thomas son of Hugh, Roger son of Thomas de Strete, Thomas his brother[1]. (*Serlby Hall Muniments*, No. 26).

Hemsworth.

262. Release and quitclaim by Ellen, widow of Gilbert de Macun of Himleswrth, to William son of Alan son of Adam of the same, his heirs and assigns, of all right in all that land with a toft and a croft and all other appurtenances which Matilda, the grantor's mother once gave to Richard de Soyewel; to hold to William, his heirs and assigns, of the grantor and her heirs and assigns, freely in perpetuity. Warranty. Sealing clause. Witnesses: Dom. Adam, chaplain of Himleswrth, Jordan de Ker of the same, Geoffrey de Scoley of the same, William son of Petronilla of the same, John *le plumber* of the same, Alan son of Adam of the same, Alan the clerk. (*Serlby Hall Muniments*, No. 27).

263. Friday, St. Peter ad vincula [Aug. 1], 1298. Grant by Gregory son of John de Hymleswrth to John de Hymleswrth, his father, and Margaret, his wife, and Cecily, their daughter, in return for a sum of money, of all the lands and tenements with appurtenances which the said John and Margaret once gave to the grantor in Hymleswrth, Hyndelay, Hoderode and Roston le Wode[2], in lordships, woods, rents, wards, reliefs, escheats, plains, grazings and pastures, with all appurtenances without reservation; to hold to the grantees and to the lawfully begotten heirs of Cecily, of the chief lords of the fee, freely and in peace. Should Cecily die without lawful issue, remainder to John, the grantor's father and his heirs and assigns. Warranty. Sealing clause. Witnesses: Adam de Wanneruyle, John de Flynthull, Jordan de Kerre, Godfrey de Scollay, Adam del Rodes, Robert de Pull' of Cuthewrth, Hugh Bayard of the same. At Hymleswrth. (*Ibid.*, No. 28).

264. Grant by Margaret, daughter of William de Bosco, of the parish of Himmelesworth, to John son of John de Hinmelesworth,

[1] Dorso. Carta pro redd' Willelmi Renberght de Collow.
[2] Hodroyd (par. Felkirk) and Royston.

of all her tenement which she had by hereditary right after the death of the said William, as well in le Wode in the said parish as in the vills of Hyndelay, Roreston, Hoderode and Himmelesworth, without reservation, in return for a sum of money given to her by the said John; to hold to John, his heirs and assigns, of the chief lords of the fee, with all appurtenances, liberties and easements. Warranty. Sealing clause[1]. Witnesses: Adam de Wannerwile, Walter de Sutton, bailiff of Osgoter and Stayner[2], William de Toueton, Jordan de Ker, William son of Petronilla de Himmelesworth, Alan called Almoth of the same, Adam le Wilede, William Cosin. (*Ibid.*, No. 29).

265. Grant by Margaret daughter of William de Bosco in her free widowhood, to John son of John de Hymelesworth, of all the tenements which she had by hereditary right after the death of William, in the vills of Hyndeley, Rorestona, Hoderode and Hymelesworth, without reservation, in return for a sum of money; to hold to John, his heirs and assigns, of the chief lords of the fee. Warranty. Sealing clause[3]. Witnesses: Adam de Wannerwile, Walter de Sutton, bailiff of Osgotecros and Stayncrosse, William de Toueton', Jordan del Ker, William son of Petronilla de Hymelesworth, Alan called Almot of the same, Adam le Wylde, William Cusyn. (*Ibid.*, No. 30).

266. Grant and quitclaim by Thomas son of William son of the rector of Camsale to John son of John de Himleswrth and his heirs and assigns, of all right in all that tenement which the said John once had of the gift and feoffment of Margaret daughter and heiress of William de Bosco in the fee of Himleswrth and Hindelay. Warranty. Sealing clause[4]. Witnesses: Adam de Wanneruil, lord of Himleswrth, Jordan de Ker of the same, Godfrey de Scolay of the same, William son of Petronilla of the same, John *le plumber* of the same, John the carter (*le careter*) of the same, Alan the clerk. (*Ibid.*, No. 31).

267. Sunday after St. James the Apostle, 13 Edward son of Edward [July 29, 1319]. Grant in her pure virginity and lawful power by Margaret, daughter of John le Carter of Hymlesworth to William son of Robert de Baddesworth, for a sum of money, of a rood and a half of arable land with appurtenances and the adjoining meadow just as it lies in the east field of Hymlesworth, between the land of John son of John Byset on the east and the land of Gregory, son of Petronilla on the west; to hold to William, his heirs and assigns, freely and in peace, of the chief lords of the fee. Warranty. Sealing clause. Witnesses: John son of John Byset,

[1] Remains of an oval seal of white wax; a fleur-de-lis.

[2] Osgoldcross and Staincross.

[3] Vesica shaped seal of dark green wax, $1\frac{3}{8}$ x $\frac{7}{8}$ in.; afleur -de-lis; ✠ S' MARG'T DE BUSCO.

[4] Vesica shaped seal of dark green wax, $1\frac{1}{2}$ x 1 in.; a fleur-de-lis; * S' TH'E FIL' WIL' PS'A CA'OL.

John de Wode, Gregory son of Petronilla de Hymlesworth, Gregory son of John of the same, John de Ledebeter of the same, John son of Robert of the same, John del Rodes. At Hymlesworth. (*Ibid.*, No. 32).

268. Sunday after Holy Trinity [June 4], 1327. Grant by Gregory son of William de Hymlisworthe to Thomas, his son, for his faithful service, of an acre of arable land in the field of Hymlisworthe in the place called Wheterode, which lies in length and breadth between the field of Kyrkeby on one side, and the land of Hymlisworthe on the other, and abuts at one end on the land of the rector of the same, and on the other above the land of John son of Robert; to hold with all appurtenances, commodities and easements to Thomas, his heirs and assigns, of the chief lords of the fee. Warranty. Sealing clause[1]. Witnesses: John Biset, John del Rodes, John son of Robert, William son of Alan, Gregory son of John de Hymlisworthe. At Hymlisworthe. (*Ibid.*, No. 33).

269. Monday before St. Mary Magdalene, 3 Edward III [July 19, 1329]. Grant by Richard son of William Nodeson of Himleswort, to Hugh son of Adam Kinge of Kynneslay, of one messuage, just as it stands enclosed, which lies in the vill of Himleswort, between the garden of John son of Robert de Himleswort on the east and the garden of William Nodeson on the west; to hold to Hugh, his heirs and assigns freely and in peace, with all liberties and easements, within and without the vill, of the chief lords of the fee. Warranty. Sealing clause[2]. Witnesses: Adam de Wannerwill, John Byset, John de Burton, Gregory son of Petronilla, John son of Robert. At Himleswort. (*Ibid.*, No. 34).

270. Sunday after St. Gregory, 5 Edward III [March 17, 1330-1]. Grant by Thomas son of Gregory de Hymleswrth to John del Rodes and Alice, his wife, of 3 acres and half a rood of arable and pasture land in the vill and territory of Hymleswrth with appurtenances, which the grantor had of the grant of Gregory, his father, in the said vill, of which 1½ roods lie in Rissefurlong in the east field between the land of Adam Wanirwille on the south and the land of William son of Alan on the north and the western headland abuts above Colepitlane; and 1½ roods lie above Brecheckoft between the land of John Ledbeter on the north and the land once of William Node on the south, and abut above Feldwelle towards the west; and 1½ roods lie in the north field of Hymleswrth between the land of William son of Alan on the west and the land of the said lord on the east, which is called Cordlande and which abuts above the land of the said Gregory towards the north; and 1½ roods lie in the same field between the land once of Robert Scotton on the west and the land once of William son of Node on the east, and the

[1] Seal of brown wax, diam. ½ in.; a hare; legend undeciphered.
[2] Seal of dark brown wax; a pierced heart; legend undeciphered.

north headland abuts above the land of the said Gregory; and 1 rood lies at le Watyrslacke between the land of the said Adam on the east and the land of Robert Franckelayne on the west and the north headland abuts above Flekewelleslatte; and 1½ roods lie at Yhickewelle in the west field between the land of John Ledbeter and John Secker on both sides, and the north headland abuts on the highway going through the middle of the village; and 1½ roods near Cortdyke lie between the lands of John Beset and John Ledbeter on both sides and the western headland abuts above the land of Adam Wanirwille; and 1½ roods lie above le Wetesehaghfurlang between the land of the said Adam which is called Cortland on the east, and the land of the rector of the church of Hymleswrth on the west, and the southern headland abuts above Presterodewelle; and half a rood lies above le Buttes between the land of William son of Alan on the north and the land once of William Node on the south; and half a rood lies in the same place between the lands of John Ledbeter and the land once of William son of Node on both sides, and abuts on the common moor towards the east; to hold to John and Alice, freely and in peace, of the chief lords of the fee. Warranty. Sealing clause. Witnesses: Adam Wanirwille, John de Burton, Robert Seriant, Alan de Scholay, Gregory son of John, John son of Robert, William son of Alan. At Hymleswrthe. (*Ibid.*, No. 35).

271. Assumption of the B.V.M. [Aug. 15] 1329. Grant by Gregory son of William son of Petronilla, to Thomas his son, of 3 acres and one and a half roods of arable land in the fields and territory of Hymlesworth, of which one and a half roods lie above le Rissiforelang, one and a half lie in the place called Mapel and one and a half in a place called Prestrodewelle, and one and a half abut above le Schaghe near the dike which is called Cortedike, and one rood lies in Yohkwelleforelang, and one and a half extend on bothe sides of the path leading to the dwelling once belonging to Jordan del Ker, and one and a half roods lie in a place called Thurkelheued abutting on the assart of the grantor, and one rood lies in the place called Watirslak; to hold to Thomas freely and in peace, of the chief lords of the fee. Warranty. Sealing clause. Witnesses: Adam de Wannerwille, lord of Hymlesworth, Dom. Simon de Baldiston, John de Burton, Geoffrey de Staynton, John Byset. At Hymlesworth. (*Ibid.*, No. 36).

272. Whitsunday [May 27], 1352. Grant by Thomas de Skolay to Margaret, daughter of John del Rodes, for a sum of money, of a toft with a croft adjacent, in Hymmesworthe which lies between the tenement of Margaret Almot on the west and the tenement of John Gudhayr on the east; to hold to Margaret, her heirs and assigns, of the chief lords of the fee, freely and in peace with all appurtenances, liberties and easements. Warranty. Sealing clause[1]. Witnesses:

[1] Fragment of a seal of yellow wax, blurred.

Adam Wanneruill, lord of Hymmesworthe, Robert Tupper of the same, John de Staynton del Redyng, John de Walton of Hesyll, John Ameas of the same. At Hymesworthe. (*Ibid.*, No. 37).

273. Tuesday April 23, 1359. Grant by Margaret, daughter of Thomas de Skollay in her pure virginity, to Alice, daughter of Robert Tuppe of Hymmesworth, of all that toft with adjacent croft in the vill of Hymmesworth, which she had of the gift of Margaret daughter of John del Rodes [*as in the preceding deed*]; to hold, of the chief lords of the fee, freely with all liberties and easements. Warranty. Sealing clause[1]. Witnesses: Adam de Wanneruill', John de Staynton, John de Walton, John de Amyas, Robert Tuppe. At Hymmesworthe. (*Ibid.*, No. 38).

274. Sunday after the Nativity, 35 Edward III [Dec. 26, 1361]. Indenture[2] whereby William de Sapinton, rector of the church of Hymmesworth grants to William de Tankerslay and Cecily, his wife, all the lands and tenements which he had of the gift and feoffment of the said Cecily, with all appurtenances in Hymmesworth, to hold to William and Cecily, freely, of the chief lords of the fee, and after the death of Cecily, remainder to Joan Roberddoghtir Wanneruill and Ellen Roberddoghtir Wanneruill, their heirs and assigns. Warranty. Sealing clause[3]. Witnesses: John de Steynton, Robert Tupper, Thomas de Scollay, Elias Coly, John son of Cecily. At Hymmesworth. (*Ibid.*, No. 39).

275. Wednesday before the Conversion of St. Paul, 43 Edward III [Jan. 23, 1369-70]. Appointment by Thomas Baylle, rector of the church of Hykelton, of Edward de Dronsfeld to deliver seisin to John son of William de Wynteworth of Burghwaleys, of all the lands and tenements, meadows, woods, rents and services in the vills of Hymmesworth, le Wode, Thwong', Ryhill, Hyndelay, Smeton, Balne and Wrangbrok, in accordance with the indenture granting the same to the said John. Sealing clause. At Northelmsall. (*Ibid.*, No. 40).

276. Jan. 20, 13 Henry IV [1411-2]. Indenture whereby Dame Isabel, widow of William de Burton, and Richard her son, grant and demise to John Coly and William Coly, his brother, a close in the fields of Hymmesworth, containing in estimation 22 acres of land and meadow, just as it stands enclosed by fences (*sepibus*), which John Hobson lately held, together with free entry and exit for their carts along a certain path between their land and the meadow of Nodestede, in length from the . . .[4] of Kynneslay as far

[1] Oval seal of red wax; a standing figure holding a gridiron, presumably St. Laurence, flanked by leaves and a star; SAVN . . . . AVRENC.

[2] Also counterpart of the indenture.

[3] Broken seal of white wax.

[4] Document rubbed.

as the aforesaid close; to hold to John and William from Martinmas next following these presents for the full term of 20 years, paying yearly to Dame Isabel and Richard 18*s*. sterling in equal parts at Whitsuntide and Martinmas and boon service of one reaping (*unam precariam unius messoris*) in the autumn for all services. Should the rent be in arrears for a week, power to the grantors to enter and retain the close. The said John and William are to repair and keep up the hedges and ditches of the said close at their own cost and expense without waste (*uasto*) in so doing. Warranty. Alternate seals. At Kynneslay. (*Ibid.*, No. 41).

277. June 5, 16 Henry VI [1438]. Release and quitclaim by Thomas Arch', son and heir of John Arch', to Thomas Marton, son and heir of Simon Marton, of the full possession of a tenement, 3½ acres and half a rood of land with appurtenances in Hymmesworth, which tenement lies between the tenement recently belonging to John Seccar on the west and the tenement of Robert Tuppe on the east. Warranty. Sealing clause. Witnesses: William Scargill, esq., Robert Neuyle, esq., Richard Burton, John Scolay, John Wod. At Hymmesworth. (*Ibid.*, No. 42).

278. Martinmas [Nov. 11], 1454. Grant and demise by John Wentworth of Northelmsall, esq., to John Ruke of Hymesworth, husbandman, of a messuage with buildings thereon, near the end of Hymesworth, with a bovate of land which lies in divers places in the territory of Hymesworth, and a close called Gillrode and another called Grysepeghell with another called Dobynrode; to hold the said messuage, lands and closes to John, his heirs and assigns for the full term of 30 years next following Martinmas, 1454, paying yearly to the grantor 20*s*. and 40*d*. during the said term, for all services. Alternate seals. At Northelmesall. (*Ibid.*, No. 43).

279. Jan. 14, 35 Henry VI, 1456[-7]. Indenture whereby John Wenteworth of Northelmsall, Joan, his wife and Thomas, their son, grant and demise to John Roke of Hymesworth lands [*as described in the preceding deed*]; to hold to John Roke, his heirs and assigns for the full term of 60 years from Martinmas next following, paying yearly to the grantor 20*s*. 4*d*. at the usual terms; and John shall maintain at his own expense and cost everything relating to the said messuage except roofing and stonework during the said term, and he and his heirs shall have thorntrees (*spinas*), brushwood (*rumos*) and heath (*dumos*) to a reasonable degree, without impediment. Warranty. Sealing clause. At Northelmsall. (*Ibid.*, No. 44).

280. Jan. 6, 21 Edward IV [1481-2]. Grant by Thomas Marton of West Teryngton to John, his son, of all that tenement with a croft called Archethyng in the vill of Hemysworth, with all the lands, meadows, grazings and pastures and appurtenances,

which lie between the land of Thomas Rooke on the east and the land of Robert Sekkar on the west; to hold to John, his heirs and assigns, of the chief lords of the fee. Warranty. Appointment of John Skolay and John Ressheworth as his attorneys to deliver seisin. Sealing clause[1]. At Hemysworth. (*Ibid.*, No. 45).

Hensall (Snaith).

281. Grant by Adam son of Reginald son of Wace de Hethensale to William son of Hugh de Balnehecca, his heirs or assigns, of a croft in the territory of Hethensale[2] as inclosed by hedges and dikes (*fossatis*), lying by the field of Hethensale towards the vill of Hecca; namely, the croft which Reginald son of Robert de Hethensale had assigned to the grantee by the charter which Reginald son of Wace, the grantor's father, had given to the said Reginald son of Robert; to hold of the grantor and his heirs, with all easements; rendering 2*d*. yearly at Michaelmas for all secular service, as the charter which the grantor's father gave to Reginald son of Robert witnessed. Witnesses: Sir Thomas de Pouclingt[on], John de Hecca, Henry de Goldale, Hugh his brother, Ralph de Ruhale, William Vendiloc, William de Mora, John the fowler (*ancupe*), William son of Hugh son of Osbert, Roger son of Edusa, Hugh son of Walter. (*E. G. Millar, Esq.*).

282. Grant by Henry son of Henry de Vernulle to Thomas de Snayt, clerk, his heirs or assigns, of all his tenements in the vill of Hethensale, with his freemen, rents, villeins and their sequels and their movable and immovable goods, suits of courts, homages, reliefs, feudal services (*feotis*), mercheats (*merchetis*), escheats of all kinds, and all other appurtenances, commons in woods, meadows, moors, turbaries, waters, pastures, and all liberties and easements, both in services and demesnes, belonging to the said tenements and rents within the vill of Hethensale and without; for a sum of money given beforehand; to hold of the grantor and his heirs or assigns, rendering yearly to the lord of the fee or his assigns the service due, and to the grantor and his heirs or assigns ½*d*. at Christmas, for all services, suits of courts, and demands. Warranty. Witnesses: Sir Thomas de Metham, Sir John de Hetona, knts., Henry de Heck, William de Camera, Edmund[3] de Goldale, William Golding of the same, William le Tanur of Snayt, Philip the clerk[4]. (*E. G. Millar, Esq.*).

283. Grant by Henry son of Henry de Vernoyl to the same, for a sum of money given beforehand, of the service and rent of

[1] A blob of brown wax; a geometric device.
[2] Balnehecke so spelt.
[3] Eadm'do; and Eadmundo in the next deed.
[4] Endorsed in a medieval hand: Carta Henr[ici] de Vernoil de ten[ementis] in Heth'.

one bovate of land with appurtenances in the vill of Hethensale; namely, the bovate which Thomas Fraunceos and his ancestors had held of the grantor and his ancestors; and a bovate of land with appurtenances which Adam Prest formerly held in bondage of Henry, the grantor's father, in the same vill, with all Adam's, sequel not signed; also grant of John son of Adam Prest, his villein, with all his sequel and chattels, Roger brother of the said John, and Henry and Osbert his brothers, his villeins, with their sequels and chattels and movable and immovable goods: to hold of the grantor and his heirs or assigns, with all liberties, commons, easements, homages, services, reliefs, escheats, merchets, suits of courts of all kinds, and all other appurtenances in woods, meadows, feedings, pastures, moors, marshes, turbaries, both in services and demesnes, belonging to the said tenements and rents; rendering [*etc. as in previous deed*]. Warranty. Same witnesses[1]. (*Ibid.*).

284. Grant by John son of Ralph de Ruhale to Thomas de Snayt, clerk, his heirs or assigns, for a sum of money given beforehand, of a rent of 12*d*. yearly on St. Laurence's day; namely, 6*d*. from Adam son of William at the well (*ad fontem*) of Hethinsale and his heirs, for a toft with buildings, lying between the tofts formerly belonging to Henry at the well and to Nicholas respectively in the vill of Hethinsale, and 6*d*. from Millicent sister of Henry son of William at the well and her heirs, for a toft with buildings in the same vill, lying between the tofts formerly belonging to the said Nicholas and to Avice daughter of John the fowler; which rent the grantor's father had sold to Henry son of William at the well of Hethinsale and issued a charter [therefor]; to hold of the grantor and his heirs, with homages, reliefs, approvements and escheats, belonging both in respect of the tofts and rent; rendering yearly a rose at the feast of St. John the Baptist for all services, suits of court and forinsec service. Witnesses: Sir John de Hetona, knt., Henry de Heck, John de Goudal, Thomas Fraunsays of Hethinsale, William Vendiloc of the same, William del Wardrop.[2] (*Ibid.*).

285. Quitclaim by John son of Thomas de Snayth, clerk, to William son of Roger Prest of Hethensale, his heirs or assigns, of all right in a messuage, one bovate of land and one quarter (*quarterio*) of land, with appurtenances in the vill and territory of Heuensale, saving a rent of 12*d*. to him and his heirs, half at Whitsuntide and half at Martinmas; rendering yearly to the chief lord 2*s*. at the usual (*statutos*) terms in the soke of Snayth. Witnesses: William de Wynteword, Laurence de Heck, William de Couwik, Jordan Auyn of Snayth, John son of Thomas of the same, Simon the clerk. (*Ibid.*).

[1] Endorsed in a medieval hand: Carta Henr[ici] Vernoil de servic[iis] in Hethensale.

[2] Seal: greenish-brown wax, round, small; a device including something resembling a fish with foliage in its mouth; ✠ . . . . IOH'I.

286. April 10, 20 Richard II [1397]. Release[1] by Master John de Newton, treasurer of the cathedral church of St. Peter of York, John Ameas of Chitlyngton, Nicholas Norfolk of Naburn, William Rosselyn of Cotenais, Nicholas Rosselyn of the same, Sir John Pygot, clerk, and John Pigot the younger, to John Daunay, his heirs and assigns, of all right in a windmill in the field of Hensall with its site, which they lately had of the grant and feoffment of Adam son of Roger de Wentworth of Snayth. (*Ibid.*).

Hesselton.

287. March 10, 9 Henry V [1421-2]. Indenture whereby Matilda, widow of William Carter of Neuton' granted and demised to Robert Rynoscow a tenement and 4 acres of land in Esilton; to hold to Robert for the term of his life on the following condition; namely, that he shall repair the said tenement sufficiently at his own expense, and he shall pay for the first 4 years next following, ½*d.* at Martinmas and thereafter to Matilda or her executors or attorney, 3*s.* yearly in equal portions at Martinmas and Whitsuntide and performing the due and accustomed services. Power to Matilda to enter and distrain should the rent be in arrears, wholly or in part, until satisfaction is obtained. As guarantor for this agreement Robert Cabayne binds himself on Matilda's behalf in the sum of 40*s.* Alternate seals.[2] Witnesses: John de Neuton', gentleman (*domicello*), ... Bowhys, John Bolton, At Bedal. (*R. Lee, Esq.*).

South Hiendley.

288. Sunday after SS. Philip and James, 6 Henry VI [May 2, 1428]. Grant by John Jenkynson of Shafton to John Mershall atte Well, of 20 acres of land and meadow with appurtenances in Southhendley in the parish of Felkirk; to hold to John Mershall, his heirs and assigns, of the chief lords of the fee. Warranty. Sealing clause[3]. Witnesses: John Heyron of Southhendley, Robert de Watton, John Chapman of the same, John [Watton] of the same, Robert the clerk of Hodrod. At Southhendley. (*Serlby Hall Muniments*, No. 46).

289. Monday the Invention of the Cross, 6 Henry VI [May 3, 1428]. Grant by John Mershall atte Well to John Jenkynson of Shafton, of 20 acres of land and meadow in Southhendley, in the parish of Felkirk; to hold to John Jenkynson and his lawfully begotten heirs, of the chief lords of the fee. Sealing clause[4]. Witnesses: [*as to preceding deed*]. At Southhendley. (*Ibid.*, No. 47).

[1] Apparently a draft or contemporary copy, not executed.
[2] Two blobs of red wax on tongues cut from the bottom of the deed.
[3] Seal of red wax, diam. ⅞ in.; a squirrel; * . . . RA . E.
[4] Seal as to preceding deed.

290. May 20, 1461. Grant[1] by William Verley of Athewyk to John Jenkynson, junior, son and heir of John Jenkynson of Shafton, of all the lands and tenements, meadows, woods and pastures, with all appurtenances in Southendley which the grantor recently had of John Jenkynson, senior; to hold with all appurtenances to John, of the chief lords of the fee. Warranty. Sealing clause[2]. Witnesses: Robert Chapman of Southendley, John Walton of the same, Thomas Gest of the same. At Southendley. (*Ibid.*, No. 48).

291. Feb. 24, 5 Edward IV [1465-6]. Release and quitclaim by Robert Toy to Thomas Jenkynson, of all right in the lands, tenements, rents and services with appurtenances which he recently held with John Fryston, John Watton and Robert Watton, now deceased, of the gift and feoffment of John Jenkynson, uncle of the said Thomas, in the vill and fields of Southhendley. Warranty. Sealing clause[3]. Witnesses: Richard Wageor, John Smyth, John Elyot, John Johnet, John Day. At Southhendley. (*Ibid.*, No. 49).

292. Jan. 29, 7 Henry VII [1492-3]. Grant by Henry Jenkynson, son and heir of Thomas Jenkynson of Southyndley, to Robert Scoley of Hauercroft and John Scoley, chaplain, brother of Robert, of all the messuages, lands and tenements, rents and services in Southyndley and elsewhere in co. York, excepting only a messuage in Shafton, lately held by William Huthon with all the lands and meadows pertaining to the said messuage; to hold to the grantees, their heirs and assigns, of the chief lords of the fee. Warranty. Sealing clause. Witnesses: John Wageor, John Norfolk, John Watton, At Southyndley. (*Ibid.*, No. 50).

293. July 1, 23 Henry VII [1508]. Demise by John Scoley, chaplain, to Henry Jenkynson, son and heir of Thomas Jenkynson, recently of Southyndley, of all the messuages, lands and tenements, rents and services in Southyndley and elsewhere in co. York, which the grantor lately held in conjunction with Robert Scoley, late of Hauercroft, his brother, now deceased, of the gift and feoffment of the said Henry, to hold to Henry, of the chief lords of the fee. Appointment of John Wageor as his attorney to deliver full and peaceful seisin of the above. Sealing clause. (*Ibid.*, No. 51).

Houghton (Castleford).

294. Sunday after St. Michael and All Angels [Oct. 5], 1337. Grant by Alice, daughter of Martin de Hoghton', wife of Henry son of Alexander de Sutton, to John Otur of Castelford and Custance, the grantor's daughter, of a certain half acre of arable land with

[1] Blob of red wax; IHS.

[2] Same date. Appointment of Nicholas Verley, son of William Verley, as attorney to deliver seisin. Same seal. (*Ibid.*, No. 48a).

[3] Small seal of dark brown wax, the letter I.

appurtenances which lies in the field of Hoghton' in a place called Sutcliff, between the land of John le Day on both sides, and which abuts on the highway leading towards Pontefract; to hold to John and Custance, their heirs and assigns, freely [*etc.*] of the chief lords of the fee. Warranty. Sealing clause. Witnesses: John de Crinyune[?] of Hoghton, Hugh son of Osbert de Castelford, William son of William Bate of the same, John son of Roger de Castleford of Qwittewode. At Castelford. (*Y.A.S.*, Md. 161, No. 12).

Howden.

295. June 16, 17 Edward IV [1477]. Agreement[1] between Ellen Monkton of Cavill widow and Robert, her son, of the one part, and Robert Lucas of Houeden and Jennet, his daughter of the other, whereby Robert Monkton agrees to wed Jennet; Robert Lucas to *make cost of aray* of Jennet at the day of the marriage also the cost of the dinner, and Ellen to meet the *cost of aray* of Robert on the said day; Robert Lucas and Ellen each to give his or her child 6 marks and Robert Lucas to give Robert and Jennet their *burde, mete, drynk, horsemete, hay and letter* for 6 years; he also binds himself at his death to give Jennet as much of his goods as to both Agnes Donyngton and Elizabeth Pertryke. Both parties bind themselves in the sum of 200 marks. Sealing clause. Witnesses: Sir Marmaduke Constable, Robert Shefeld, Thomas Dalayron. At Houeden. (*Serlby Hall Muniments*, No. 52).

296. July 20, 22 Edward IV, 1482. Indenture whereby Ellen Monkton and Robert, her son, grant to Robert Marler all their lands and tenements in Hoveden, Belby, Thorp Kylpyn, Duncotes, Balcome[2], Newlands, Tornefeld Dike, Benetland, Grenakholme[3], Drewton, Southcave, Neswik, Brakyn, Estrington, Lathome and Melborne with all appurtenances, which belonged to William Moston and Joan, his wife; to hold to Robert for the term of his life and after his death to Thomas his son and Joan his wife and their lawfully begotten heirs; and in default of issue remainder to 1) Alice Vavesor and Margaret Marler, sisters of Thomas Marler, and their lawfully begotten heirs, 2) to the right heirs of William Moston and Joan, his wife. Warranty against the abbot of Westminster and his successors. Appointment of Thomas Cotnesse and William Mylner as their attorneys to deliver seisin. Alternate seals[4]. (*Ibid.*, No. 53).

297. Oct. 18, 24 Henry VII [1508]. Grant by John Nelson, son and heir of Hipolitas Nelson, late of Houeden, to Henry Dave of Houeden, of a messuage in Houeden, lying in the place called

[1] In English, paper draft or copy of deed.
[2] Balkholme.
[3] Greenoak.
[4] Two blobs of red wax, on the first a fleur-de-lis.

Halegat between the messuage once of Peter del Hay now held by Mary Thwats on the east and the tenement of Thomas Metham esq., on the west, together with 8 acres of land and meadow belonging to the said messuage, which lies in divers places in the fields of Houeden on the south side of the said vill, all of which came to the grantor by hereditary right after the death of Hipolitas, his father; to hold to Henry, his heirs and assigns, of the chief lords of the fee. Warranty. Sealing clause. Witnesses: Dom. Elverdo Richardson, chaplain, Richard Kyghlei, John Robson, Thomas Lawton, John Cott. At Houeden.[1] (*Ibid.*, No. 54).

Dorso: Seisin delivered before Robert Allanson, Luke Holand, Robert Atkinson, Richard Berne, Robin Beswyk, the day within written.

Hunshelf.

298. St. Luke, 1 Henry V [Oct. 18, 1413]. It is agreed by Richard Oxsprynge, John son of William Brounhede and Jordan Marchall, that whereas they have received by his charter of feoffment, all the goods, moveable and fixed, of Thomas Greve, they now depute to the said Thomas full power and licence in respect of the goods for the administration therof to their use and profit, and they entirely hand them over until they shall jointly revoke this present warrant. Sealing clause.[2] At Hunschelfe. (*Y.A.S.*, Md. 244, No. 10).

Hutton-Lowcross.

299. 1383. Agreement between Hugh son of Richard de Hoton and Walter son of John de Thorp whereby Hugh grants to Walter in perpetuity, common pasture for all his animals except goats between Crosgates and Langesty, where the way goes down from Crosgate to Holgryp, also from Langesty as the wood of Othenclvue extends to the close of Thynghoudale, with the grazing of Nesse when it is not sown, similarly with common pasture for the said animals of Walter in the moor of the said Hugh de Hoton, namely, from le Pykedhowe towards the south, just as it is found in the wood of Restanes. Hugh also grants to Walter 3 cartloads of the trunks and 4 cartloads of branches to be taken from his wood of Hoton at the Lord's Nativity and 30 bundles (*trussa*) of heather at the same time each year, in perpetuity. Should it happen that in the time of pannage, that Walter's pigs in seeking grazing cross the path of Crosgate towards the north as far as the woods of the said Hugh, Walter shall give to Hugh or his heirs better . . .[3] grazing in the time of pannage. Hugh may

[1] Endorsed, the dede of ye mese and lands late of ye heres of Hippolyte Neleson, belongyng to Henrie Dave of Hoveden.

[2] Seals: three, of black wax, all on one tongue cut from the bottom of the deed. (1) and (3), similar, the letter R between sprays of leaves, (2) blurred, the letter W.

[3] Document badly rubbed.

make a park or enclose at his will over and above his manor of Hoton, and for the grazing of his animals on the moor of the said . . . of Pykedhowedale, Walter shall pay ½*d.* for each animal yearly, and he shall [grind his corn] at Hugh's mill to the sixtieth measure; paying yearly to the said Hugh and his heirs a pound of pepper a pound of cummin and 1*d.* at the Nativity for all secular services and demands. Warranty. Sealing clause[1]. [Witnesses illegible]. (*R. Lee, Esq.*).

Kepwick.

300. Monday after the Invention of the Holy Cross, 14 Edward son of Edward [May 4], 1321. Release and quitclaim by John son of Thomas son of Robert de Kepuwyk, to Thomas son of Walter de Leke, of all right in a toft with a croft in the vill of Kepuwyk and in 7 strips of land adjacent in the field of Kepuwyk, which toft, croft and land he had of the gift of Thomas and Cecily, his father and mother. Warranty. Sealing clause. Witnesses: Ingram Knut, Thomas de Leke, Oliver de Silton, Walter de Leke. At Kepuwyke. (*Newburgh Priory Muniments*, No. 8/31).

Kilham.

301. Grant by William son of Geoffrey Attehowe of Killum to Dom. Ralph son of William Dunsour of Pokethorp, chaplain and his heirs and assigns, of a messuage and 3 bovates of land with appurtenances in Killum, and of a toft with buildings thereon and half a bovate of land with appurtenances in Hugat, which the grantor had by hereditary right after the death of William Attehowe, his father; to hold to Dom. Ralph, of the chief lords of the fee. Warranty. Sealing clause. Witnesses: Geoffrey Randolph, Walter Tanur, William de Langetoft, Richard Textor, Thomas le Carter. (*N. G. Hyde*, No. 16).

Kinsley.

302. Grant by Thomas son of John de Kineslay to Adam de Castilford, of his capital messuage and a bovate of land with appurtenances in the vill and territory of Kynneslaye, which bovate lies in divers places throughout the field of Kynneslay towards the south, namely, one acre in Cinderforlandis between the land of Alexander Munte and William Suete, and half an acre is in le Burhys, one acre in Wetlandis, half an acre in le Bretlandis, two half acres as they lie in Ryecroft, one acre at Kyrkebrige, half an acre in Kyrkeforlange, one acre in le Halye, one acre in Thereplandis, half an acre above Baldewinhil, one acre called Lyttilacre, one acre in le Westmor, one acre at Lauerhende and one acre in Longeforlandis between the grantor's lands, and a croft which belongs to the said capital messuage; in return for a sum of money given to Thomas by the said Adam; to hold to Adam, his heirs and assigns, of the

[1] Probably a draft or copy as there is no evidence of a tongue or seal.

chief lords of the fee, freely, quietly and in peace, with all liberties and easements as held by the grantor; performing the due and accustomed services and paying to the grantor 1*d.* at the Purification of the B.V.M. for all secular services. Warranty. Sealing clause. Witnesses: Sir Robert de Saham, Thomas de Hoperton, William de Toueton of Kinneslaye, William Olyuer of the same, Richard de Wodehuses, Richard Lesquier of Dunedale. (*Serlby Hall Muniments*, No. 55).

303. Grant and quitclaim by Robert son of William de Pontefracto to William de Toueton, his heirs and assigns, of all right which he has in 6 acres of land with appurtenances in Kineslay, which he had of the gift and feoffment of Thomas de Kynneslay; to hold to William, his heirs and assigns, of the chief lords of the fee, in return for 20*s.* of silver which the grantor received from him. Sealing clause. Witnesses: Jordan del Ker, John le Plomer, William Rok, Adam de Castelford, William Olyuer. (*Ibid.*, No. 56).

304. Michaelmas, 11 Edward son of Edward [Sept. 29, 1317]. Grant by Simon de Baldreston to John de Burton of Kynnesley, of 5 tofts in the vill of Kynnesley with 4 acres and a rood of land in the adjacent crofts towards the north; he also grants 4 acres and a rood of land, of which 2 acres and a rood lie in the same field which abuts above Lececroft, and 2 acres with a meadow adjacent lie in le Wodelandes; which tenements the grantor had of the gift and feoffment of the said Adam de Wanneruyle in exchange for lands and tenements once belonging to Martin the clerk in Hymlesworth; to hold to John, his heirs and assigns, freely and in peace of the chief lords of the fee. Witnesses: Sir Adam de Wanneruyle, knt., William de Migeley, Godfrey de Steynton, John Daungerous, John del Wode. At Kynneslay. (*Ibid.*, No. 57).

305. Friday before St. Hilary, 14 Edward son of Edward [Jan. 9, 1320-1]. Grant by John de Hesill to John de Burton of Kenislay, of an assart in the territory of Kenislay which is called Hylbertrode and which lies in length and breadth between the land of the lord Adam de Wannirwyll on the south and the old road which leads to Pontefract by way of Cawysgrewe on the north and abuts above the land of the said Adam on the west and the stream which flows through the land of John de Brakenyll and the said assart towards the east; to hold to John, his heirs and assigns, of the chief lords of the fee, with all woods, meadows, pastures and appurtenances belonging to the said assart, within and without the boundaries of Kenislay, freely and in peace in perpetuity. Warranty. Sealing clause[1]. Witnesses: Sir Adam de Wanirwyl, knt., Godfrey de Staynton, William de Megelay, John Hesill, junior, John le Arche of Ryhyll, Hugh le Nodderer, John de Bosco of Suthyndelay. At Hylbertrode. (*Ibid.*, No. 58).

[1] Seal of dark brown wax; an animal; ✱GILLA. OSS . . OSE.

306. Nov. 20, 1 Henry V [1413]. Indenture whereby Dame Isabel de Burton and Richard de Burton grant and demise to William Scolay and Alice, his wife, all the lands and adjacent meadows which lie in a certain field of Kynneslay called le Wollay between Holynwell and Wollaybrig, also the pasture and arable land of Ilberdroyde, with one parcel of land adjacent above le Westmore next to the highway; to hold to William and Alice from Martinmas next for the full term of 19 years, paying yearly to the grantors, 10*s.* 8*d.* at Whitsuntide and Martinmas in equal portions. Power to the grantors to enter and distrain should the rent be in arrears for 15 days, either wholly or in part, until full satisfaction is made, and should it be in arrears for so long as a month, power to the grantors to enter and retain, this indenture notwithstanding. William and Alice shall entrench the western boundary and the northern side (*costam*) of the said parcel of land above le Westmore, and shall surround with a quick hedge (*viua sepe*) all the lands which they shall dig at their own cost. And they shall not part with or demise the said lands during the said term. Warranty. Sealing clause.[1] (*Ibid.*, No. 59).

307. Oct. 10, 37 Henry VI [1458]. Indenture whereby William Medylton of Stokhylld, esq., and John Wynter, clerk, release and quitclaim to Richard Burton of Kynneslay, esq., a close called Jakeroyd with the adjacent meadow abutting above Carhouseyherd which they recently had of the gift and feoffment of Henry Burton, the father of Richard; to hold to Richard, his heirs and assigns, with all liberties and easements, during the lifetime of John Burton, brother of the said Richard; should Richard die while John is living, remainder to the grantors. Alternate seals. Witnesses: Thomas Medley, Thomas Whyppy, clerk, Robert Burton, John Wodhouse, John Scoley. At Kynnesley. (*Ibid.*, No. 60).

308. Oct. 10, 1474. Will of Henry Burton of Kynnesley. Being of sound mind and sane memory he commits his soul to Almighty God, Blessed Mary and All Saints, and his body to be buried on the south side of the choir of the church of Hymmesworth. He leaves:—Item: his best animal as his mortuary. Item: to Edward Hally 3*s.* 4*d.* Item: to William Mylner 3*s.* 4*d.* Item: to Robert Jonson 3*s.* 4*d.* Item: to John Proktor 3*s.* 4*d.* Item: Alice his wife to find a candle for the sepulchre of our Lord at Easter, and to find a candle yearly to burn before the image of Blessed Mary in the chapel of the B.V.M., called Burton Chapell. Item: to the priest who performs his exequies 12*d.* Item: to Dom. William Homet, 3*s.* 4*d.* Item: to Robert Harper 2*s.* Item: to John Walton 2*s.* The residue of his goods he leaves to Alice, his wife, for the payment of his debts, and he makes her his executor. He appoints William Ashton, prior of St. Oswald of Nostell and John Wynter, rector of the parish

[1] Small blob of brown wax on one of two tongues cut from the base of the deed.

church of Ackworth as supervisors for the carrying out of this will. Witnesses: William Homet, chaplain, William Mylner, Robert Johnson, Enfeoffment of James Hamerton, Henry Pudsey, Nicholas Medylton and William Serlby of all his lands and tenements.[1]

Probate granted to Alice at York, Jan. 13, 1474[-5]. (*Ibid.*, No. 61).

Kirkby Fleetham.

309. [1241] Indenture witnessing an agreement between the abbot and convent of St. Agatha of the one part and Sir Roger de Stapeltun of the other, whereby the abbot and convent release and quitclaim to Sir Roger all right in all that parcel of land meadow and wood of Kyppling' which is between Kyreby and the course of the water of Suale as it flows on the day of the Annunciation of the B.V.M. [Mar. 25], 1241; and for this release Sir Roger quitclaims to the abbot and convent all right in all that other parcel of land, wood and pasture with appurtenances which is between the said water of the Suale and the vill of Kippling'. Should the Suale by chance change its course either towards the part belonging to the abbot and convent or towards that of the said Roger, then which ever party suffers shall be compensated according to the said division. It is also agreed that if the demesne animals of the abbot and convent or those of Sir Roger, shall by chance cross the said bounds, then they shall not be impounded but driven back unharmed to their own land, and recompense made for any damage done to meadows or crops (*segetibus*). Moreover either party may strengthen its bounds against the said waters without contradiction, provided that neither party removes stones nor anything else to the detriment of the other's land, for the strengthening of his own. Alternate seals. Witnesses: Sir Brian son of Alan, Sir Roald the constable, Sir Alan son of Brian, Brother Richard de Thorneton, Precentor of Cuton[2], Sir Adam de Nayrford, Sir Adam de Magneby, Sir Adam de Aluerton, bailiff of Richemund, Richard de Nortf', Sir Thomas de Lasceles, Robert de Ayndeby. (*Y.A.S.*, Md., 40, No. 1).

310. Sunday after St. Lucy the Virgin, 14 Edward son of Henry [Dec. 14, 1281]. Indenture whereby William Gyffard grants and quitclaims to Sir Nicholas de Stapelton all his land in Fletham with appurtenances and with all his villeins, their sequel and chattels, and with the homage and service of all free tenants, except the service of Sir Brian son of Alan; namely, all the land which Sir Nicholas holds of him in the same vill, for a term of years; to hold to Sir Nicholas, his heirs and assigns in fee and hereditarily without reservation and in perpetuity, paying yearly to the grantor and his heirs, a rose at the Nativity of St. John the Baptist for all secular

[1] Fragment of an oval seal of dark brown wax; a kneeling figure; legend undeciphered.

[2] Cowton.

services, suit and demands, and performing the services due and accustomed to the chief lords of the fee. Warranty. Alternate seals. Witnesses: Sirs Robert de Lasceles of Langethorn, William de Skargyle, Henry de Watlous, knts., Robert de Hertforth, seneschal of Rychemund, Harsculf de Cleseby, bailiff, Hugh de Langegon' [sic], John de Colingham, Nigel de Saundrevile, Richard de Wyndefors, William de Makkene, Manser de Morton, William de Ridale, At Northmorton.[1] (*Ibid.*, No. 2).

311. Indenture witnessing an agreement between the abbot and convent of St. Agatha, the occupiers, and Juliana widow of Roger de Stapelton and Nicholas son and heir of the said Roger and Juliana, plaintiffs, relating to two parts of wood and pasture lying between the vill of Kirkeby and the course of the Suale in the territory of Kippling, and to the dower which the said Juliana was seeking to obtain in the woodland and pasture of the wood of Kippling on the other side of the river Suale, namely between the vill of Kippling and the said river, of which lands Roger her husband had been seised. Wherefore the said abbot and convent agree to surrender the two parts of wood and pasture to Nicholas, to be held of them, so that Juliana, his mother, should maintain them for his use until he reached lawful age, paying yearly at the fair (*nundinas*) at Richemund, a gilt spur to the said abbot and convent for all services; and Juliana, for her part, quitclaimed to the abbot and convent all right in the said dower of wood and pasture near Kipplyng, and for this release the abbot and convent granted to her, two parts of the two bovates of land with appurtenances in the vill of Kipplying which Roger, her husband once held of Sir Roald, until the attainment of lawful age of the nearest heirs of Roger de Stapelton, in respect of which Juliana should perform the forinsec service pertaining to the same, and should pay yearly to them a rent of half a mark in equal portions at Whitsuntide and Martinmas. Should the animals of either party stray across the boundaries they were not to be impounded but chased back unharmed, and compensation given for any damage to the meadows or crops. Alternate seals. Witnesses: Sir Roald son of Alan, Sir Pygote de Lasceles, Robert de Stapelton, Thomas de Lasceles, Thomas de Hoterington, Adam de Alurton, Alan de Crakehale. (*Ibid.*, No. 3).

312. Indenture between Sir Miles de Stapelton and Dame Juliana, prioress of Marrigg,[2] whereby Juliana with the assent of the convent and chapter, grants and quitclaims to Sir Miles, all the lands, woods and tenements which she has in Fletham in a certain place and which have been enclosed by the said Sir Miles and which adjoin his manor in Kirkebyfletham; to hold to Sir Miles, his heirs and assigns in his severalty (*in suo seperali*), of the chief lords of the fee; she also quitclaims all right in a pond in the close, with the

[1] For the Stapleton connection with North Moreton, Berks., see Y.A.J., Vol. VIII, p. 86 *et seq.*

[2] Marrick.

common pasture or woodland which may be brought in by extension of the said enclosure. In exchange for this release, Sir Miles grants and confirms to the prioress and convent, 3 acres and half a rood with appurtenances in Fletham; to hold to the prioress and convent in pure and perpetual alms. Alternate seals. Witnesses: Sirs Brian son of Alan, Thomas de Rychemund, Harsculf de Cleseby, knts., Henry le Scrop, Henry son of Conan, Richard de Bernyngham. (*Ibid.*, No. 4).

313. Wednesday, St. Nicholas, 30 Edward son of Henry [Dec. 6, 1301]. Grant by Henry le Scrope to Sir Miles de Stapelton, of his land with a parcel of wood and waste, namely that land with wood and waste which lies adjacent to the manor of Sir Miles at Kirkeby in the place between the lands, woods and waste which Sir Miles had of the gift of Henry son of Conan and the prioress of Marrig', namely, all and so much as shall belong to the grantor within a certain area defined and measured out by one plough-team (*tractatum per unam carucam*), with the consent of the said Henry son of Conan and the prioress of Marrig'; to hold to Sir Miles and his heirs of the chief lords of the fee. Warranty. And because the said Miles has other lands, woods and waste of the gift of Henry son of Conan and also of the prioress, in a place adjoining the other boundaries within the said area, Henry grants that Sir Miles and his heirs may enclose all those lands, woods and waste with appurtenances within and next to the said area, by a wall, fence or hedge; to have and hold them in his severalty in perpetuity. Warranty. Sealing clause. Witnesses: Sirs Brian son of Alan, Harsculf de Cleseby, knts., Hugh de Colingham, Robert de Aynderby, Adam de Kirkeby, Adam son of John, John son of Adam. At Fletham. (*Ibid.*, No. 5).

314. Wednesday, St. Nicholas, 30 Edward son of Henry [Dec. 6, 1301]. Grant and quitclaim by Miles de Stapelton and Henry son of Conan de Fletham to Henry le Scrope, of the right to enclose and completely appropriate to himself all that piece of land which lies outside the old gateway of the said Henry le Scrope towards the north, in the vill of Fletham, together with all the water which flows through the same piece of land, starting from the corner of the byre of the same Henry towards the east, which is situated above the plot of land which Henry had of the gift of Petronilla de Conyers, and continuing towards the west as far as the messuage of Henry Payne. Warranty. Sealing clause[1]. Witnesses: Hugh de Colingham, Adam de Kirkeby, Adam son of John, John son of Adam. Henry Payne. At Fletham.[2] (*Ibid.*, No. 6).

315. Sunday after St. Nicholas, 30 Edward son of Henry [Dec. 10, 1301]. Indenture whereby Sir Miles de Stapelton grants

[1] Tongues for two seals; (1) fragments of an oval seal of white wax; (2) fragment of an armorial seal; a cross fusily; legend undeciphered.

[2] Endorsed in a contemporary hand, Relaxac' de Stapilton et Henricus fil' Conani de ten' in Fletham.

and confirms to Henry le Scrop', all his wood of Fletham and all the waste pertaining which he has anywhere within the confines of the vill, without reservation; to hold to Henry with all the common pasture which Sir Miles has in the woods of Henry son of Conan and the prioress of Marrigg in the territory of Fletham, just as held by the said Sir Miles; to hold to Henry, his heirs and assigns, freely [*etc.*], of the chief lords of the fee. Warranty. Release and quitclaim of the same with warranty clause. Moreover Sir Miles agrees that Henry may enclose the same when he wishes and hold it in his severalty, and should it happen that Henry or his heirs are able by any means to obtain those woods or part of them which belong to the prioress and Henry son of Conan, they may similarly be enclosed by Henry, when and how he wishes, without impediment from Sir Miles or his heirs; and for this grant Henry agrees that the cattle of Sir Miles shall not be interfered with or impounded in the said wood or waste in the open season (*tempore aparto*), until such time as the said wood and waste should be enclosed by Henry or his heirs. And it is agreed for all time that Henry, by reason of, and in accordance with the terms of this grant may enclose in the said woods and waste, and in the other woods which he may abtain, when and in what way he wishes without hindrance or impediment. Warranty. Alternate seals.[1] Witnesses: Sirs Brian son of Alan, Harsculf de Cleseby, knts., Hugh de Colingham, Adam de Kirkeby, Adam son of John, John son of Adam. At Fletham. (*Ibid.*, No. 7).

316. Final concord at Westminster three weeks after Easter-day, 9 Edward son of Edward [May 2, 1316], before William de Bereford, Lambert de Frikyngham, John de Benstede, John Bacun, John de Mutford, justices, and others, between Henry le Scrop', *quer.* and Nicholas de Stapleton, *imped.* concerning Nicholas's promise to present a suitable priest to the church of Kirkeby Fletham, which is vacant; in respect of which an agreement was made between the two in this same court, whereby Henry granted to Nicholas the presentation to that church during the vacancy; for which concession Nicholas agreed for himself and his heirs that in the case of a vacancy from death, dismissal, resignation or removal of the clerk presented by him, then Henry, his heirs or assigns should make the next two successive presentations without hindrance; and Henry granted that when the living became vacant for any of the above reasons after the two presentations, then Nicholas, his heirs or assigns should make one presentation without impediment; and so the said Nicholas shall have one presentation to the church and Henry shall have two, and so forth in perpetuity.[2] (*Ibid.*, No. 8).

317. Tuesday before St. Barnabas the Apostle, 2 Edward III [June 7, 1328]. Release and quitclaim by Henry de Kirkeby to Sir

[1] Oval seal of white wax; undeciphered.

[2] Endorsed, A fyn of ye patronag of kyrby fletham.

Nicholas de Stapelton, knt., of all right in two closes with appurtenances in Kirkeby Fletham, namely in that close behind the garden belonging to Sir Nicholas, and that close lying adjacent to the garden which once belonged to William de Wyndhill, which closes Miles de Stapelton, father of Nicholas caused to be enclosed; to hold to Nicholas, his heirs and assigns in perpetuity. He also releases all actions and whatever secular demands he has against the said Nicholas, by reason of debts, contracts [*etc.*], from the beginning of time until these presents. Warranty. Sealing clause[1]. Witnesses: Sirs John de Stapelton, Thomas de Rokeby, knts., William Basset, Thomas de Fencotes, William de Scurueton. At York. (*Ibid.*, No. 9).

318. Wednesday before St. Barnabas the Apostle, Edward III [June 8, 1328]. Indenture whereby Nicholas de Stapleton, knt., son and heir of Miles de Stapleton, grants to Henry de Kirkeby a toft and a bovate of land with appurtenances in Kirkeby Fletham, namely, the toft which lies between the land of the said Henry on one side and the land once belonging to William de Wyndhill on the other, and the bovate of land which Thomas, son of Juliana once held; to hold to Henry and his lawfully begotten heirs, of the grantor and his heirs, paying yearly 2*s*. of silver in equal portions at Whitsuntide and Martinmas for all services. Warranty. Should Henry die without lawfully begotten heirs, reversion to the grantor. Alternate seals[2]. Witnesses: John de Stapelton, Thomas de Rokeby, knts., William Basset, Thomas de Fencotes, William de Scurueton. At York. (*Ibid.*, No. 10).

319. Saturday, St. Andrew the Apostle, 10 Edward III Nov. 30, 1336]. Release and quitclaim by Elias de Fletham and Elizabeth, his wife, to Nicholas de Stapelton, knt., of all right in the common pasture of a certain place called Kyrkebyclos in the vill of Kyrkebyfletham, namely, as much as pertained to their free tenancy in the said vill. Warranty. Sealing clause. Witnesses: Henry de Kyrkeby, Adam del Spens, Thomas Folet, John Folet, John son of Adam. At Kyrkebyfletham. (*Ibid.*, No. 11).

320. Thursday the vigil of SS. Peter and Paul, 15 Edward III [June 28, 1341]. Grant by Robert son of Richard Russell of Kirkeby to William Hildon of Willey, of a messuage in Kirkeby, lying between the toft of Edmund Perepount on one side and the toft of William Goguerifeld on the other, and a piece of land called Gospitelwong lying in the field of Herthwik in Kirkeby, between the land of the lord of Kirkeby on one side, and the land of the rector of the church of Kirkeby on the other, with all appurtenances; to hold to William, his heirs and assigns, of the chief lords of the fee. Warranty. Sealing

1 Seal of red wax, broken and undeciphered.
2 Fragment of a seal of red wax.

clause. Witnesses: Sir John de Anesley, knt., Reginald de Anesley, William de Selston, Thomas de Langton, Robert de Lyndeby, William son of Gilbert de Kirkeby, Gilbert son of Matilda of the same. At Kirkeby. (*Ibid.*, No. 12).

321. Jan. 20, 23 Edward III [1349-50]. Indenture whereby Miles de Stapelton, knt., grants to Thomas son of Henry de Kirkeby and Isolde, daughter of John Vauasour and their lawfully begotten male heirs, of common pasture for two cows in the wood of Kirkeby-fletham, lying near the Swale; should Thomas and Isolde die without heirs, then the grant to lapse. Warranty. Alternate seals[1]. Witnesses: Sir Thomas de Haslarton, John Vauasour, John de Kirkeby, William de Hollethorp. At Hathelsey. (*Ibid.*, No. 13).

322. Friday before the vigil of the Assumption of the B.V.M., 29 Edward III [Aug. 14, 1355]. Grant by John de Kirkeby of Wygenthorp to Miles de Stapelton, knt., of all his lands and tenements with appurtenances in Kirkebyfletham which he had of the gift and feoffment of Sir Nicholas de Stapelton, father of Milo; to hold to Miles, his heirs and assigns, of the chief lords of the fee freely and quietly in perpetuity. Warranty. Sealing clause[2]. Witnesses: Richard le Scrop', Thomas de Fencotes, knts., Richard de Richemond, John de Fletham, Thomas de Kirkeby. At Kirkeby.[3,4] (*Ibid.*, No. 14).

Langton (N.R.).

323. Tuesday the morrow of St. Thomas the Apostle, 33 Edward son of Henry [Dec. 22, 1304]. Quitclaim by Geoffrey son of Thomas de Gormyre to Sir Milo de Stapelton, knt., of all right in 4 acres of meadow with appurtenance lying in the meadows of Mickellangeton in the place called Mickeldale, which 4 acres the said Milo had of the gift and feoffment of Thomas the grantor's father; to hold to Milo, his heirs and assigns of the chief lords of the fee, freely and in peace. Warranty. Sealing clause[5]. Witnesses: Sirs Thomas de Lascels, Thomas de Coluyle, Robert de Cleseby, knts., Henry Lescrope, Roger de Ask, Hugh de Langeton, Robert de Windehil, Henry de Windehil. At Mickellangeton. (*Y.A.S.*, Md. 40, No. 16).

324. Monday before the Nativity of St. John the Baptist [June 22, 1338]. Indenture whereby Nicholas de Stapelton, knt.,

[1] Tongues for two seals; on the second, a broken seal of white wax, IHS beneath a spray of leaves; legend undeciphered.

[2] Seal: brown wax, diam. $\frac{7}{8}$ in.; in a cusped border a shield of arms; a lion rampant to the dexter; * IOHIS DE KERKEBY.

[3] Endorsed: Carta J. de Kirkeby Miloni de Stap'chr facta.

[4] Appointment of Thomas de Fencotes, clerk, to deliver seisin. Same day, same seal. (*Ibid., No.* 15).

[5] Seal: brown wax, diam $\frac{1}{2}$ in.; a bird holding a twig; S'ROB'FIL. WIL . . . . LL.

quitclaims to Mag. William de Langeton, clerk, a messuage with a croft adjacent in Magna Langeton super Swale, which William holds for the term of his life of the demise of the said Nicholas; to hold to William, his heirs and assigns of the chief lords of the fee, paying yearly to Nicholas, his heirs and assigns, 3*s*. of silver in equal portions at Whitsuntide and Martinmas. Power to Nicholas to enter and distrain if the rent should be in arrears either wholly or in part. Warranty. Alternate seals. Witnesses: Henry de Kirkeby, John de Kirkeby, Robert de Midelham, Thomas de Hukerby, John Brian, clerk. At York. (*Ibid*., No. 18).

Leake.

325. St. Lawrence the Martyr, [Aug. 10], 1294, 22 Edward. Grant by John son of Ralph de Leek to Dom. John Brayzwith, called Leek, clerk, of all his manor of Leekraiynel with all appurtenances in the same vill, without reservation; to hold to Dom. John, his heirs and assigns, freely and in peace, of the chief lords of the fee, in perpetuity. Warranty. Sealing clause[1]. Witnesses: Sirs Richer de Wussand and Oliver de Buscy, knts., Adam de Leek, Walter de la Pomeray, of the same, John de Bolteby in Scilton Paynel, Robert son of Gote of the same, Edmund de Couseby, Henry de Ouerscilton, Henry, junior of the same, Roger, brother of Michael de Berouby, Otuy de Moubray of the same, Robert de Foxholes. At Leek. (*Newburgh Priory Muniments*, No. 1/10).

326. St. Lawrence the Martyr [Aug. 10], 1294, 22 Edward. Grant by John son of Ralph de Leek to Dom. John de Brayzwith, called de Leek, of all his meadow of Keepwyk, namely that which lies near Penigbekk at the head of Holsik, with all appurtenances; to hold to John, of the chief lords of the fee. Warranty. Sealing clause[2]. Witnesses [*as to the preceding deed but with the omission of the first two*]. (*Ibid*., No. 1/12).

327. July 20, 22 Edward IV [1482]. Indenture whereby Ellen Monkton and Robert Monkton, her son, grant to James Danby, son and heir of John Danby, all the lands and tenements with meadows adjacent in Leke and Brawath in co. York, which recently belonged to William Moston and Joan, his wife; to hold to James, and his lawfully begotten heirs, with remainder in default of issue to the right heirs of William and Joan. Confirmation to Ellen and Robert of James's right, title and possession of the said lands. Warranty of the same against the abbot of Westminster and his successors. Appointment of Thomas Cotnesse and William Laton to deliver seisin. Alternate seals[3]. (*Serlby Hall Muniments*, No. 62).

[1] Seal of yellow wax, broken; a lion; . . OHIS FIL' RADVL . . . .

[2] Seal as to preceding deed.

[3] Seal of red wax on one of two tongues; undeciphered.

Lebberston.

328. Conversion of St. Paul [Jan. 25], 1359[-60]. Indenture whereby William de Playce, knt., grants and demises to John son of Geoffrey de Kayton of Lebriston the northern part of a certain messuage, part of a place now lying waste and 4 bovates of land with appurtenances in Lebriston, which the grantor has and holds in the said place, of the gift and feoffment of the abbot and convent of Rievall'; to hold to John for the term of his life, of the grantor and his heirs, paying yearly 20*s*. of silver in equal portions at Whitsuntide and Martinmas for all services and demands. Warranty. Alternate seals. Witnesses: Robert Barde, Thomas de Kilwardby, William son of Robert de Kayton, William Baty, John Cresk. At Neuton near Wynteringham. John shall maintain all the houses and buildings on the said lands in as good condition as when he received them. (*E. Stanley Jones*, No. 23)

Old Malton.

329. Sunday after St. Gregory the Pope [Mar. 13], 1322[-3]. Quitclaim by Sir John Torny, knt., to Sir Gilbert de Aton', knt., of all right in all the lands, tenements, rents and services of free tenants, villeins, their sequel and chattels, which Gilbert has of his grant in the vills of Old Malton, How and Wycomb, which the grantor first had of the gift of the said Gilbert. Warranty. Sealing clause[1]. Witnesses: Walter Perchhaye, Thomas de Boulton, Simon Lund, knts., John Moryne, John de Birdesden, William de Apelton, William de Swynton. At Malton. (*J. B. Payne*, No. 2).

Menston.

330. Sunday after All Saints, 23 Edward son of Henry [Nov. 6, 1295]. Grant by Richard Cartis and Helewise, his mother, to William Attebeck of Mensington, his heirs and assigns, of a piece of land in the field of Mensington in the place called Langetoft, with the exception of the adjacent meadow, and which lies between the land of the said William and the land which once belonged to Matthew de Mensington, also a rood of land lying in the place called Greneland between the land of William and that of the said Matthew, also a strip lying in the place called Hoppedrydding between the land of William and that of Gilbert son of Beatrice; to hold to William, his heirs and assigns, of the chief lords of the fee; and the said Richard shall warrant the lands by a piece of land in the field of Mensington in a place called Dowayngayl between the land of Alexander de Mensington and the land which once belonged to Gilbert son of Michael, also a rood of their (*nostre*) land lying in the place called Greneland between the land of Alexander de Mensington and that of

[1] Seal: red wax, diam. 1 in.; a shield of arms surmounted by three feathers; a chevron between three oxen [?]. S.IO . . . IS DE TORNY.

Matilda, widow of Robert de Burlay, and a butt of land lying in the place called Mellebutte between the land of Alexander de Mensington and the land once of Gilbert son of Michael. Sealing clause. Witnesses: Walter de Midelton, Walter de Haukeswrd, Walter, his son, John de Schelleray, Michael de Raudon, Alexander de Mensington, Thomas del Rodes, Michael le Kellar, Henry son of Matthew de Mensington, William de Ottelay, clerk. At Mensington. (*Farnley Hall Muniments*, No. 105).

331. Grant and quitclaim by William son of Thomas de Menstone and Walter son of Walter de Haukeswrd, of all the land and meadow with a toft and a croft and buildings and all other appurtenances without reservation, which he once held of Walter in the vill and territory of Menstone; also a certain annual rent of 3*d.* from Richard de Merbeck and his heirs for an acre of land lying in two parts called Norcroft and Aldicroft; namely 1*d.* at Martinmas and 1*d.* at Whitsuntide, and with the homage, reliefs and wardship of the said Richard, his heirs and assigns, and ½*d.* [*sic*] in respect of forinsec service; he also quitclaims 1*d.* from William son of William Stute at Whitsuntide for an acre of land in places called Goldicroft and Ragenildcroft with his homage [*etc.*]; to hold to Walter, his heirs, and assigns, with all liberties and easements within the vill of Menston and without. Warranty by William in return for the 8 marks sterling which Walter gave to him in his great need. Sealing clause. Witnesses: Robert de Stopham, Ralph Mansel, William de Lascelles, knts., Robert de Pouil, Matthew de Brame, Hugh de Berwik, Michael son of Peter de Menston, Matthew of the same, William de Haukeswrd, Thomas Francais of the same. (*Ibid.*, No. 106).

332. Grant by Matilda, widow of Robert de Burgelay of Mensington to Adam, son of Germain de Mensington and Agnes, his wife, of half an acre of arable land in the field of Mensington in a place called Foweleskerridding towards the southern part, and half an acre of land and meadow lying above Wateridding towards the southern part, and 3 strips lying in le Wraridding towards the eastern part, and one strip lying above Grenelandes, and one strip above Goldicrok, and a piece of meadow next to Grenelandside, and a piece of meadow above Bistalbutte and Plumtesbuttes lying above Croftes, and a strip called Ringgelaygatelandes; to hold to Adam and Agnes, their heirs and assigns, of the chief lords of the fee, with all liberties and easements. Warranty. Sealing clause. Witnesses: Walter de Midelton, Walter de Heukeswortd, Alexander de Mensington, Michael Keller of the same, William Attebec of the same, Robert de Seuerbi of the same, Henry son of Matthew of the same. (*Ibid.*, No. 107).

333. Grant and confirmation by Richard son of Godewyn de Menston, to Simon son of Michael Barn of Burley, for his homage and service and for a certain sum of money, of half that bovate of

land and of a toft and croft with appurtenances which he had of Ralph Maunsel in the vill of Menston; to hold to him and his heirs with all liberties and easements [*etc.*] within the vill and without, in the same manner as the grantor held of Ralph Maunsel, paying yearly to the grantor and his heirs, 19*d.* in equal portions at Whitsuntide and Martinmas, for all service except forinsec service of the King, pertaining to the said half bovate. Warranty. Sealing clause. Witnesses: William Ward, Walter de Haukesworth, Alexander de Menston, Matthew his son, Hugh son of Richard de Burl', Michael son of Peter de Menston, Robert de Burnhage, Michael Barne of Burlay. (*Cartwright Memorial Hall, Bradford*).

Mitton.

334. Monday before the Nativity of St. John the Baptist [June 20], 1362. Will of Thomas Sotheron[1]. *In primis*, he leaves his soul to God, Blessed Mary and all Saints and his body to be buried in the church of Mitton, and his best draught animal to go before his body as his mortuary (*principali*). Item: he leaves to the high altar of Mitton 40*d.* Item: to be distributed among the poor, 15*s.* Item: to the brethren of Lancastre, 12*d.* Item: to the brethren of Weryngton, 12*d.* Item: to the brethren of Preston, 2*s.*, and to the brethren of Appilby, 2s. Item: he leaves the remainder of his goods not otherwise bequeathed, and after his debts have been paid, to his children (*liberis*). John, his son, and William, vicar of Mitton, to be his executors.

Proved before the sequestrator in the archdeaconry of York at Skipton, on June 26, 1362. (*Farnley Hall Muniments*, No. 108).

Menthorpe.

335. Thursday the eve of the Purification of the B.V.M., 49 Edward[2] III [Feb. 1, 1374-5]. Release by Robert de Haldanby and Alfred (*Aluueredum*), vicar of the church of Athelingflet, to John Dayuill of Wythmore, of all right in all the lands and tenements which they had of the grant and feoffment of the said John in the vill of Menthorp and Wythmore[3], together with the right of passage[4] (*passagis*) in Menthorp. Menthorp[5]. (*Y.A.S.*, Md. 135, No. 8).

336. Whit Monday, 6 Richard II [May 11, 1383]. Indenture between Thomas Daunay of Escryk and Thomas de Northiby of

[1] See *Yorks. Deeds*, IX, p. 126, for an indenture which appears to relate to the goods and chattels of Thomas Sotheron, *alias* Thomas le Surreys.

[2] The King's name is omitted.

[3] For details about this property and the family of d'Eyville see Raine, *Hemingbrough*, pp. 237, 289; Whitemoor is a farm in the township of Cliffe; Thomas Dawnay of Escrick acquired the property from John d'Eyville in 2 Richard II (*Ibid.*).

[4] Clearly a right of ferry over the Derwent is intended (*Ibid.*, p. 238).

[5] Two seals of yellow-brown wax, each on a tongue of the parchment; broken or blurred.

Menthorpe witnessing that whereas the latter had granted to the former, his heirs and assigns, a messuage, two bovates of land and four acres of meadow with appurtenances in Menthorpe, and had bound himself to warrant the same. Thomas Daunay granted that neither Thomas de Northiby nor his heirs should lose anything by the said warranty, because he could have the warranty of William Dayuill of Laxton and his heirs as the assign to the said Thomas de Northiby in respect of the said tenements. Alternate seals. Menthorpe. (*Y.A.S.*, Md. 141, No. 13).

Newton-le-Willows.

337. Grant by Elias son of Arnaldus de Neuton' to Roger, his brother, of the same vill, of half a rood of land and 6 perches in the territory of Neuton', lying in Stedlandis, for the services which he performed and for the 3*s*. of silver which he gave to the grantor in his great need (*in maximo negocio*); to hold to Roger, his heirs and assigns, with all appurtenances and easements, of God and the church of Blessed Patrick of Brunton', in free and perpetual alms, paying yearly to the said church, ½*d*. at the Nativity for all secular services and demands. Warranty of the said alms to the church. Sealing clause[1]. Witnesses: Robert de Camera, William Torpina, Robert son of Robert, Robert son of Walter, William de Louersale, William de Clifland. (*R. Lee, Esq.*).

338. Monday before St. Martin in the winter [Nov. 8], 1322. Indenture whereby Elias de Brumpton' grants to Alice, daughter of William de Rand, his brother, a messuage with a toft, a croft and 2 acres of land and the reversion of 2 acres of land which Emma widow of the said William holds in the name of dower and which should come to the grantor by inheritance, after the death of Emma, with all appurtenances in the vill and territory of Neuton near Patrickbrumpton'; to hold to Alice and her lawfully begotten heirs, of the grantor and his heirs, with all liberties and easements within and without the vill, paying yearly to the grantor and his assigns during his lifetime 7*s*. of silver in equal portions at Whitsuntide and Martinmas, and performing the due and accustomed services. Warranty. Alternate seals[2]. Witnesses: Roger de Lyns, Peter de Thornhill', William Tortmayn, Thomas de Swyinitwayt, Robert Norman. At Neuton'. (*Ibid.*).

339. April 30, 22 Richard II [1399]. Release and quitclaim by Agnes, widow of William Cabayn, to Robert Cabayn of Newton, of all right in a third part of all the lands and tenements with appurtenances in Newton, which belonged to the said William Cabayn on the day of his death and which third part came to her as her dower;

[1] Seal of green wax, diam. 1¼ in.; an eight pointed device; ✠SIGILL' ELIE FIL ARNALDI.

[2] Seal of brown wax, diam. ¾ in.; probably a hare; legend blurred.

to hold to Robert and his heirs, in perpetuity. Sealing clause[1]. Witnesses: John Norton', Robert Norton', John Rick, John Fletham, William Pechi. At Newton. (*Ibid.*).

340. March 4, 5 Henry VI [1426-7]. Appointment by Christopher Conyers, John Bone of Midilhame, Thomas Snape and William Ulthwayt of Crake, of John Wawane of Newtone as their attorney to take seisin of all the lands, tenements, meadows, rents and services with appurtenances in the vill of Newtone, according to the form of a certain charter of Robert Rynnyschow and Isabel his wife. Sealing clause. (*Ibid.*).

341. May 9, 12 Henry VI [1434]. Grant by Robert Rynnyscouh' of Hunton', and Isabel, his wife, to Robert de Warcopp of Westmorland, William Vyncent of Smythton, esqs., William de Balk, John de Houyngham of Byland, Robert Dayuell' of Byland, Thomas Barbur of Thriske, *yomen*, and Juliana de Newton of Crayke, the grantor's sister, of a messuage and 5 acres of land with appurtenances in the vill and fields of Newton near Patrikbrumton'; they also grant that other messuage and 4 acres of land in the vill and fields of Hesilton which they had of the gift and feoffment of Robert Cabayne; to hold to the grantees, of the chief lords of the fee. Warranty. Sealing clause[2]. Witnesses: William Nichollson of Newton, John Robynson of Newton, Thomas Porter of Newton. At Newton. (*Ibid.*).

342. Dec. 28, 15 Henry VI [1436]. Release and quitclaim by Robert Cater of Newton near Patrikbrumton to Robert Warcopp of Westmorland, William Vyncent of Smythton, esqs., William de Balk, John de Houyngham of Byland, Robert Dayuell of Byland, Thomas Barbur of Thryske, *yomen*, and Juliana de Newton of Crayke, of all right which he has in a messuage with a croft adjacent and 5 acres in the vill and fields of Newton near Patrikbrumpton. Sealing clause[3]. Witnesses: Robert Thornton of Newton in Rydale, John de Duffeld of Byland, Richard Dayuell. At Byland. (*Ibid.*).

343. St. Hilary, 17 Henry VI [Jan. 13, 1438-9]. Grant by Matilda Carter and Robert Cabayn, her son, to William Barker of Newton, of all the lands and tenements which belonged to Robert Cabayn, Robert's father; namely 2 messuages with appurtenances in the vills and territories of Newton and Hesilton; to hold to William for the term of his life, of the chief lords of the fee. Warranty. Sealing clause. Witnesses: Christopher Conyers, Thomas Momford, Robert Norton', William Aiscogh, Christopher Norton'. At Newton. (*Ibid.*).

[1] Small seal of red wax, blurred; probably the letter R between sprays of leaves.

[2] Broken seal of red wax, probably the letter R beneath a crown; the impression on the second seal appears to have been made by a ring.

[3] Broken seal of red wax, the letter R and sprays of leaves.

344. Dec. 24, 21 Henry VI [1442]. Grant[1] by Robert Carter of York, *Baxkster*, to William Barker of Newtonmorker near Patrikbrompton, of all the lands, tenements, rents, services, possessions and reversions which have come, or ought to come to the grantor, in the vill and territory of Newtonmorker, by inheritance after the death of Matilda Carter, his mother, daughter and heir of Robert Cabayne, late of Newton Morker; to hold to William, his heirs and assigns, of the chief lords of the fee. Warranty. Sealing clause[2]. Witnesses: Christopher Conyers, Thomas Mountfort, William Routh, esqs., Christopher Norton, Henry Tosdale. At Newton Morker. (*Ibid.*).

345. Oct. 24, 34 Henry VI [1455]. Release and quitclaim by Robert Carter of York, *Baxster*, to Robert Danby, justice of the lord king, Christopher Conyers of Horneby, William Burgh', senior, esqs., and Laurence Welson, chaplain, of all right in all the lands, tenements, rents, services, possessions and reversions in Newton Morker, which came to him by inheritance after the death of Matilda, his mother, daughter and heir of Robert Cabayn. Warranty. Sealing clause. Witnesses: John Conyers, Thomas Mountfort, knts., Christopher Norton, At Newton Morker. (*Ibid.*).

Otley.

346. 7 Kalends of December, 26th year of the episcopate of Walter de Gray, archbishop of York [Nov. 25. 1241]. Grant by Walter de Gray, archbishop of York, to Mag. Hugh de Ottelay, of a toft in Ottelay, namely, that which lies between the land which Geoffrey Pirtenote holds towards the east and the land which William the carpenter holds towards the west, which toft lies above the watercourse (*ductum*) called Skiterik on both sides of the said watercourse; to hold to Hugh and his heirs, of the grantor and his successors, freely, quietly and in peace, paying yearly to the grantor, 6d. in equal portions at Whitsuntide, and Martinmas, for all services. Sealing clause. Witnesses: Mag. Robert Haget, archdeacon of Richemund, Sewalo de Bouill' canon of York, Mag. William de Senedon, Walter de Call'ell, chaplain, Dom. G. de Bekland, canon of Beverley, William de Widindon, Alan de Hegel and Reginald de Scowa, clerks. At Cawod'. (*Farnley Hall Muniments*, No. 109).

347. Indenture whereby William Faukes of Newall grants to Richard de Wyginton and Beatrice, the grantor's daughter, 3 messuages, 10 bovates of land and 7 acres of meadow with appurtenances in Newall, an acre of meadow in Ottelay and a messuage and 16 acres of land and 6 acres of meadow and an acre of wood with appurtenances in Snaudon in Askwich; he also grants to Richard

[1] Quitclaim of the same to the same, dated 31 Dec., 1442. Same witnesses. Broken seal of red wax, the letter T. (*Ibid.*).

[2] Broken seal of red wax.

and Beatrice the service of Henry Vauassour and an annual rent of 4*s*. 6*d*. from 8 acres of land which the said Henry holds of the grantor in Pouelholm, also the service of Matilda, widow of Nicholas de Horton, with 4*s*. annual rent from a messuage held of the grantor by Matilda in Newall; also the service of William de Caue and 3*s*. rent from a toft, croft and 5 acres in Denton lying between Skirefare and Bollebec, which William holds of the grantor; also the services of Thomas Paylene with a rent of 7*d*. from 1½ acres lying in le Storthes in the field of Otteley which Thomas holds of the grantor; and the service of Isaac the cobbler with 2*d*. rent from an acre of land lying in Mygelay in the field of Ottelay; and the service of Robert son of Gilbert, with 4*d*. rent from an acre of land in Wymenecroft in the field of Farnelay; to hold to Richard and Beatrice and their lawfully begotten heirs with all liberties and easements in wards, reliefs, escheats and services of the said free tenants, of the grantor and his heirs, paying yearly to the grantor for the term of his life, 10*li* of legal money, in equal portions at Whitsuntide and Martinmas, and after the grantor's death paying yearly a rose at the feast of SS. Peter and Paul [June 29] to his heirs for all services, and performing the due and accustomed services. Warranty. Should Richard and Beatrice die without lawful issue, reversion to the grantor and his heirs. Alternate seals. Witnesses: Walter de Middelton, William de Farneley, William son of Elias de Castelay, William son of Hugh of the same, Henry le Vauassour of Lethelay, Richard Gafaire of the same. (*Ibid.*, 110).

348. Court of the manor held at Otley, Jan. 31, 10 Henry VII [1494-5]. At the said court Nicholas Medilton surrendered into the hand of Robert Michell, in the presence of Laurence Broune, James Scalwrey and other tenants, 3 messuages and 3 bovates of land and meadow, of which, one rood of meadow lies at Styfote, one rood of meadow in Littelromer and the other rood of meadow also there; also an acre of land once of Henry Mitton, half an acre once parcel of a certain bovate of land recently belonging to John Hogg, with appurtenances in Otteley, all to the maintenance of John Fawkes esq., and Nicholas Fawkes his son and heir apparent, and his heirs. John and Nicholas came to the said court and there received of the lord the said lands, to hold according to the custom of the manor, and they paid to the lord 16*s*. 8*d*. as fine, were admitted and did fealty. (*Ibid.*, No. 111).

Osbaldwick.

349. Court of William Potman, doctor of law, held at Strensall, Dec. 4, 1478, 18 Edward IV. To this court came John Bawde and Isabel, his wife, and surrendered into the lord's hand, a messuage and 2 bovates and 2 acres of land in the vill and territory of Osbaldwyk, within the jurisdiction of this court, to the use of Thomas Middelton. And Isabel swore at the same court that the said surrender was made

spontaneously, of her own will and without compulsion of her husband, John Bawde. And to the court came Thomas Middelton and received the said land for himself and his heirs from the lord's hand for the rent and services due and accustomed. He did homage, was admitted and gave to the lord for entry as is shown in the heading. (*Y.A.S.*, Md. 59/18, No. 30).

Oxton.

350. Sunday before St. Hilary, 40 Edward III [Jan. 10, 1366-7]. Grant by Thomas de Midelton, knt., to Dom. John de Midelton, rector of the church of Kyrkeby Rauenwath, Hugh de Kaily and John May, chaplains, of a messuage and 3 roods of arable land with appurtenances in the vill of Oxton near Taddecastre, which the grantor had of the gift and feoffment of Thomas Spayn; to hold to John, Hugh and John, their heirs and assigns of the chief lords of the fee. Warranty. Sealing clause[1]. Witnesses: William Vynter of Taddecastre, John de Kyrkeby, bailiff of the same, Robert de Bilton, Roger de Saxton, Thomas Teron[2]. (*Y.A.S.*, Md. 59/18, No. 4).

Pannal.

351. Grant by Walter de Stokeld to Elias son of John de Halton' and his heirs, of the service and homage of Alexander son of Walter de Panhale and his heirs, namely, form half a carucate of land in Panhale, with all appurtenances, liberties and easements within the vill and without, which Alexander holds of the grantor, freely, performing the forinsec service which pertains to half a carucate where 12 carucates make a knight's fee. Warranty. Sealing clause. Witnesses: Henry de Percy, John de Hauton', William de Arches, William de Hebeden, William de Stiueton, Godfrey de Alta ripa, Hugh de Hauton', Adam de Lelay. (*Y.A.S.*, Md. 59/18, No. 5).

Patrick Brompton.

352 July 21, 21 Henry VII [1506]. Indenture whereby Christopher Conyers, son and heir of Brian Conyers of Pynchynthorpe, gent., and Alice, his wife, grant and demise to William the abbot and the convent of St. Agatha near Richmond, all their lands and tenements in Brompton on Swale; to hold to the abbot and convent and their successors from Martinmas last for the term of 99 years, paying yearly to Christopher and Alice and their heirs 11*s*. sterling in equal portions at Martinmas and Whitsuntide; should the rent be in arrears for 40 days power to enter as well into the above named lands as into all the other lands of the said abbot and convent

[1] Seal: greenish wax, diam. 1 inch; in a cusped border a shield of arms; fretty, a canton; T . . . ON.

[2] Endorsed: Oxton iuxta Fenton.

in Brompton until satisfaction for the rent and arrears is obtained. Alternate seals.[1] (*R. Lee Esq.*).

Penistone.

353. April 15, 17 Edward IV [1477]. Appointment by Richard Donyng of the parish of Bradfeld, of Richard Sotheran of the same parish as his attorney to deliver seisin and possession to Thomas Scorer of Dogmanton in co. Derby, of a tenement in the parish of Penyston, called Donnyghowes, with appurtenances, according to the form of a charter to Thomas. Sealing clause. Witnesses: Richard Waynwright, John Ellys, John Adamson. (*Y.A.S.*, Md. 244, No. 11).

Pickhill.

354. Grant by Elias, rector of Pikehale, to Andrew de Magnebi' to hold of the grantor and his heirs in fee and hereditarily, 5*s*. annual rent in his mill of Pikehale, in equal portions at Martinmas and Whitsuntide, for a quitclaim of the plea between them in the king's court at York concerning the pool of the said mill at Pikehale. Warranty. Witnesses: Roger de Baduent sheriff of York[2], Richard Malebisse, Walter de Buuington, Ralph son of Ralph de Neshaim, Ralph de Muleton, Thomas de Midelton, William de Laceles, Arnald de Upsale, Geoffrey Fossard, Ralph de Laceles, Hugh de Magnebi, Halnath de Halnathebi, Nicholas de Stapelton, Alan de Holteby.[3] (*Y.A.S.*, Md. 59/18, No. 7).

Pinchingthorpe.

355. Octave of St. Hilary, 13 Edward son of Edward [Jan. 21, 1319-20]. Final concord before William de Dereford, knt., between John de Bradeleye and Adam de Thorp concerning the manor of Pynchunthorp with appurtenances, whereby it was agreed that Adam recognised the manor as the right of the said John which he had of the gift of the said Adam. For this recognition John granted to Adam the said manor and handed it over to him in the same court; to hold for his life and after his death remainder to Walter son of John de Thorp and Margaret, his wife, and the heirs of their bodies, and thereafter to the right heirs of Walter in perpetuity.

Be it held in remembrance[4] that an indenture was made between the said Walter, son of John, and the prior of Gisborne touching the attornment of the said Walter, by reason of a fine levied by John de Hoton concerning the manor of Hoton, dated Thursday before St. John the Baptist, [June 22], 1340. (*R. Lee Esq.*).

[1] Fragment of the conventual seal, red wax.
[2] Deputy-sheriff from 1194-98. *E.Y.C., Vol.* vi, p. 125.
[3] Seal of white wax, diam. 1½ in. broken; a geometric design; ✠ S. . . ELI.
[4] In French in a later hand.

356. Friday after St. Andrew the apostle, 18 Richard II [Dec. 4, 1394]. Grant by John Conyers and Robert Wyrssale to Thomas de Boynton' knt., John Conyers of Tollesby and Thomas de Ullethornes of their manor of Pynchonthorpp' with appurtenances, and all other their lands, tenements, rents and services in the same vill; to hold to Thomas, John and Thomas, their heirs and assigns in perpetuity, of the chief lords of the fee. Warranty. Sealing clause[1]. Witnesses: Ralph Bulmer, John Cauill', knts., John Percy of Kyldale, James de Toucotes, Laurence de Semer. (*Ibid.*).

357. Sept. 6, 13 Edward IV [1473]. Appointment by John Conyers, knt., of William Jakson and Robert Wederhird as his attorneys to take full and peaceful seisin from Christopher Conyers of Sokburn, knt., Robert Danby, knt., Thomas Witham, esq., Ralph Surties, clerk, Ralph Dodisworth, esq., John Middelton, esq., John Yarom, John Shirewynd' and Laurence Wilson, clerks, of the manor of Pynchynthorp with appurtenances and of a messuage and 4 acres of land and meadow in Newton near Brompton, recently the property of a certain William Barker and now held by Christopher Nicholson, according to the form of their charter to the said John Conyers. Sealing clause. (*Ibid.*).

358. Sept. 10, 13 Edward IV [1473]. Indenture[2] whereby John Conyers, knt., grants and demises to Brian, his brother and Elizabeth, his wife, daughter of Thomas Nelson of York, merchant, his manor of Pynchynthorp, a messuage and 4 acres of land in Newton near Patrikbrompton, now held by Christopher Nicholson; to hold to Brian and Elizabeth on the following terms, namely, for the term of their lives and for that of their lawfully begotten heirs, by the service of the fourth part of a knight's fee and performing the due and accustomed services without further payment to John, provided always that should it happen that Brian alienate all or any part of the said lands, or if Brian and Elizabeth die without issue, then John may re-enter upon the said lands and hold them as before, this indenture notwithstanding. Appointment by John of William Braderyng and William Caldbeck as his attorneys to deliver seisin. Alternate seals.[3] (*Ibid.*).

359. Nov. 14, 10 Henry VIII [1518]. Bond by William, prior of Gisburne to Christopher Conyers of Pynchynthorpe esq., in the sum of 100*li.* sterling payable to the said Christopher or his heirs or assigns at Michaelmas next following.

[1] Seals: (1) red wax, a small gem, a maunche between two words, undeciphered; (2) missing; (3) a blob of brown wax, blurred.

[2] A similar indenture of the same date with the additional proviso that Brian and Elizabeth perform suit of court at Horneby. Appointment of William Braderyng and Adam Lyghtfote as attorneys. (*Ibid.*).

[3] Small seal of red wax; an eagle displayed.

The condition of this obligation is that if the said prior and convent agree to abide by the arbitration of Sir Robert Brudenell', knt., one of the king's justices, and Anthony Fitzherbert, sergeant at law, in the matter of the right title and possession of all the land, meadow, pasture, heath, moor, ground rents and services in Pynchynthorp and Hoton, now in dispute between the said parties, and also in all other matters now at variance between them, so that the decision of the said arbitrators is made and given before Sunday next, then this obligation is to be null and void, otherwise to stand in full strength[1]. William, prior of Gisburn. Cristofor Conyers. (*Ibid.*).

360. June 24, 4 Elizabeth [1562]. General release by Cuthbert Chylton of Locketon, co. York, gent., to George Conyers of Pynchynthorpe of all actions, debts, demands, [*etc.*], which he has against the said George. Sealing clause.[2] Cuthbert Chylton.
Dorso: Witnesses: Thomas Smeton, Robert Smeton, John Foster, Thomas Whiett, John Clerkson, William Whiett, Richard Kyrkby (*Ibid*.).

361. April 6, 39 Elizabeth [1597]. Indenture[3] whereby Roger Lee of York, doctor of *Phissycke* and William, his son, in return for a sum of money duly paid, grant to Andrew Yonge and his wife Dorothy, daughter of the said Roger, the capital messuage, lands, tenements and hereditaments belonging to the site and manor of Pynchinthorp in co. York, with the orchard and gardens and divers closes, namely, Pondgarthe, Bowsse close, West close, Dayle close, Awderson close, Somerfeild, Claygaite, Berkegarth and other closes in and above the *bancke*, and of a close called the Newe Intacke, all in the town and territory of Pinchinthorp on the south of the Quenes waye there; they also grant a cottage and croft with appurtenances in the same town, lately held by Richard Lambe and 3 closes of ground called Busshoppgarthes, with common pasture on the moor there; to hold and remain to the use of the said Roger for the term of his life without impeachment of waste and after his death to the use of William Lee for his life and after his death, 1) to his sons in tail male and general, and in default of issue, 2) to his daughters in tail general, 3) to the right heirs of Roger Lee. Alternate seals[4]. Andrewe Younge. Dorethe Young. (*Ibid.*).

362. Oct. 9, 9 James I, [1611]. Final concord before Edward Coke, Thomas Walmysley, Peter Warburton and Thomas Foster, justices, between John Whitbye, *quer.*, and John Skorth and Ann, his wife, and Thomas Coverdill and Philida, his wife, *def.*, concerning a messuage, 3 acres of land, an acre of meadow and common pasture

[1] Small broken seal of red wax; a bird.
[2] Small hexagonal seal of red wax; B.C.
[3] In English.
[4] Two blobs of red wax, both blurred. *Dorso:* Witnesses by Francis Killingbeck, notary public, John Spence, Edward Wood.

for all their animals in Pinchinthorpe, whereby it was agreed by John, Anne, Thomas and Philida that the said lands belonged to the said John Whitbye which he had of the gift of the said John, Ann, Thomas and Philida, who now quitclaimed the same to John Whitbye and his heirs in perpetuity; they also warrant the same against the heirs of Ann, as do Thomas and Philida against the heirs of Philida. For this recognition, quitclaim and warranty, John Whitbye gave to John, Ann, Thomas and Philida 41*li*. Sealing clause[1]. E. Coke. At Westminster. (*Ibid.*).

Plumpton.

363. Friday St. Peter ad vincula, 17 Edward III [Aug. 1, 1343]. Release and quitclaim by Eustachia, widow of Peter de Middelton, knt., to Sir William de Plumpton, knt., of all right in all the lands, tenements and rents with appurtenances in the vill of Plumpton and in the field of the said vill, which is called Rufferlington, which once belonged to Henry Beaufitz, knt. Warranty. Sealing clause. Witnesses: Robert Ros of Ingmanthorpe, John son of William de Moubray, Walter de Kereby, John de Middelton, Richard de Middelton. At Plumpton.[2] (*Y.A.S.* Md. 59/18 No. 8).

Polkthorpe.

364. Grant by Thomas de Plumstede and Alice, his wife, to Richard their son, of a toft and a bovate of land with appurtenances, except for 3 acres and a rood of land, in Pokethorp, which toft and bovate except for the 3 acres and rood the grantor had of the gift of Alice who was the wife of Peter Brid; to hold to them and their lawfully begotten heirs in fee and hereditarily in perpetuity, of the chief lords of the fee. Warranty. Sealing clause. Witnesses: Richard de Torny, William de Midelton, Henry Damyot, Robert son of Walter de Pokethorp, Nicholas Gilyot, Robert Brid, William de Hamerton. (*N. G. Hyde*, No. 17).

365. Grant by Juetus son of the late Lambert de Pokethorpe to Richard, his son, his heirs and assigns, of an acre and 3 roods of land in the fields of Pokethorpe, namely, one rood at Kelddail from the path which leads towards Kyllum to the ditch of Kyllum, and half a rood at Schorthbuttes from the headland of Gerbedail as far as the boundary between the fields of Pokethorpe and Nuerton[3], and one a half roods at Kyrkedail from the vill of Pokethorpe as far as the highway, and one rood above le Buttes from the headland of Langdail as far as the boundary of Driffeld, and one rood at Wrangdale from the path which leads towards Cotum as far as the boundary of Driffield, and one and a half roods in Rydail from the path leading

[1] Fragment of a seal of brown wax.
[2] Endorsed: Plompton. Rughfarlyngton.
[3] Nafferton.

from Cotum as far as the ditch of Kyllum, and which lies on both sides of the land of Robert Brid of Pokethorpe; also part of the grantor's toft in the vill of Pokethorpe which came to him by hereditary right and which lies between the toft of Beatrice, daughter of Geoffrey son of Lambert de Pokethorpe on one side and the toft of Matilda, daughter of the said Geoffrey on the other; to hold to Richard or to whomsoever he wishes to assign or give it, of the grantor and his heirs, freely and in peace, in fee and hereditarily with all liberties and easements within and without the vill of Polkthorpe in perpetuity; paying yearly to Robert Brid and his heirs 3½d. in equal portions at Whitsuntide and Martinmas for all secular services, suits and demands. Warranty. Sealing clause.[1] Witnesses: Robert de Bouelton', Walter de Raygat, Nicholas Gylot, William son of Humphrey, Robert son of Walter Barthum of Kaython[2], Robert Crosseby, clerk. (*Ibid.*, No. 19).

Pollington.

366. Agreement[3] between John de Lascy, earl of Lincoln and constable of Chester, and Sir Rades de Duffeld, knt., and Emma his wife, by which John de Lascy granted to Rades and Emma and their heirs sixty acres of land in Fippin', measured by the perch of twenty feet, of which ten were of standing wood and fifty of copse in Fippin' towards Pouelington. For this Rades and Emma quitclaimed to John all their right and claim in the said wood of Fippin' and in Almholm', saving to Rades and Emma, their heirs and men, two ways, one beginning at Cuwik through the middle culture of Sir John de Lascy as far as the south field (*sudcampum*) at the head of Almholm' towards the east, and the other way extending between the wood which Sir John had granted them above and his own wood as far as the south field towards the west, of a breadth of two perches. Alternate seals. Witnesses, Sirs Henry de Notingham, rector of Rowell [Rothwell], Adam de Nereford, John de Crigel', steward, Thomas de Polington, Henry de Goldhal', Mag. Roger de Bodham, Walter de Ludham, Walter de Hauuill', Michael de Tonett', Osbert the clerk.

367. Sept. 11, I Henry V [1413]. Release by Isabel late wife of William de Wyntworth, in her widowhood, to John Daunay, Nicholas Norffolk, William Rosselyn, and William Darthyngton, chaplain, and the heirs and assigns of the last three, of all rents and services with appurtenances belonging to her as of her manor of Polyngton, in respect of any lands or tenements of John Daunay or those which had lately belonged to John Warner in the soke of Snaith; together with all right and claim in the said lands or tenements.

[1] Fragment of green seal on a tongue of twisted parchment.
[2] Cotham.
[3] For the full text, see Appendix: illustrated in the Frontispiece.

Witnesses, Thomas Reresby, knt., Thomas and William his sons, Ralph de Wyntworth, Richard Burgoyne, Thomas Dilcok the elder, Thomas Dilcok the younger. Thribergh.[1] (*Y.A.S.*, Md. 135, No. 9).

Pool-in-Wharfedale.

368. [1236]. Indenture whereby the lord Walter de Gray, archbishop of York, grants, demises and quitclaims to Robert son of William Briton' of Pouel, custody of the land and the heirs of Richard de Monte of Farnele together with the rights pertaining to the free holding of Pouel, also the profits pertaining to the said wardship. And as the archbishop handed over to Robert seisin of the said custody of the land and heirs in his full court at Ottel' by Paul de Neuhale and Elias de Rauenth', his bailiffs, namely on Monday before the Annunciation of the B.V.M. [March 24], 1236[-7], an agreement was made between the said Robert of the one part and Henry de Pouel of the other, whereby the said Robert granted and demised to Henry and his heirs the custody of the said lands and heirs of Farnele for the full term of 3 years, also the said custody from that day until the feast of St. Michael next following, so that Henry may fully enjoy the profits of the wardship and the crops from the said lands from autumn last until the said day; to hold to Henry, his heirs and assigns, freely [*etc.*], with all liberties in woods, fields, plains, meadows, mills, ways, paths, waters, pastures, grazings and in all customs pertaining to the said holding. Henry shall maintain the custody, the heirs and the buildings fully and in the same state and condition as he found them, and he shall not give the heirs in marriage, to their disparagement, unless it be with the assent, counsel and agreement of the parents on both sides. Robert for his part shall, for the term of 3 years, warrant the said custody to Henry, and if he is unable to do so, shall allow to Henry, his heirs and assigns the value of the wardship and custody from his free tenement in Pouel in exchange and it shall remain to him freely until the term is complete. At the conclusion of the term reversion of the wardship to Robert, without contradiction. Alternate seals. Witnesses: Sir Nicholas Wrad', William le Wauassur, William de Widendon, Paul de Neuhale, Hugh de Lelay, Elias de Rauenther, German Mansel, John de Calli, William de Lindelay, Thomas Hurtechy, Richard de Ledes, Adam de Neuhale. (*Farnley Hall Muniments*, No. 112).

369. Thursday after the Invention of the Cross, 10 Edward son of Edward [May 5, 1317]. Release and quitclaim by Peter son of William de Middelton to John de Caylli and his heirs, of all right in all that meadow which Sir Adam de Myddelton, the grantor's uncle, once sold to Henry de Caylli and Henry son of Paul de Pouel and Christiana, mother of the said Henry, and which lies in the field of Pouel. Warranty against all men, but saving to the grantor an annual

[1] Seal: red wax; no distinct impression.

rent of 1*d*. at the Nativity. Sealing clause. Witnesses: Walter de Middelton, Peter del Stode, William de Fernelay, William Faucus of Newale, Thomas de Preston', Thomas de Scalwra. At Stubbum. (*Ibid.*, No. 6).

370. The morrow of St. Martin the Bishop, 21 Edward son of Henry [Nov. 12, 1293]. Grant by Walter de Middelton to William Faukes of Newall of 4*s*. 6*d*. rent with appurtenances in Pouell, from 10 acres of land and meadow in Pouel Holme, from Henry le Vauasur and Matilda, his wife and the heirs and assigns of the said Matilda, in equal portions at Whitsuntide and Martinmas, with all the gift of the same tenement in homages, reliefs and escheats and with all else pertaining to the said lordship; to hold to William, his heirs and assigns, freely and hereditarily in perpetuity. Warranty. Sealing clause.[1] Witnesses: Richard de Galeway, Paul Ketel, Adam Payllene, Henry Bonefant, William Payllene, William son of Roger the Sutor, John le Sauser, William son of Paul the clerk. At Otteley. (*Ibid.*, No. 113).

Potto.

371. Thursday after Corpus Christi, 13 Edward III [June 20, 1339]. Indenture stating that since Thomas *in ye* Wylyes of Pothow has granted to Sir William Malbys, knt., his heirs and assigns, a certain annual rent of 12*s*. from all the grantor's lands and tenements in the vill of Pothowe, as described in a certain writing, now the said Sir William has granted for himself, his heirs and assigns that if they may hold and enjoy a messuage and 2 bovates of land with appurtenances in Skalton, which he has in exchange for a bovate of land in the marsh of Clifland, of the gift and feoffment of the same Thomas and Agnes, through the said Agnes, then the said writing and annual rent of 12*s*. shall be of no virtue, but if the said Agnes, her heirs and assigns retain and enjoy the said 2 bovates then this writing to remain in full strength. Alternate seals.[2] At Skalton. (*Newburgh Priory Muniments*, No. 8/32).

Ribston.

372. Quitclaim and sale by Walter son of Nigel de Stockelde to Nigel de Plumton, of all that tenement pertaining to one knight's fee which the grantor holds of Nicholas Basset for 40 marks of silver . . .[3] namely, all that tenement which he has within the vill of Ribbestain and without, and one carucate of land in Ranes with appurtenances which he holds of the Countess of Warewic,[4] and all

[1] Broken seal of white wax, beneath a canopy, the Virgin and Child.

[2] Seal of red wax, diam. 1 in.: a shield of arms couchee beneath a helm and mantling; a chevron between 3 hinds heads . . . LLELMI MALBYS.

[3] Holes in deed.

[4] In 1175 the inheritance of William de Percy was partitioned between the husbands of his two daughters, one of whom was Maud, wife of William, earl of Warwick. (*Complete Peerage* X, p. 444).

that dwelling which he has in Koletorp and Hornington,[1] and moreover (*praeterea*) Sadewelle; to hold to Nigel and his heirs, with all men, homages, services and other easements, of the said Nicholas, and the said carucate in Ranis, of the countess and her heirs, freely [*etc.*] as held by the grantor. Warranty. Witnesses: Robert Vauassore, Mauger his brother, Walter de Perci, [Henry] his brother, Hugh de Leleia, Robert his brother, . . . Lardin', Robert his brother, R . . . God . . . Robert de Wiuelestorp, Thomas de Dihton, Nigel the butler, Adam the butler, Robert son of Wekeman . . . Robert Outhanebi, John Beugrant, Alexander de Witheton, Alan son of Elias.[2] (*Y.A.S.*, Md. 59/19, No. 1).

373. Grant by Walter son of Nigel de Stockeld to Robert son of Huckeman de Plumton, for his homage and service, of a toft with an orchard (*pomerio*) in Ribbestain, namely the toft which Robert son of Hulfkil holds, and an acre of land in the fields of Ribbestain which William Strangald holds and which lies between the path which leads from Ribbestain to Spofford and the water called Crempel; to hold to Robert and his heirs, of the grantor and his heirs, freely [*etc.*], with all liberties and easements within the vill and without, with the exception of a bovate of land to which this toft and acre pertain paying yearly two barbed arrows for all services, at Martinmas. Warranty against all men, and if the grantor and his heirs are not able to warrant the toft and acre they will give to Robert and his heirs a like amount of land in the same vill in exchange. Witnesses: Nigel de Plumton, William de Luuetot, Ralph son of Baldwin, Hugh de Lelai, Alexander de Witheton, Matthew de Bram, Henry de Screuin, Robert son of Henry, Walter de Folifait.[3] (*Ibid.*, No. 2).

374. Grant by Walter son of Nigel de Stockeld' to Robert son of Huckeman de Plumton, for his homage and service, of 5½ acres of land in the fields of Ribbestain; one which Robert son of Yllkil holds and which is beyond the road leading from Ribbestain to Spotford . . .[4] to the south, and 2 acres which Ulf son of Ber . . . holds which lies next to Frodesbeki on the east, and 2 acres which Godwin holds . . . which extend above the aforesaid acres; to hold to Robert freely [*etc.*] in woods, plains, meadows, and pastures, paying yearly to the grantor and his heirs two [silver] spurs for all services [and demands]. Warranty. Witnesses: Nigel de Plumtun, Hugh de Lelay, Ralph son of Baldwin, Alexander de Wicton, Richard son of Nigel, Gilbert Lardinarius, Robert son of Henry, Henry de Screuayn, Richard son of Alexander, Walter son of Robert, Walter de Morpathe, Robert Beugraunt, Adam the clerk.[5] (*Ibid.*, No. 3).

[1] Cowthorpe, Hornington, parish of Bolton Percy.
[2] Fragment of green wax on a pink silk braid.
[3] Large seal of green wax, broken.
[4] Deed torn and rubbed.
[5] Endorsed: Carta Walteri Fil' Nigelli de Stockeld de quinque acras et dim' in Ribbestan.

375. Grant by Nigel de Plumton to Peter his son, for his homage and service, of a carucate of land in Ribbestain, with appurtenances within and without the vill, namely that carucate which lies between the fields of Sadewelle and Spofford, except church lands and the lands of Robert son of Uckeman; he also grants all the land which lies between the ditch of John Beugrant and Crempel,[1] also 7 acres of land which Richard son of Beucelius holds in Brunigecroft and 2½ acres of land which extend as far as the road from Bram to Lidgate, and an acre and a rood which extend as far as the said road towards the west, and 1½ acres which Walter the carpenter holds and which extend towards the road to Spofford, and 2 acres which Richard Pilemor holds and which stretch towards the said road to Spofford, and half an acre which Richard Pickehauere holds below Lund, and an acre which Dolfin the smith holds and which extends towards the road to Bram, and 2 tofts which lie between Walthef Crisp' and Walter the carpenter and the toft which Thomas the baker (*pistor*) holds, and the toft which Mauger holds and the toft which Hugh son of Ulf holds and the toft which William Bekan holds; to hold with all liberties and easements, paying yearly to the grantor a pair of white gloves at Easter for all services. Witnesses: John de Daiuile, Robert de Wiuestorp, William de Luuetot, Elias de Marten', William de Karleuile, Robert son of Uckeman, Henry Luuel, Gilbert Lardener.[2] (*Ibid.*, No. 4).

376. Grant by William son of William de Ribbestain, to Robert son of Huckeman de Plumtun, of half an acre of land in the fields of Ribbestain in the east of Ribbestain, namely in Brunrigcroft; to hold to Robert and his heirs, of the grantor and his heirs by hereditary right, for 12*s*. which he paid to the grantor, and paying an halfpenny for all services at Martinmas; and let it be known that the grantor assigns the payment of the halfpenny at the said term to William Beugrant and his heirs. Witnesses: Nigel de Plumtun and Peter, his son, Matthew de Bram, Hugh son of Apolitus, Ralph de Waddesielf, Robert son of Henry, Waucalin brother of Matthew de Bram, Walter de Aiketun.[3] (*Ibid.*, No. 5).

377. Grant by Adam de Ribestayn to William de Plumton, for his homage and service, and to the increase of the tenements which he holds of Adam, of an acre of land with appurtenances in the field of Ribestayn, namely in Fulsicriding next to Rauulriding adjoining the land of Henry the clerk of Ribestayn towards the north; to hold of the grantor and his heirs, freely and quietly, paying yearly 1*d*. at Easter for all services and demands. Warranty.

[1] Crimple beck.

[2] Seal: light brown wax; diam. 1 7/8 in., a mailed equestrian figure to the sinister; ✠ SIGILL . . . VS D . . . A.

[3] Endorsed: Carta Will' filii Will'mi de una acra terre et dim' in Ribbestan. xxxiij.

Sealing clause.[1] Witnesses: Nigel the butler of Dicton', Robert de Wyueton, Adam de Wyton', Mathew de Braham, Jolan de Ayketon, Robert de Stiueton, Thomas de Ribestain, Henry his brother, William le Bengraunt, Richard Dagun. (*Ibid.*, No. 6).

378. Grant by Adam son of Robert de Ribestayn to William the steward of Plumton, for his homage and service, of a toft which Walter the grantor's brother held of him [the grantor] in the vill of Ribestayn at Sandlaydes, and half an acre in the field of Schadewelle which extends above Scheshepol, also the homage and service which the said Walter and Robert the grantor's brothers are accustomed to perform; to hold to William freely and quietly, paying yearly to the grantor 1*d.* at Easter for all services, customs and demands. Warranty. Sir John Maloleporarius, Sir Alan de Kirkeby, Sir Thomas de Arches, Nigel the butler of Dicton, Jolan de Ayketon, Richard Dagun, Robert de Stiueton, Thomas de Ribestayn, Henry his brother, Walter de Braham.[2] (*Ibid.*, No. 7).

379. Martinmas [Nov. 11], 1234. Indenture witnessing an agreement between William the steward of Plumton and Everard de Ribestain whereby William leases (*dimisit ad firmam*) to Everard a toft and a croft in the vill of Ribestain for the term of 14 years, namely that toft and croft which Walter the son of Robert held; to hold to Everard and his assigns, of William and his heirs, freely, with all liberties and easements, paying yearly to the grantor and his heirs, 5*s.*, half at Whitsuntide and half at Martinmas, for all services. Warranty. Alternate seals. Witnesses: Nigel the butler of Dicton, Robert son of Nigel, Reginald the dispenser (*dispensatore*), William son of Thomas de Dicton, Robert de Stiueton, Thomas de Ribestain. (*Ibid.*, No. 8).

380. Grant by Peter de Hornington to William de Plumpton for his homage and service, of 2 acres of land with appurtenances in Ribbestain in his assart, which land extends above the marsh and continues by way of the marsh for the breadth of the 2 acres as far as the ditch towards the south of the marsh; to hold to William and his heirs, of the grantor and his heirs, in fee and hereditarily, freely and without reservation, paying to the grantor a pair of white gloves yearly at the Nativity, for all services. Warranty. Witnesses: Nigel the butler of Dicton, Robert his son, William de Dicton, Robert de Wycton, Roger his brother, Adam de Wycton, Thomas le Lardener, Jolan de Ayketon, Henry de Bram.[3] (*Ibid.*, No. 9).

[1] Good impression of a seal of light brown wax; diam. 1¼ in.; a fabulous animal; ✠ SIGILL' ADE FILII ROBERTI.

Endorsed: Carta de una acra in Ribbestan xxvj.

[2] Seal of green wax, as to the preceding deed.

Endorsed: Carta Ade fil Rob' de Ribbestan de uno tofto una acra et dim' de terra in Ribbestan. xxxiiij.

[3] Seal, a fragment of red wax; . . . HO. Endorsed: Carta Petr' de Hornington de duabus acr' terre in Ribbesta' xxxvij.

381. Grant by Peter son of Dolfin to William son of Robert de Plumton, for his homage and service, of a toft and a croft with appurtenances in Ribbestain, lying between the toft of Hobekin and the toft of Richard son of Bencelin; to hold to William and his heirs, of the grantor and his heirs, in fee and hereditarily, freely [*etc.*], in woods, plains and with all liberties and easements within the vill and without, paying yearly to the grantor a pair of white gloves at Easter for all services and exactions. Warranty. Witnesses: Adam de Witon', William de Bram, Henry his brother, Jollan de Ayketon, Robert son of Suain'.[1] (*Ibid.*, No. 10).

382. Grant by Robert de Plumton to Henry, the clerk, son [?] (*fil*) of Ribbestain, for his homage and service, of a toft in the vill of Ribbestain and an acre and a rood of land in the fields of the same vill, namely, the toft which the grantor had of the gift of Thomas, brother of the said Henry, and the acre and rood lie adjoining Henry's land at Holegate; to hold to Henry and his heirs, of the grantor and his heirs, in fee and hereditarily, with all easements pertaining, paying 2*s*. yearly for all services and demands, in equal portions at Whitsuntide and Martinmas. Warranty. Witnesses: William de Hebbeden, William de Stiveton, Richard de Goddelesburgh, Nigel, the butler of Dicton', William de Plumton, Thomas de Stokeld, Roger de Hubi, Robert his brother, Jolan de Hayetun.[2] (*Ibid.*, No. 11).

383. Grant by William the steward of Plumton to Isabel his daughter, in free marriage, and to her heirs, of 2 bovates of land in the territory of Schadewell, with all appurtenances; he also grants a dwelling (*domum*) with appurtenances in the vill of Ribbestayn which Martin of the same vill holds of him; to hold to Isabel and her heirs, of the grantor and his heirs, freely with all liberties and easements within the vill and without, paying yearly to the grantor and his heirs 12*d*. in equal portions at Whitsuntide and Martinmas for all services and demands. Warranty. Sealing clause. Witnesses: Sir Alan de Alfeld, Sir Patrick de Westwic, Sir Richard de Brerton, Sir John de Hamerton, Henry de Ribbestayn, Matthew de Bram, William de Beugrant, Robert de Dicton, Nigel his brother, Thomas de Ribbestayn, Ralph de Scotton, Richard de Scotton, Roger de Scotton, Adam de Tows', Peter de Burton. (*Ibid.*, No. 12).

384. May 1, 5 Richard II [1382]. Indenture[3] between Sir William de Ribston and Sir Peter Mauleuerer, by the arbitration of Sir Ralph Ypers, Sir Richard Tempest, Alan de Cattall, Richard Banastre, witnessing that whereas discord had arisen between Sir

[1] Seal: vesica shaped, of white wax; a spray of leaves; ✠ SIILLGVM P . . . OLFIN. Endorsed: Carta Pet' filii Dolfini de uno tofto & crofto cum ptu' in Ribbestain. xxxix.

[2] Tongue for seal but seal missing; tied in with the tongue are a number of knotted linen strands and fragments of paper.

[3] In French.

William and Sir Peter over certain tenements and rents with appurtenances which Sir Peter claimed from Sir William as of the lands & tenements which he holds of him [Peter] in the vill of Haghenlath,[1] namely that which the said William and his heirs and assigns pay yearly to Sir Peter, his heirs and assigns at Whitsuntide and Martinmas in equal portions, being 66*s*. 8*d*. for lands and tenements in the vill of Haghenlath and 62*s*. 8*d*. for lands and tenements in Ribstan, which Sir William holds of Sir Peter; now it is agreed between them that if the rents shall be in arrears wholly or in part for 40 days after any of the terms, Sir Peter and his heirs or assigns may distrain on the lands in Haghenlath until the rent and arrears are paid, and if the rent is in arrears for a quarter of the year after any of the terms, he may enter and occupy without hindrance from William; and it is also agreed that if the lands at Heghenlath should be recovered by force . . . [2] any man or woman . . . of the possession of Sir William . . . claim the right as it was before the day of the seizure . . . Alternate seals.[3] (*Ibid.*, No. 13).

385. Beheading of St. John the Baptist [Aug. 26], 1296, 24 Edward son of Henry. Grant[4] by John de Sikelinghale and Alice his wife to Agnes, daughter of Robert son of Henry de Parva Ribbestain, of all their part of a toft lying between the toft once belonging to Robert son of Roger de Parva Ribbestain and the toft of Gilbert son of Alduse of the same, which part of the toft came to Alice by hereditary right after the death of Alice, widow of Henry the clerk, her grandmother; they also grant a rood of land with appurtenances in Little Ribbestan, in a place called le Riddingg' between le Dernewath on one side and le Kerende on the other; to hold to Agnes, her heirs and assigns, with all appurtenances within and without the vill, performing the due and accustomed services to the lords of the fee and paying yearly to the grantors a rose in the season of roses if demanded. Warranty. Sealing clause.[5]

[1] Hanlith.

[2] Document blurred and illegible.

[3] Seal of brown wax on a tongue cut from the deed; diam. 1 in.; in a border of chevrons a shield couchée below a helm; 3 greyhounds courant . . Petri Mauleue . . .

[4] Precisely similar grants to Agnes by 1) Joan, her sister. Same date and witnesses. Seal of green wax; diam. 7/8 in., an animal and a spray of flowers; ✠S' IOHANNE FIL' ROB' (*Ibid.*, No. 15). 2) Rosa, her sister. Same date and witnesses. Seal of green wax; diam. ½ in., a hand holding a bunch of flowers; S'ROSE FIL'E ROB'TI (*Ibid.*, No. 16). 3) Cecily, her sister. Same date and witnesses with the addition of John de Sikelinghale. Seal of green wax; diam. 7/8 in., a small animal below a spray of leaves; ✠S' CECILIE FIL'E ROB'TI (*Ibid.*, No. 17). 4) John son of Elias Hardy of Cotingham and Margaret, his wife. Dated Sept. 9, 1296. Same witnesses. Two seals of dark green wax; a) diam. 7/8 in., a rose; ✠ S'IONIS FIL' EL' HARDY; b) diam. 1 in., an eagle on a rock; ✠S'MARGAR'FIL' ROB'TI (*Ibid.*, No. 18).

[5] Two seals of green wax; a) diam. 1 in., a star above a crescent; S'IONIS DE SICLINGHA; b) oval, 1 in. × ½ in., a chalice covered by a veil; ✠S' ALICIE FIL'E ROB'TI.

Witnesses: Sir Richard de Stockeld, knt., Thomas Golyas, Nicholas de Dighton, Robert le Boteler of Dighton, Robert Dagun, Roger Dagun, Nicholas de Parva Ribbestain, Robert Broun of the same, Gilbert son of Alduse de Ribestain, Thomas de Dighton, Adam Warde of Colthorp, Richard the cook (*Coco*) de Parva Ribbestain. At Little Ribbestain.[1] (*Ibid.*, No. 14).

386. Grant, demise and quitclaim by Joan daughter of Robert son of Henry of Little Ribstan, in her virginity to Robert son of Roger of the same vill, of all right in all the meadow and cultivated land called Rogercroft which lies in two places in the same croft, namely one part lies on the south of the said croft and the other extends above Portamcroft of the said Roger; paying yearly to the grantor and her heirs a rose during the quindene of St. John the Baptist for all services. Warranty.[2] Sealing clause. Witnesses: Sir Richard de Stockeld, Thomas Golias of the same, Mathew de Stodefald, Matthew son of Elias de Bram, Robert de Sutton, Robert Brun of Ribstan, Thomas son of William ad moram of the same, William de Faxflet of the same. (*Ibid.*, No. 19).

387. Grant by Thomas Fonne of Little Rybestain to Robert del Hil in Sicklinghale and Alice, his wife, of half an acre of arable land with appurtenances in the east field of Little Rybestain, of which one rood lies above Nedellandes, between the water of the Nidde and le Litheyat, and two half roods above le Toftes extending towards le Engbuttes; to hold to Robert and Alice, of the chief lords of the fee, freely, [*etc.*], paying yearly to the grantor, his heirs or assigns, a rose at the Nativity of St. John the Baptist for all services. Warranty. Sealing clause.[3] Witnesses: William de Bilton in Wetherby, Richard de Stiueton, Henry Blome, William Connel, king's bailiff, of Clarehou, John the proctor (*procurator*). (*Ibid.*, No. 20).

388. Grant by Robert son of Robert de Parua Ribstayn to Robert de Le Hyl in Siclinghal and Alice, his wife, of half an acre of land with appurtenances lying in the grantor's croft and abutting above his garden to the south, with free entry and exit through his garden, also an annual rent of 3*d.* in Little Ribston, also half an acre of land lying at Foulsyke on the south next to the land which Richard Mauleuerer once held, also 3*d.* annual rent from Robert son of Roger the tanner of Spofford and Agnes, his wife; to hold to Robert and Alice freely and without reservation, paying yearly to the chief lords of the fee, a red rose at the Nativity of St. John the Baptist for all secular services, exactions and demands, Warranty. Sealing clause.[4] Witnesses: Richard de Stiueton,

[1] Endorsed: Carta Joh' and Margar', and in a later hand, Tent' in Sokagio.
[2] In the warranty clause the grantee is described as Robert son of Roger son of Adam de Parva Ribstan.
[3] Seal: part of an oval seal of white wax; a spray of flowers; . . . RVL.HI.
[4] Oval seal of brown wax, blurred and undeciphered.

Nigel de Wetherby, William de Bilton, Thomas del Hyl in Siklinghal, John the proctor of Little Ribston. (*Ibid.*, No. 21).

389. 7 Edward III [1333]. Grant[1] by Henry Blome of Little Ribstan to Robert de Hylle of Syckelynghale, dwelling in Little Ribstan, and Alice, his wife, and the heirs and assigns of Robert, of 4 strips of arable land in the field and territory of Little Ribstan attefulesyk, which lie in length and breadth between the land of Richard de Sutton on the north and the land which Robert del Hylle bought from Robert son of Robert de Parua Ribstan on the south, abutting towards the east on the land of Robert de Goldesburg; to hold to Robert and Alice with all liberties and easements, freely in perpetuity of the chief lords of the fee. Warranty. Sealing clause. Witnesses: Sir William de Plompton, Sir Peter de Mydelton, knts., Robert de Goldesburgh, Matthew de Brame, William de Byrkyn, John de Dyghton, Robert son of Robert de Parua Ribstan. At Ribstan. (*Ibid.*, No. 22).

390. Sunday after Easter, 8 Edward III [April 3, 1334]. Grant by Robert de Parua Ribstan to Robert del Hyll and Alice, his wife, and their lawfully begotten heirs, of a strip containing half an acre of arable land which lies in length and breadth of the grantor's croft between the land of John the proctor (*procurator*) on the north, and the land of the said Robert del Hylle which once belonged to the grantor on the south, and one end abuts towards the east and the other towards the west; to hold with all liberties and easements in the vill and territory of Little Ribstan, of the chief lords of the fee, with free entry and exit by way of the grantor's garden. Warranty. Sealing clause. Witnesses: Sir William de Plompton, Sir Peter de Myddelton, knts., Matthew de Bram, William Birkyn, Thomas Golias of Stokyld, Robert de Goldesburgh of Little Ribstan, Henry Blome. At Little Ribstan. (*Ibid.*, No. 24).

391. Jan. 18, 1381[-2], 4 Richard II. Grant[2] by John son of Henry Blome of Little Ribstan to Thomas de Kilburn of York, *Draper*, of a messuage and 8 acres of land and meadow with appurtenances which came to the grantor by hereditary right after the death of Henry, his father, in the vill and territory of Little Ribstan, and which is held of the grantor by John de Horsford; to hold to Thomas, his heirs and assigns, of the chief lords of the fee. Warranty. Sealing clause.[3] Witnesses: Roger Fulbaron, Robert de Bilton,

[1] Quitclaim of the same to the same by William son of Henry Blome, dated Sunday after the Purification of the B.V.M., 1333 and 8 Edward III [Feb. 6, 1333-4]. Witnesses the same except that Thomas Gullead replaces Robert de Goldesburgh. (*Ibid.*, No. 23).

[2] Indenture made on the same day whereby Thomas agrees that if during the term of 10 years, John shall pay to him or to his attorney at York, 10 marks sterling, then the above charter to be null and void, otherwise to stand. Seal as to the grant. (*Ibid.* No. 26).

[3] Seal: red wax, diam. ½ in.; pseudo armorial, three crosses; *S' IACOBI LA . . .

William de Dighton, Robert Starkbayn, Thomas de Galway. At Little Ribston. (*Ibid.*, No. 25).

392. Thursday, the Ascension [May 23], 1392. Grant by Thomas de Kylburn, *Draper*, of York, to John Bouay of Little Ribstan, his heirs and assigns, of a messuage and 8 acres of meadow with appurtenances in Little Ribstan; to hold to John, his heirs and assigns of the chief lords of the fee. Warranty. Sealing clause.[1] Witnesses: Roger Fulbaron, Robert his son, Robert de Bilton, junior, Richard Popeler of Dyghton, Richard de Lynton, Peter de Dyghton, Thomas Galway. At Little Ribston. (*Ibid.*, No. 27).

393. Thursday before Septuagesima, 3 Henry IV [Jan. 19, 1401-2]. Grant by William son of Richard Hykson of Little Rybstone to Nicholas de Mydylton, knt., of a messuage in the vill of Little Rybstan, lying between the messuage of John Bottelar of Spofforth on one side and the messuage of John Bylson of Little Rybstan on the other, with an acre and a half of arable land lying between Little Rybstan and Loxlay on the east with certain strips of land[2] (*ranis*) abutting (*habuttant'*) on the said messuage which extend in length on the western side towards Loxlay; to hold with all appurtenances to Nicholas Mydelton, his heirs and assigns, of the chief lords of the fee. Warranty. Sealing clause.[3] Witnesses: Robert de Plwmton, Robert Rosse and Robert de Bylton. At Stokeld. (*Ibid.*, No. 28).

394. [1471-2]. This bill indentid made the xxiij day of March the yer off the reigne off Kynge Edward the iiijth betwene Thomas Middilton on the on partie and Harre Botelar on the other partie, witnes that the sayd Harre hath borowyd off the sayd Thomas Middilton xl*s*. to be payd unto the sayd Thomas at the fest off Seynt Michell the archangell next comynge and yff it happyn the sayd Harre Botelar that he pays not the sayd xl*s*. unto the sayd Thomas or ellis yff it happyn the sayd Harre to de afor the sayd fest of Seynt Michell, the sayd Harre wills and graunteth be this his present writynge that it sall be lawfull unto the sayd Thomas Middilton to entre into, have and reteigne all the lands and tenementes, rentes, reversions and services that late wer Robert Botelar his fadir whoo heir he is, in Litill Ribbiston, accordyng to a feffement made the first day off June the yer off the reigne off Kinge Edwarde the iiijth the xj, be the sayd Harre Botelar unto Richard Middilton and William Havksworth feffeth unto the use off the sayd Thomas Middilton. In witnes wheroff as well the forsayd Thomas as Harre Botelar enterchangeable hath set to ther seals. Wretyn and deliveryd the yer and the day above wretyn. (*Ibid.*, No. 29).

[1] Seal: red wax, a device, possibly a bee; legend undeciphered.

[2] *rana*, a strip of land or unploughed baulk. *Wright's Dialect Dict.*

[3] Seal: red wax, diam. 7/10 in.; a sheaf of corn between a star and a crescent; * S' DE . . . RICC DE SHEFFELD.

395. [1473]. This bill indentide made the ij day of Novembir the yer of the reigne off Kynge Edward the iiijth the xiij, witnes that Harry Botelar hays resavyd off Thomas Middilton xxvj marke of lawfull mone off Ingelonde in partie off payment off l marke that the sayd Thomas ought hym for a mes and certen lande that he hath bought off hym in Litill Ribbistone off the wych xxvj marks the sayde Harry knowlege to be fully content ande payd and the sayde Thomas to be acquit and distchargide be this my writynge, in witnes wher off I the sayd Harre have sett to my seall.[1] Writyn and deliveryd the yer and the day abovesayde. (*Ibid.*, No. 30).

396. May 16, 15 Edward IV [1475]. Release and quitclaim by Henry Butteler, son and heir of Robert Butteler late of Barowby, to Thomas Middilton, Richard Middilton, and William Hawkkisworth, their heirs and assigns, of all right in a messuage and all lands, tenements, rents and services with appurtenances in Little Rybstane. Warranty. Sealing clause.[2] Witnesses: William Plompton, Richard Hamerton, John Norton, knts., Robert Roos, Nicholas Middilton. (*Ibid.*, No. 31).

397. March 6, 17 Edward IV [1476-7]. This indentur made the vj day of March the yer off the reigne of Kynge Edwarde the iiijth the xvij betwix Thomas Middilton on the one partie and Harre Botteler on the other partie, witnes that I the sayd Harre Botteler knowlege me to have resavyd and to be fully content and payd off l mark off lawfull mone be the hande off the sayd Thomas Middilton to me due for a mes and certen landes and tenementes with their appurtenances in Litill Ribbistone, that I sold unto the sayd Thomas his heirs and assigns for evermore for the same aforsayd, the sayd Thomas Middilton to be dischargid be this my present writyng off the some of l mark aforesayd, and over this I wilt be this my present writynge that Edmond of Thwates, Harre Arthyngton and Robert Sek' qwam the feffers now lyffynge of Robert Bottelar mye fadir qwas heir I the sayd Harre Bottelar am; to the use on me, my heires and assignes, release by this dede to Richard Middilton and William Haukkisworth their heirs and assignes al the right, clame and titel that they have in Litill Ribbistone for evermore, wych Richard and William are feffeth, to the use of the sayd Thomas Middilton his heirs and assignes. In Witnes wher of I the sayd Harre Botteler has set to mye seal.[3] Wretyn and deliveryd the yere and day above sayd. (*Ibid.*, No. 32).

398. Jan. 29, 22 Edward IV [1481-2]. Indenture whereby Thomas Houlden of Thryske, *smyth*, confirms and ratifies to Thomas

[1] Seal: red wax, appended directly to the bottom of the deed, undeciphered, possibly a fleur-de-lis. Imbedded in the wax and surrounding the device is a twist of straw.

[2] Seal: blob of red wax; two interlacing triangles.

[3] Seal: red wax, the letter R. Surrounding the seal is imbedded a twist of straw.

Medilton and Joan, his wife, and to their heirs and assigns, their title to, and possession of, a messuage with appurtenances in the vill of Little Ribbystane in which John Coward lives, also in a cottage with appurtenances in the same vill, in which James Hyrdson lives, and also in all the lands, tenements, rents and services which belonged to Edmund Garton, otherwise called Edmund Marshall, of all of which Thomas and Joan have peaceful possession and seisin at the time of the making of these presents. Warranty. Sealing clause.[1] Witnesses: Robert Plompton, Peter Medilton, knts., William Hakkysworth, Richard Saxton, John Bekyrton. (*Ibid.*, No. 33).

Ripon.

399. Thursday before St. Bartholomew, 21 Edward III [Aug. 23, 1347]. Grant by John son of William de Doncastre of Rypon, to William Mauleuerer, knt., and Alice, his wife, and the heirs and assigns of William, of all that piece of land with buildings thereon in Ploxmaygate in Rypon which he had of the inheritance of Agnes, his mother; to hold freely and in peace, with all liberties and easements, paying yearly to the lords of Ryplay, 3*s*. of silver in equal portions at Whitsuntide and Martinmas for all services. Warranty. Sealing clause. Witnesses: Peter de Richemounde, seneschal of Rypon and seisin delivered by Roger de Clitherum, bailiff of Rypon, John de Schirwode, Adam de Skoton, Thomas Burdon, Nicholas Warayner. At Rypon. (*Y.A.S.*, Md. 59/19, No. 34).

400. Sunday after the Nativity of the B.V.M. [Sept. 13], 1360. Release and quitclaim by William son and heir of Adam de Sallay of Rypon, to Agnes, his sister, her heirs and assigns, of all right in that piece of ground with buildings thereon in Ploxmayngate in Rypon, which lies between the burgage of Hugh the tanner (*pellipar'*) of Westgate on one side and the burgage of Robert de Suerygg, which once belonged to John de Shirburn on the other. Warranty. Sealing clause. Witnesses: Nicholas Hubert, Richard Barry, John de Ilketon, Robert de Suerygg, Walter de Holgill. At Rypon. (*Ibid.*, No. 35).

401. Thursday, St. Scholastica the Virgin, 36 Edward III [Feb. 10, 1361-2]. Grant[2] by John de Shirwod to Dame Alice Mauleuerer, widow of Sir William Mauleuerer, knt., of a tenement with appurtenances in Rypon, in Hertstretgate, which lies between the tenement of Robert de Tanfeld on the north side and the tenement of Nicholas Hubert on the south; to hold to Dame Alice, her heirs and assigns, freely, etc., of the chief lords of the fee. Warranty. Sealing clause. Witnesses: John de Clutherom, Roger de Clutherom, Robert de Brunhous, Thomas Scot', Richard de Richemund. At Rypon. (*Ibid.*, No. 36).

[1] Fragment of red wax.

[2] Same date. Appointment of Henry Dreuet, chaplain, to take seisin. At Rypelay. (*Ibid.* No. 37).

402. Sunday after St. John the Baptist, 47 Edward III [June 26, 1373]. Indenture whereby Perot Mauleuerer grants and demises to John Blakburn of Rypon and Joan, his wife, a tenement with a garden in le Horsfair, lying between the tenement of Nicholas Hubard and the tenement of Robert de Tanfeld, for the term of their lives or for the lifetime of the survivor; paying yearly to the grantor 16*s*. and to lord Marmyon 12*d*. for all services, in equal portions at Whitsuntide and Martinmas. John and Joan grant for themselves and their executors and assigns that they will during the said term maintain and repair all the houses (*domos*) in the tenements and leave them in a proper and fit condition at the end of the term. Perot binds himself, his heirs and executors to carry out this grant, and John and Joan find as securities for their maintenance of the agreement, John Stow and Thomas de Ilketon. Alternate seals.[1] At Ryppelay. (*Ibid.*, No. 38).

403. [1524]. The Estret of Subsidie graunted to Oure Soueraign lord Kynge Henry the viijth in the xvth yere of his Reign, William Myddilton Knyght and John Pullyn, two of the Comissioners of oure said Soueraign lord the Kyng by devysyon, to William Frank of Ripon, gent., Thomas Condall of Monkton, yoman, and Thomas Fawcett of Nydde, grettyng. We will and charge you to leve and geder all somes of monys here after wryttyn, and to delyver theym Indiltale to Richard Aldeburgh of Aldeburgh, Esquyer, John Ratclyff of Hewik, esquyer, and Richard Paver of Dray . . . , high Collectors theyr.

Ripon

John Dest for goods		12*d*.
Roland Wilson for goods		12*d*.
Christifer Ulithorne for a childs porcon of goods ...		12*d*.
William Robson for goods		12*d*.
Richard Turrs for goods		12*d*.
Robert Stavely for goods		18*d*.
Abram Combland for goods		12*d*.
Henry Warwyk for goods		12*d*.
Robert Playn for goods		12*d*.
Robert Baron for goods	3*s*.	6*d*.
Robert Wardrop for goods	3*s*.	6*d*.
William Frankysh for lande	3*s*.	4*d*.
Nyman Jacob, a Duchman, for goods	2*s*.	
Ralph Cook for goods		12*d*.
Robert Holme for goods		18*d*.
Myles Rondale for lande		12*d*.
William Nicholson for goods	2*s*.	6*d*.
William Dromester for goods	2*s*.	6*d*.
Cristofer Watson for goods		18*d*.

[1] Seal of brown wax, diam. 8/10 in.; in a cusped border a shield of arms: on a bend three lozenges; *SIGILL' RICARDI DE DISCEFORD.

John Bland for goods	2*s*.	6*d*.
William Tanner for lande		12*d*.
William Whitside for goods		12*d*.
William Seyll for goods	22*s*.	
Thomas Monkyn for goods	6*s*.	8*d*.
Steven Loksmyth for goods	2*s*.	
William Saddeler for goods		12*d*.
Thomas Burton for goods		12*d*.
William Askewith for Vag'		6*d*.
William Kettylwell for goods		12*d*.
Robert Ward for goods	2*s*.	
Robert Kettylwell for goods	20*s*.	
Thomas Jakson for goods		12*d*.
Mabell Ripley, widow, for goods		12*d*.
Isabel Malory, widow, for lande		12*d*.
Robert Gepson for goods		12*d*.
Thomas Drawn for goods		12*d*.
John Myddylton for goods		12*d*.
Robert Goldesburgh for lande	2*s*.	
Dame [blank] Musgraue, wedowe, for lande ...	2*s*.	
Thomas Staueley for goods	20*s*.	

Markyngton cum Hamellh'[1]

William Atkynson for goods		16*d*.
Thomas Atkynson for goods		12*d*.
Henry Atynson for goods	2*s*.	
*Elyn Scotyswoman		8*d*.
*Margaret Scotyswoman		8*d*.
Richard Lemyng for goods		12*d*.

Hewyk ad pontem

John Ratclyf, esquyer for lande	20*s*.	
John Dikson for lande	2*s*.	
Thomas Brown for goods	2*s*.	6*d*.
William Bargh for goods	2*s*.	6*d*.

Monkton

John Lawson for goods	5*s*.	
Thomas Cundall for lande		16*d*.
William Sharo for lande		16*d*.
Myles Cundall for goods	2*s*.	6*d*.

Asmunderby cum bondgate

John Newton for goods	3*s*.	4*d*.

[1] With hamlets.

Sharo

John Woddall for goods		3*s.*	6*d.*
John Byndloys for lande			12*d.*
Thomas Wodd for goods			12*d.*
Robert Pacok for goods		2*s.*	
Thomas Monketon for lande			12*d.*
John Gibson for lande			12*d.*
George Woddall for goods			12*d.*

Nidd

John Vauasor for lande		20*s.*	
Katterina Grymston, wid' for goods			12*d.*
Richard Wilks for goods			12*d.*

Bishopside

Thomas Emson for lands		2*s.*	
Wife of George Colzer for lande			12*d.*

Skelton

Thomas Steyll for lande			12*d.*

Bishop Thornton

Thomas Halyday for lande			20*d.*
Richard Mylns for goods			12*d.*
William Diconson for goods			12*d.*
James Bicroft for goods			12*d.*

Thorpe iuxta Ripon

Thomas Alanson for lande			20*d.*

Whiteclyff

William Walworth for goods		5*s.*	

Gevyndale

John Redeshawe for goods		2*s.*	6*d.*
(*plus in dorso*)			

Bishopton cum Clotherom

John Norton, esquyer, for land	3*li.*	6*s.*	8*d.*
William Hogeson for goods			12*d.*
Richard Carhyll for goods			12*d.*
Hogs [blank] to John Norton for wage			6*d.*

Newby cum Mulwath

John Warde for goods		2*s.*	6*d.*
Edward Withes for goods		2*s.*	6*d.*
Katerin Scot, vid', for goods			16*d.*

Scleynyngford cum Staynley

Henry Kirkby for wages ... ... 6*d.*
Myles Staveley for goods ... ... 4*li.*
John Lofthouse for goods ... ... 8*s.*
John Staveley for goods ... ... 6*s.* 8*d.*
Thomas Steyll for goods ... ... 12*d.*

Westwyk

Rauff Wythes for goods ... ... 20*s.*
John Withes for goods ... ... 3*s.*

Nunwyk cum Sutton Holgrave

Cristofer Tedd for goods ... ... 7*s.* 6*d.*
John Byndloys for goods ... ... 20*s.*

Magna Staveley

William Malory, esquyer, for lande... ... ... 20*s.*

Summa libertatis de Ripon ... 22*li.* 6*s.*

William Myddilton, knt. ... ...John Pulleyn (*Ibid.*, No. 39).

Rishworth.

404. July 26, 4 Edward IV [1464]. Indenture[1] whereby Thomas Wilkynson, vicar of Halifax, John Lacy, esq., John Brodelegh, chaplain, Richard Shagh' and Richard Waterhous grant to John Sayuill, junior, son of John Sayuyill esq., late of Copley, all their messuages, lands and tenements, meadows, woods, pastures, rents and services with appurtenances in Northland, *hammelett* of the vill of Rysshworth, which they recently held jointly of the gift and feoffment of the said John Sayuyll esq.; to hold to John Sayuyll, junior, and his lawfully begotten heirs male, of the chief lords of the fee, and in default of issue 1) to Humphrey Sayuyll, brother of John and his lawfully begotten male heirs, 2) to the right heirs of John Sayuyll, their father. Alternate seals.[2] Witnesses: Robert Milner, Robert Clay, William Rayner. At Northland. (*Y.A.S.*, Md. 260/1).

Rogerthorpe (Badsworth).

405. Sept. 27, 10 Henry VI [1431].[2] Indenture whereby Richard de Burton grants to Richard de Balderston 2 parcels of land

[1] Also a precisely similar indenture, but larger in size. (*Ibid.*, No 2). Also appointment by the same of Robert Pek and Thomas Ecclysley to deliver seisin of the same. There is evidence of only 4 seals to this document, all are blurred. (*Ibid*, No. 3).

[2] Five small seals of red wax, (1) an animal, possibly a unicorn, (2) a pelican in her piety; legend undeciphered, (3) undeciphered, (4) a man's head, (5) the letter R below a crown.

called Mabbezorde and Huttrellynge, which he recently had of the gift and feoffment of the said Richard Balderston in Rogerthorp; to hold to Richard, his heirs and assigns of the chief lords of the fee in perpetuity, on the following condition, namely, that the said Richard, his heirs, executors or assigns, severally or in common, shall not disturb, inconvenience or molest Thomas Northorp, perpetual chaplain of the parish church of Hemmesworth, or his successors, without their consent, by entering into and occupying a messuage, toft and virgate of land in Hemmesworth which the said Richard Balderston once had of the gift of Richard de Walton, rector of the church of Hemmesworth and John Smyth of Baddesworth and which once belonged to John de Hill, son and heir of Richard son of William del Hill; in this event, or if he should deprive the said Thomas or his successors of the profits and issues of the said messuage, toft and lands, or of any part of them, then it shall be lawful for the grantor or his heirs to re-enter and to hold the 2 parcels notwithstanding this indenture. Warranty. Alternate seals.[1] Witnesses: Thomas Sayvell, knt., William de Gayrgreve, John Banastre of Newhall, John Banastre of Walton, Edward del More. At Rogerthorp. (*Serlby Hall Muniments*, No. 63).

Scarborough.

406. Thursday after the Sunday on which is sung *Quasi modo geniti* [April 22], 1316. Grant by John son of Thomas Coupcorn of Scardburgh, to Juliana daughter of Adam, forester of Gylingmore, of 3 roods of arable land lying in the field of Scardburgh, in length from Grengate on the east as far as Hengrist on the west and in breadth from the land once of John de Pycheford on the south as far as the land of the grantor on the north; to hold to Juliana, her heirs and assigns, of the chief lords of the fee. Sealing clause. Witnesses: Robert Waweyn and Adam de Pykering, bailiffs of Scardburgh, Adam de Heplerthorpp', Adam de Semer, Geoffrey de Folketon, Hugh de Wandesford, John de Seterington. At Scardburgh. (*N. G. Hyde*, No. 19).

407. Eve of St. Martin [Nov. 10], 1301. Indenture between Henry de Ruston of Scardburgh of the one part and Richard called the tailor and Matilda, his wife, daughter of Roger Randolf, of the other, whereby Henry grants to Richard and Matilda that portion of land which belonged to the capital holding (*capital' mans'*) of Roger Randolph and which lies in the old town of Scardburgh in length 21 paces from the highway on the south as far as the land of John de Hundmanby of Scardburgh on one side and the land of the said Henry on the other on the north, and in breadth 12 paces from the land of the said John on the west, as far as the land of Henry on the east; to hold to Richard and Matilda to the end of their lives,

[1] Blob of red wax; an ivy leaf.

freely and in peace, of the chief lords of the fee, paying to Henry, his heirs and assigns 1*d.* at Whitsuntide for all services. Warranty. And if the said Richard shall absent himself from the vill of Scardburgh for half the year through the death of Matilda if he outlives her, Henry may repossess himself of the lands and dispose of them as best suits him. Richard and Matilda shall maintain the lands with all necessities. Sealing clause. Witnesses: Robert Wawayne, bailiff of Scard', Philip de Hornbury, Adam de Ruston, Robert Coroner, Adam de Heplerthorp, Adam de Semer, John de Setterington, Simon Burton. At Scardburgh.[1] (*Ibid.*, No. 20).

Scawton.

408. Thursday after St. James the apostle, [July 26], 1291. Indenture witnessing that whereas contention had arisen between Richard de Kereby on the one hand and Sir Richard de Malebys on the other, concerning the common pasture of the said Richard de Kereby belonging to his free tenement in the vill of Scalton, namely in 6 acres of arable land lying within the park of the said Richard in Scalton and in 5 acres of meadow in the same vill, and similarly concerning a certain dyke raised up to the detriment of his said free tenement, now it is agreed on the Thursday after St. James, 1291 in the manner following, namely, that the said Sir Richard grants to Richard de Kereby, his heirs, his common in the said meadow after the harvest has been fully gathered in, also that he is allowed to lay flat the said dyke at the harvest time and that his harvest on the far side of the dyke may be carried without intervention from Richard or his heirs; but it shall be permitted to the said Sir Richard after this harvest has been gathered, to raise up the dyke at his will; Sir Richard also grants to Richard de Kereby a rood of land lying in . . .[2] which Alice Hudy once held; and for this grant Richard de Kereby quitclaims for himself and his heirs all right in the common pasture in the 6 acres of land lying in the said park, in perpetuity. Warranty. Alternate seals. Witnesses: Sir William de Harum, Sir John de Fauken[burgh], Sir William Burdun, James de Holme, John de Yelaund, Bernard de Berke, Adam de Thorny, William de Scipton.[3] (*Newburgh Priory Muniments*, No. 8/21).

409. Thursday after the Translation of Blessed Thomas the martyr [July 13], 1312. Indenture whereby an agreement was made between Sir Richard Malbys, lord of Skalton of the one part and Stephen de Cantelay, Matilda, his wife, Juliana de Besingby and William de Besingby of the other, namely, that the said Sir Richard granted and confirmed to Juliana and Matilda, her sister, an acre,

[1] Endorsed in a contemporary hand, Thomas Sergent; in a later hand, Ubi Thomas Douler manet, and later, W. Loksmyth habet nunc.

[2] Document stained.

[3] Dorso: Inter Ricardum Mal' e R. de Kereby de communa pasture de Scaltona.

a rood and 10 perches of land and appurtenances in the territory of Skalton, which lie in the place called Pedinbanke on the east and extend from the path called Kerbysti to le Wayngate which is in the higher part of Pedinbanke; and the said Stephen, Matilda and Juliana grant to Sir Richard an acre, a rood and 10 perches with appurtenances in the territory of the same vill which lie in 2 places in a field called Biyondepedinkeld, this being in exchange for the aforesaid land granted by Sir Richard; to hold the said acre, rood and 10 perches in Pedinbanc to Juliana and Matilda and their lawfully begotten heirs, of the chief lords of the fee, freely and in peace, and should they die without such heirs, remainder to the right heirs of William de Besingby in perpetuity. Sir Richard is to hold the said acre rood and 10 perches in Byondepedinkeld for himself and his heirs in perpetuity. Mutual guarantees. Moreover William de Besingby grants to Richard and his heirs the said acre, rood and 10 perches in Biyondepedinkeld in exchange in perpetuity, and the said William, Stephen, Matilda and Juliana agree that Sir Richard and his heirs may enclose with hedge, wall or ditch the lands in Biyondepedinkeld and also the place called Cuontesdale, namely from the park of Pedyn as far as Kuontesdale and from Kuontesdale for 18 roods in the wood of le Holt towards the north where it rises up to the oak near the path del Holt, and so from the said oak to Wayngate of Holtslake and from Holtslakke to the wall of the said park belonging to Richard, so that neither William, Stephen, Matilda nor Juliana shall have common pasture or any other right within this enclosure; but if it should happen that any of their animals should at any time stray into the enclosure, by reason of defective fencing, then they shall not be impounded but driven back without harm. Alternate seals. Witnesses: Sir John de Barton of Friton, Sir Robert de Bolton, Sir William de Harum, knts., William de Sproxton, William de Apilton, John de Butterwyke, Roger Rabot. (*Ibid.*, No. 8/22).

410. Grant by Richard de Kerby son of Richard de Kerby to Sir John Malbys, knt., of a meadow in Skalton with appurtenances which is called the little meadow and lies near the mill, just as contained within its bounds; to hold to Sir John, his heirs and assigns, of the chief lords of the fee. Warranty. Sealing clause. Witnesses: Sirs John de Barton of Fryton, Robert de Boulton, William de Harum, knts., William de Sproxton, William de Thorneton, William de Besingby. (*Ibid.*, No. 8/23).

411. June 1, 13 Edward III [1339]. Indenture whereby Thomas *in ye* Wyches and Agnes, his wife, of Pothow, grant and demise to Sir William de Malbys a messuage and 2 bovates of land with appurtenances in the vill and territory of Scaleton, lying near the manor and tenement of the said Sir William; to hold to Sir William, his heirs and assigns, of Thomas and Agnes, freely and in peace for the term of the life of the said Agnes, and paying 12*s*.

yearly, in equal portions at Whitsuntide and Martinmas, and should the said Sir William continue to hold the messuage and 2 bovates after the death of Agnes, then he and his heirs shall pay 30*s*. yearly at the two terms to the right heirs of Thomas and Agnes. Warranty. Alternate seals. Witnesses: John Gouwer of Sexhowe, Nicholas his son, Laurence Gouwer, Thomas Moubray, William de Pothowe, Robert de Gouton, At Scaleton. (*Ibid.*, No. 8/24).

Sessay.

412. Friday after St. Katherine the Virgin, 10 Edward II [Nov. 26, 1316]. Grant and quitclaim by John le Spenser of Ceszay to John the carpenter of Ceszay, his heirs or assigns, of a messuage with croft adjacent, 6½ acres of land, and all his meadows belonging to two bovates of land which he had had in the vill and territory of Ceszay, with all easements in moors, plains, feedings, pastures and woods, so that the grantees should give nothing for their share (*proporc'*), but have free entry and exit in the woods of Ceszay without payment [?] (*take*) or any such demand, to hold as freely as John, the grantor's father, had held the premises; rendering yearly to the chief lord of the fee[1] a rose in the time of roses if demanded, for all secular services, except forinsec service. Witnesses: John Darell of Cessay, Marmaduke Darell, John Boumte, Richard Wigot, John de Thormotby. Ceszay. (*E. G. Millar, esq.*).

413. Wednesday after Whitsunday [June 4], 1343. Grant by William Darell of Ceszai, knt., to John his son of a close called Newhengbank with a plot adjacent outside the close for building a house, and eighteen acres of land with appurtenances in the territory of Ceszai, of which six acres lay in Thwersurflat on the east, two acres on Layrberghflat on the west, two acres on Thistelflat, six acres in *le Brek* on the east, and two acres on Ownamflat; to hold for the grantee's life and one year more, rendering yearly 34*s*. sterling for all services, half at Whitsuntide and half at Martinmas. Alternate seals. Witnesses: Robert de Newbi, Edmund ad funtem [*sic.*], John the carpenter. Ceszai.[2] (*Y.A.S.*, Md. 141, No. 14).

414. Thursday after St. Botulph the Abbot [June 18], 1349. Grant by Thomas Darell son of Sir William Darell, knt., to John son of John Outi of Ceszay and Alice his wife and the heirs of their bodies, of two messuages and 10½ acres of land with appurtenances in the vill and territory of Ceszay; with remainder to John son of John Outy and his heirs. Witnesses: John Darell, William Darell, John the forester, William son of Hugh, John Corpe. Ceszay. (*E. G. Millar, esq.*).

[1] Spelt *pheodi*.

[2] Seal: yellow wax, round, 7/8 in.; within a cusped and indented border a shield of arms, a lion rampant. *SIGILLVM IOHANNIS DAREL.

415. Jan. 26, 23 Henry VII [1507-8]. Release by Ralph Darell of Byland (*Bellalanda*), gent., to Guy Dawnay, esq., and Joan his wife, sister and heir of Thomas Darell, late of Sessey, esq., of all right in the manors and lordships of Sessey, Eldemer, Tirryngton, Liuerton, Dalton, Thurkelby, Crakehall, Heton, and Broddesworth, and in all other lands and tenements, meadows, feedings, pastures, rents, hereditaments and services, lately belonging to Thomas Darell, esq., in co. York and elsewhere. Witnesses, John, abbot of Byland, Robert Crower of Cawton, gent., Richard Barreye of Sessey, gent., John Barsworth, gent., of Thornmanby.[1] (*Y.A.S.*, Md. 135, No. 10).

Shafton.

416. March 1, 2 Richard III [1484-5]. Release and quitclaim by John Lound, rector of the church of Hymmysworth, John Wynter, rector of the church of Acworth, John Morley, Henry Brygg, to John Toy, of all right in a croft containing a rood of land and 3 acres and a rood of land in the vill and fields of Shafton, which they lately had of the gift and feoffment of the said John Toy. Warranty. Sealing clause.[2] Witnesses: John Thomson, vicar of the church of Felkirk, William Coppull, Thomas Lomealx, Robert Ward, William Huchonson. At Shafton. (*Serlby Hall Muniments*, No. 64).

417. Nov. 4, 24 Henry VII [1508]. Indenture whereby John Holylee of Shafton grants to John Beaumont of Mirfeld, Richard Dalton of Dalton, Richard Grethedde and Peter Rouse all his closes, lands and tenements and meadows with appurtenances in Shafton; to hold to the grantees, of the chief lords of the fee. Warranty. Sealing clause.[3] (*Ibid.*, No. 65).

Snaith.

418. Thursday after Michaelmas, 22 Richard II. [Oct. 3, 1398]. Grant by John de Monkefryston, chaplain, dwelling in Snayth, to Richard de Somersete, taverner of Snaythe, of a messuage with all the buildings thereon in Snaythe, lying in length and breadth between the messuage formerly of John Lambard on the south, and the messuage formerly of Robert Cade on the north, and abutting on the road leading towards the marsh at the eastern end

[1] Fragment of seal of red wax.

[2] Four small seals of brown wax; on the first a man's head, the others undeciphered.

March 6 [1484-5]. Grant by John Hylylegh, his heirs and assigns of lands [*as above*]. Witnesses: William Coppull, Thomas Lomealx, Robert Ward, William Huchonson, Henry Brygg. Small seal of wax; the letter T below a crown. (*Ibid.*, No. 64a).

March 8 [1484-5]. Quitclaim of the same by John Toy to John Hylylegh. Same witnesses and seal. (*Ibid.*, No. 64b).

[3] Seal of red wax, the letter M in a square frame.

and on a toft of William de Stubbs which formerly belonged to John son of Thomas the clerk, at the western end; to hold to Richard, his heirs and assigns, of the chief lord of that fee, paying yearly to the heirs of Laurence de Hek or their assigns 3*s.* 6*d.* of silver at the four annual terms appointed in the soke of Snaythe, in equal portions, for all other services, suits of court, aids and demands. Warranty. Sealing clause.[1] Witnesses: John de Lynlay, John Longe, Thomas de Cowyk, Thomas de Crulle, John Smythe. Given at Snaythe. (*Y.A.S.*, Md. 182, No. 80).

419. Sunday before the Nativity of St. John the Baptist, 4 Hen. IV, [June 17, 1403]. Indenture by which Elizabeth, widow of Thomas Daunay leases for the whole of her life, to John Neville and Alice, his wife, their heirs and assigns, all her demesne in the soke of Snath, which is called Gramoreses, with all rents, services of all tenants whether free or villein, with all their following and belongings, also courts, with all other appurtenances and easements, pertaining to the demesne; to hold of the chief lord of the fee, and paying yearly to Elizabeth for the first five years a peppercorn at the Nativity for all suits, services, etc., and paying also for the following years of her life 100*s.* at the specified terms; and if it happen that the rent be in arrears at any term for the space of 20 days, then it shall be lawful for Elizabeth or her assigns to re-enter and distrain until satisfaction is obtained for any loss or expense incurred. Warranty. Alternate seals.[2] Witnesses: Richard Burgone, Thomas Dilcok, William de Scherewod, Thomas Hobson', Richard Tancred. At Snath. (*Y.A.S.*, Md. 153, No. 23).

420. Oct. 4. 5 Hen. IV. [1403]. Grant by John Gillotson' carpenter, lately dwelling in Snaythe, to John Daunay, of all the grantor's messuage with appurtenances in Snaythe, which lies between the messuage of Collette Rugheschaghe on the east and the messuage of Thomas Frere on the west and abutting on the highway of the vill on the south, and on Stokhousgarthe on the north; to hold to John Daunay, his heirs and assigns, of the chief lords of that fee. Warranty. Sealing clause.[1] Witnesses: Nicholas Colne, receiver of the Castle of Pontefract (*receptore Castri Pontisfracti*), Thomas Hesille of Bole, John Smythe of Snaythe, John Lynlay keeper of the park of Cowik, Richard Taverner of Snaythe, William Jepok of the same, William Broun, bailiff. At Snaythe. (*Y.A.S.*, Md. 182, No. 81).

421. July 15, 7 Henry IV. [1406]. Grant by Alexander de Hek to John Daunay, his heirs and assigns, of his ruined barn (*orreum*), with the timber, the foundations and the site, with all

[1] Seal: small blob of brownish-yellow wax; Virgin and Child.

[2] Seal: red wax, diam. 9/10 in.; shield of arms in cusped border, charge and legend undeciphered.

[3] Seal: fragment of red wax, device appears to be a letter.

ways, easements and other appurtenances in the vill and territory of Snaythe, which barn lies on the south of a messuage of John Fox, butcher, next to a garden, recently of Richard de Snaythe; to hold to John Daunay, his heirs and assigns, of the chief lords of the fee. Warranty. Sealing clause.[1] Witnesses: Nicholas Daunay, John Hek of Balne, John Fox, butcher, John Rudde. At Snayth. (*Ibid.*, No. 82).

422. June 24, 11 Henry IV. [1410]. Grant by Simon de Thorneton' to John Daunay of Snaithe, senior, and William Rosselyn' of Cotenays of all that toft in Snaithe, lately of Margaret de Hek, lying between the site of the house late of Richard de Snaithe on the west, and abutting on the north and east on the messuage of John Fox of Snaith, butcher, and upon a path leading towards Goldale on the south, with the whole length and breadth as contained in the ancient charter granting the same, with all roads and other easements pertaining to the said toft; to hold to John and William and the heirs and assigns of John for ever. Warranty. Sealing clause.[2] Witnesses: Thomas Dilcock, Nicholas Daunay, John de Snaithe, Richard Lokyngtoun. At Snaith. (*Ibid.*, No. 83).

423. Whitsunday [May 15], 1418. Grant by Richard Knaresburghe and Richard Broune living in Carlton' near Snaythe to John Thornhille of Snaythe, his heirs and assigns of a piece of land in Snaythe lying between the land of the same John Thornhille, lately purchased of John Rudd' and Henry his brother, and the land of John Thornhille lately purchased of John son and heir of John Frere of Couwyk, and abutting on the highway of the vill and on a path leading to Typpynghous, and containing in width one perch; to hold of the chief lord of the fee. Warranty. Sealing clause. Witnesses: William Pulter of Snaythe, John Gilotson' of the same, carpenter, Simon Thornton' of the same, Richard Taverner of the same, William Long of the same. At Snaythe. (*Ibid.*, No. 84).

424. July 4, 1418. Grant by William, son of Robert de Daltoun, heir of Joyce Croft of Cowyk, to John Thornhille of Snaithe, his heirs and assigns, of a rood of land and meadow with appurtenances, lying in les Smalengges de Snaithe between the land and meadow of John Thornhille, formerly called Tinteland on the south, and the grantor's land on the north, and abutting on the water of Dyk on the east and on the hedge of the field of Cowyk on the west; to hold of the chief lord of that fee. Warranty. Sealing clause.[3] Witnesses: John Eland of Snaithe, William Pulter of the same, John Fox of the same, butcher, John Rudd' of Cowyk, Henry Milner of the same. At Cowyk. (*Ibid.*, No. 85).

[1] Seal: blob of brown wax; small fleur de lis.
[2] Seal: blob of green wax impressed with an instrument shaped like a trefoil.
[3] Seal: small fragment of red wax, broken.

425. Trinity Sunday [May 18], 1421. Grant[1] by John Smythe of Snaythe to John Thornylle of Snaythe and Margaret, his wife, and the heirs and assigns of John, of half a toft with buildings on it in the vill of Snaythe, which lies between the toft once held by John Lytster on the east, which once belonged to John de Couwyk, and the toft which William Bouwer holds, which once belonged to Adam, son of William Bouwer on the west, and abuts on the highway of the vill to the north, and on the highway leading below the vill on the south; with free entry and exit to the said half toft along that path which lies between the toft once belonging to Adam Bouwer and the toft once of Richard, son of Jacob Hers; also grants one butt of land with appurtenances in Snaythe lying between the garden once of Adam Bouwer, and the land which John Litester once held on the east, and between a certain pathway which once belonged to the said Adam and Richard Spenser on the west, and abuts on the common way to the south, and on the garden once belonging to Adam on the north, and contains in length 10 perches, to hold the toft and butt to John and Margaret and the heirs of John, of the chief lord of that fee. Warranty. Sealing clause.[2] Witnesses: John Daunay, Nicholas his brother, Robert Dylcok, William Pult', John Gilotson'. At Snaythe. (*Y.A.S.*, Md. 153, No. 24).

426. Tuesday before St. Margaret. 9 Henry V [July 15, 1421]. Release by Robert Watton' esq., to John Dawnay of all right which he has by a covenant with John, in a messuage and a toft with appurtenances in Snaithe, late of William Broun and William Fisseby, lying on the east of a toft lately Fish toft; to hold to John, his heirs and assigns, of the chief lord of the fee. At . . .[3] Sealing clause.[4] (*Y.A.S.*, Md. 182, No. 87).

427. June 1, 11 Henry VI [1433]. Appointment by William Daunay of Simon de Thornton of Snaythe and Richard Floter of Hensalle as his attorneys, to deliver seisin to Robert Watton, knt., Thomas de Metham, esq., William Scargyll, esq., John Daunay, his brother, Nicholas Daunay and John Schyppman', chaplain, of all the lands and meadows, pastures, moors, rents, services with appurtenances in Snaythe and Cowyk or elsewhere in the soke of Snaythe, which he had of the gift and feoffment of John Daunay, his father; as specified more fully in his charter to the said Robert, Thomas, William etc., he agrees to everything done in his name by the above attorneys. Sealing clause.[5] (*Y.A.S.*, Md. 153, No. 25).

[1] Release of the same dated the following day Two seals pendant from one tongue: (1) broken, (2) bird facing sinister, legend undeciphered (*Y.A.S. MD* 182, No. 86).

[2] Seal: red wax; diam ½ in ; a wolf or dog to the dexter

[3] Document scratched and illegible.

[4] Seal: ½ x ¾ in.; a man's head facing to the sinister.

[5] Seal on tongue cut from deed: red wax, gem bearing a boar's head with a scroll in the mouth to the dexter. The word on the scroll undeciphered.

428. St. Peter in Cathedra. [Feb. 22] 1431[-2]. Grant by William Daunay to Robert Redenesse of Polyngtonn and Alice his wife (*and the heirs and assigns of the said Robert*)—[crossed out] of a messuage built upon in Snaithe, with a toft and a croft and with free entry and exit to the same, abutting on the highway of Snaythe on the north and on a road behind the vill on the south, lying on the east side of the lane called Couwyk layne, which late was in the tenure of John Smythe, and all the lands which the same John Smythe had with the aforesaid messuage in the west field of Snaythe; to hold all the grantor's estate (*totum statum meum*) in the messuage, toft, croft and lands, to Robert Redenesse, Alice his wife, and their heirs lawfully begotten, paying yearly to William Daunay, his heirs and assigns, 13*s*. 8*d*. at Easter and Michaelmas in equal portions, and paying yearly on behalf of the heirs and assigns of John Daunay, the grantor's father, to the lord of the manor of Snayth, 3*s*. 5*d*., also paying annually to the Lord Abbot of Selby 2*s*. at the usual times; should it happen that the said rent of 13*s*. 8*d*. is in arrears in part or in whole for a quarter of a year after any term, or should it happen that the heirs and assigns of John Daunay be distrained for the rent, or should it happen that Robert and Alice or any of their heirs lawfully begotten, should in future alienate, waste, or insufficiently repair the messuage, toft, croft or land, then it shall be lawful for William Daunay his heirs and assigns to re-enter all the premises if they wish, and to hold them forever, this charter notwithstanding. Warranty. If Robert and Alice die without heirs of their bodies, then all the premises to revert and to remain to William Daunay, his heirs and assigns. Alternate seals.[1] Witnesses: Richard Burgoigne of Balne, Nicholas Daunay of Couwyk, Thomas de Balne of Snaythe, William Lynlay of Couwyk, John Rudd' of the same, Simon Thornetonn of Snaythe, William Skott' of Polyngtonn, the bailiff of the court of Snaythe. At Snayth. (*Y.A.S.*, Md. 182, No. 88).

429. Eve of St. Thomas the Apostle, 17 Henry VI [Dec. 20, 1438]. Grant by John son of Henry Milner of Cowyk to Richard Hawell of Snaythe, his heirs and assigns, of one selion of land lying in the east field of Snaythe, containing one perch in breadth, and lying between the land lately of Thomas Paynot on the west, and the land beyond the road, formerly of Henry, and now in the tenure of Nicholas Daunay, on the east, and abutting on Wrymore on the south, and on the ditch of the meadow on the north; to hold of the chief lord of the fee. Warranty. Sealing clause.[2] Witnesses: William Schipwrighte of Snaythe, Robert Burdeclener of the same, John Wygan' of the same, John Ryther of Cowyk, Thomas Hichecok of the same. At Snaythe. (*Ibid.*, No. 89).

[1] Seals: two, blobs of red wax; (1) the letter R; (2) not deciphered.

[2] Seal of red wax, the letter R surmounted by a crown, with a sprig of leaves to the dexter.

430. St. Mary Magdalene, 25 Henry VI [July 22, 1447]. Indenture by which John Daunay grants to Robert de Rouclyff of Eskryk, Nicholas Daunay of Cowyk, Richard Schirwod of Hensalle, Richard Rud, chaplain, and John Wegan' of Snaythe, all his lands, tenements, meadows, moors with appurtenances in the soke of Snaythe, which are of servile tenure (*bass' tenura*) in the fee of the Duke of Lancaster; to hold the said lands etc., to Robert, Nicholas, Richard, Richard and John, their heirs and assigns on the same terms as grantor held according to the form of a new charter of the Duke of Lancaster, from the Feast of St. Michael in the aforesaid year of the reign of King Henry VI until the termination of 51 years next following; also the lands which John has of the grant and release of various people, to hold of John, rendering to the lords of the fee the due and accustomed services of the manor. Alternate seals.[1] Witnesses: Richard Dylcok of Snaythe, Thomas Balne of the same, William Lyndlay of Cowyk, John Ryther of the same, Henry Bond of the same. At Cowyk. (*Y.A.S.*, Md. 153, No. 26).

431. St. Valentines Day, [Feb. 14] 1460[-1]. Grant by John Westryn' and John Westmorland of Carlton', junior, to John Smythe of Snaythe, senior, and Alice, his wife, for the term of their lives, of a certain messuage, with buildings in the vill of Snaythe, which lies with its whole length and breadth between the messuage recently belonging to John Litster of Snaythe, on the east; and a messuage late of William Bouwer, *schippewrighte*, on the west; and adjoining the broad way leading from Snaythe to the south; and on the highway leading from the centre of the vill to the north; also all the free land acquired through the same John Smyth at the present time, which lies in various parts of the fields of Snaythe, which messuage and land grantors recently had of the gift and feoffment of the aforesaid John. To hold to John and Alice for life, both being alive together, and the heirs and assigns of the said John, of the chief lord of the fee. Warranty. Sealing clause.[2] Witnesses: John Daunay of Snaythe, William Pulter of the same, John son of Julian Cardynalle of the same, Richard Taverner of the same, John Thornhille of the same. At Snaythe. (*Y.A.S.*, Md. 182, No. 90).

432. Penultimate day of Sept. 2 Edward IV [29 Sept. 1462]. Indenture by which William Dey of Snaythe leases to Robert Berkere, otherwise Robert Kewre and Margaret, his wife, their heirs and assigns, two acres of land of Gramerose, of which one acre lies in Mydyloxmay in the fields of Snaythe, between the land of Thomas Vendelok on the west, and the land which William Longe holds by inheritance on the east, adjoining the land of John Dawnaye on the north, and Mydiloxmay dyk on the south; the other acre of land

[1] Five small seals of red wax: 1, 4, 5, blobs; (2) interlacing strapwork; (3) undeciphered.

[2] Two seals of light brown wax: (1) Bird facing to the sinister, legend undeciphered; (2) Broken; letter R surmounted by a crown and flanked by sprigs of leaves.

and meadow in the Sowthfeld of Snaythe on the west part of Depsyk lies between the land Henry Watson' holds by inheritance on the west, and the land of William Burgon' of Balne on the east, and adjoins the enclosure (*parcam*) of Fyrpyne on the north, and the water of Went on the south; to hold to Robert and Margaret, their heirs and assigns for the term of 51 years, paying annually to William, his heirs and assigns for all suits, services and demands, the sum of 2*d*. Warranty. Alternate seals.[1] Witnesses: Richard Edinwud, Thomas Awkberewe, Thomas Thornton', Nicholas Rudde, John Mylner of Snaythe. (*Ibid.*, No. 91).

433. Dec. 5, 3 Edw. IV [1463]. Grant and surrender by Alice Dylcok, dau. of Thomas Dylcok, administratrix of the goods and chattels of the aforesaid Thos, to William Crosby, son and heir of Agnes Robinser, late of Carleton', of all the lands and tenements, meadows and moors, called Whitebarnelands, with appurtenances, in Snaythe, which Thomas had for a term of years by the demise of William. To have and to hold to William, his heirs and assigns all right and claim which she has in the lands, tenements, meadows and moors aforesaid. Sealing clause.[2] (*Ibid.*, No. 92).

434. July 5, 20 Edw. IV [1480]. Grant by Emmotte (*Emota*) Williamsonn', widow, in her pure widowhood to John Bobewythe, John Benet, senior, and Thomas Bobewythe, of half an acre of meadow in the northern meadows of Snaythe, lying between the King's meadow on the east and the meadow of Margaret Astay on the west, lately called *Anable dyk doughter thynge* and abutting on the water of Ayre on the north and on the east field of Snaythe on the south; to hold to them, their heirs and assigns of the chief lords of that fee. Warranty. Sealing clause.[3] Witnesses: John Friston', Christopher Beyn, Robert Wegan, junior, Thomas Huchenson', Robert Gerson' of Snaythe. At Snayth. (*Ibid.*, No. 93).

435. Oct. 16, 28 Henry VIII [1536]. Be it knowen unto all men to whom this present wrytynge shall come that I Lionell Percy, generall receyvor for our Soveraigne lord the kynge within the Soak of Snaith hath remytt, released, and utterly for me, my heirs and executors fro evermore haith made quyte clame unto John Dauney, knyghte, all and every action, as well reall as personall, suyts, debtts and demandes whiche I have, or by any manor of meane may have agenst the seid John Dauney, from the Begynnynge of the world unto the day of the makynge of this presemt, By reason of the gederynge of the kynge ferme within the seid Soake of Snaith. In witnes herof unto this my generall acquytaunce I the seid Lionell haith sette my seall. Dated att Snaith the xvi day of Octobre in the xxviii th yere of the reigne of our soveraigne lord the kynge Henry the eight. (*Ibid.*, No. 94).

[1] Seal: blob of reddish-brown wax; letter W.
[2] Seal of red wax; undeciphered.
[3] Seal of red wax; not deciphered.

436. Grant by George Smythe of Snathe, yeoman, in consideration of his marriage with Joan Collines, widow, of the same, to George Frankland and Thomas Tolland of Snathe, yeomen, of a toft with a croft in Snathe, now held by Agnes Samson, widow, and lying between the land of John Daunay Esq., towards the west, and the land of George Smythe on the east and abutting on the highway towards the north, and on the field of Snathe towards the south; he also grants one and a half acres of arable land lying in the different fields of Snathe and Cowik, of which half an acre lies in the west field of Snathe in le Byrkshawe, which lies between the land of the Queen on the west, and the land of John Daunay on the east; and half an acre lies between the land of Thomas Tolland, junior, on the east in the field of Cowik, and the land of Edward Coike on the west, and the common way leading to Roclyff on the south, and a rood of land belonging to William Motherby on the north; and the other half acre abuts on the land of Robert Fryston to the west and on the land hereditarily of William Tolland on the east, and on the other side towards the south, and on the land recently of John Woodhus to the north; he also grants two acres and one rood of pasture lying in the north meadows of Snath in different places there, of which one and a half acres lie between the meadows aforesaid of the Queen on the west, and the meadows of George Bowm [?] to the east, and abuts on the water of Ayre on the north, and on the fields of Cowik to the south; and three roods lie in le Smayllynges between the said fields of the Queen now held by Edmund Norton on the north, and the fields hereditarily of Richard Glendowe on the south, and abuts on the water called Turnsbrygdyk towards the east, and on le Foodesehirlls towards the west; to hold to George and Thomas, their heirs and assigns, of the said George Smythe and Joan Collines and their lawful heirs, rendering the due and accustomed services to the chief lords of the fee. Warranty. Sealing clause.[1] (*Y.A.S. Md.* 153 No. 27).

Southowram.

437. Purification of the B.V.M. [Feb. 2], 1347[-8]. Grant by John Fige and Joan, his wife, to Robert de Windhill, of a piece of land called Copeyherd, lying in the territory of Southouram between Bobrillyherd on the east and Halifaxbrok on the west; to hold to Robert, his heirs and assigns, freely and in peace, of the chief lords of the fee. Warranty. Sealing clause.[2] Witnesses: John de Northclif, John de Windibank, William Tilly, Richard Coppera, John Tilly. At Southourum. (*J. B. Payne*, No. 4).

438. Monday after St. John of Beverley [May 10], 1378. Grant by Robert Fygge of Rothwell to John Smyth of Halifax, of

[1] Seal of brownish wax, blurred and undeciphered.

[2] Tongues for two seals, on the second an oval seal of brown wax, possibly the Annunciation, but much rubbed.

half a meadow with half a dwelling and a courtyard adjacent, also a yard called Bobrilyerd in the territory of Southouram on the east of the water called Halyfaxbroke, between the path leading from the church of Halifax towards Southouram and the road which leads from the same church towards Hiperum, all of which came to the grantor by inheritance after the death of Joan his mother; to hold to John and his heirs, freely and in peace, paying yearly to the chief lords of the fee a rose at the Nativity if demanded. Warranty. Sealing clause.[1] Witnesses: Dom. Richard de Heton, vicar of Halifax, John Drak', John Milnar of Halifax, Robert Litster, Thomas de Cliffe. At Halifax. (*Ibid.*, No. 5).

439. Thursday after the Annunciation, 10 Henry IV [Mar. 28, 1409]. Since John Smythson of Halifax and Matilda, his wife, hold a messuage called Bladehous, 2 parcels of land called Bladeroides and Bladehey and a parcel of meadow called le Brodenge with appurtenances in Southouram, for the term of their lives, with reversion to Thomas Lacy del Mere iuxta Castelford and his heirs, now Thomas del Lacy grants to Henry Sayuyll of Coppelay esq., the reversion of the said lands and tenements; to hold to him after the deaths of John and Matilda, of the chief lords of the fee in perpetuity. Warranty. Sealing clause.[2] Witnesses: Thomas Sayuyll of Thornehill, Adam Mirfeld, William Mirfeld, Thomas de Methelay. At Southouram. (*Ibid.*, No. 6).

440. Oct. 26, 8 Edward IV [1468]. Indenture whereby Thomas Wylkynson, vicar of the church of Halifax, John Lacy esq., John Brodelegh, chaplain, Richard Shagh, Richard Waterhous, grant to Humphrey (*Vmfrido*) Sayvill, son of John Sayvill esq., deceased, late of Copley, all their lands and tenements with appurtenances with other lands and tenements which they recently had of the gift and feoffment of the said John in Southouram and Staynland, as more fully described in their charter; to hold to Humphrey and his lawfully begotten heirs male, of the chief lords of the fee; and in default of issue, remainder to John Sayvill and his heirs male, and in default of issue, to the right heirs of John the father of John and Humphrey. Sealing clause.[3] Witnesses: John Hemyngway, William Otes, Peter Baroclogh, John Gledehill', William Holywell'. At Southouram. (*Ibid.*, No. 7).

Tibthorpe.

441. Quitclaim by Rabot son of Walter de Bonington to Peter de Brus of all right in 2 bovates of land with a toft and croft

[1] Seal of broken white wax.

[2] Small hexagonal seal of red wax; undeciphered.

[3] Seals: 5, of red wax; all gems, 1. 3 and 5 blurred and not deciphered: (2) a unicorn and the letter T.W.; (4) R surmounted by a crown.

and appurtenances in Tibbetorp, namely the two bovates which Ralph son of Gode held in the said vill. For this release and quitclaim Peter de Brus gave to the grantor 16 silver marks. Sealing clause. Witnesses: William de Tometon', Walter de Percy, Godonis de Humeth, Robert de Munceaus, John de Aton', Richard de Hoton', Reginald de Rosel, John Malleuerer, Thomas de Giseburn', Alan the clerk, John the clerk, Alan de Percy.[1] (*Lord Scarbrough*, B2, 1).

Tickhill.[2]

442. Indenture tripartite; William Jordon, constable of the castle of Tykehill, William Dendale of Tykehill, Adam de Hertil, his man, Richard Outi, John the goldsmith, John Boter, John the porter (*janitor*) of the castle, John Chittock, John de le Hay, Richard de Stokvan in Tykehill, Richard Til, William de le Westegate, Nicholas Cole, John his son, Walter le Cres, John his brother, William son of Hugh de Harword, Thomas de Hyrton, William his son, William son of Robert son of Roys, William Greteheued, Geoffrey the baker (*pistor*), Hugh Thorif of Tykehill, greeting. Because of the cessation of the alms customarily distributed, the monks in the marsh of Tykehill are unable to live in a fitting manner on the portion once assigned to them, neither does the portion of the chaplain of the Hospital of St. Leonard at the top of the causeway (*calcete*) of Tyk' suffice for the quarter part of his maintenance, therefore it is the desire and will of the noble men, Masters John Clarel and Bertrand, stewards of the Honour and Castle of Tykehill, and of the whole community of the vill of Tyk', lest in both places, or in either one of them, the celebration of the divine mysteries should cease, that one of the said monks shall reverently celebrate in the said chapel of St. Leonard daily, when he can conveniently do so (*cum commode uacare poterit*), wherefore they assign and grant to the said monks, in respect of his work, a certain piece of meadow, just as it is enclosed with a hedge and a ditch at the time of the making of this grant, together with half of the arable land and all the rent pertaining to the said Hospital so long as one of the monks shall serve the chapel in the aforesaid manner. The members of the said Hospital or their guardian or master shall retain for their use the other half of the land and rent, also the croft adjoining the said Hospital with its buildings, and with a certain piece of meadow, as already assigned to them; but all the trees growing in the alder grove (*alneto*) next to the wood of Tornewode within the close of meadow belonging to the Hospital shall be equally divided between them and the monks, and as often as they shall be felled the price shall be settled by common agreement. The said chapel shall be maintained in all its necessities equally by the monks and by the members of the Hospital; and the latter, or

[1] Dorso: In a contemporary hand, Une quiete clamaunce de dous bouxs de tere en tılbetorp'.

[2] This section also includes some deeds relating to places in the honour of Tickhill.

their guardian may retain for their maintenance whatever alms they can obtain from any source, but of the offerings at services in the chapel they may receive and take away nothing, for these are to remain in entirety to the said monks.

And that this agreement concerning the said portions assigned in the manner aforesaid may be of full strength, the above written parties sealed it for themselves and their successors and on behalf of the whole community, as also have John Clarel and Bertrand, the principals in the matter, who have acted with their full approbation and consent. (*Ibid.*, E1, 1).

443. Grant by Richard Merwan and Sybil his wife, daughter of Roger de Weteley to William Dendal' of Tikehill, of an annual rent of 10½d. of which 4½d. is derived at the four terms of the year from a certain toft with appurtenances which is situated in Baggeley between the toft of Thomas son of Gilione and the toft once belonging to Roger *ad pratum*; and 2d. from another toft lying close to the moor towards Tikehill, also payable at the four terms, which toft lies on the east side of the road; also 1d. at the two terms, namely ½d. at Easter and ½d. at Michaelmas from half an acre of land lying next to the moor which extends beyond le Segges; and 3½d. from Elias the reeve of Bageley, at the four terms, namely at Easter ¾d., St. John The Baptist ¾d., St. Michael ¾d. and at The Nativity 1¼d., for a certain meadow and land lying adjoining the moor and the garden once belonging to William de Baggeley, which is called Merwanhengs; to hold to William Dendal' his heirs and assigns, by hereditary right, paying to the grantors and their heirs a needle at the feast of St. John the Baptist for all secular services and demands. For this grant and concession William Dendal' has given to the grantors a sum of money. If William or his heirs by reason of any loss or distraint are unable to obtain the said rents then it shall be lawful for them to distrain on the grantors' toft in the street of Sundirland which lies between the toft once of Hugh Dand and the toft of John son of Elias de Bageley until the said rents are fully paid. Warranty. Sealing clause.[1] Hugh and Adam de Misortaro, John son of Roger, William the goldsmith, William son of Robert, John Richeman, Hugh Sprad', John son of John, Roger the clerk. (*Ibid.*, B16, 1).

444. Grant by John de Basyngburne to the monks of the chapel of St. Thomas de Humberston in the marsh, there serving God, Blessed Mary and St. Thomas, for the health of his soul, and of the souls of his wife, Agnes, of his ancestors and successors, in free and perpetual alms, of all his land and pasture above Moriswra which lies between the land which his ancestors once gave to the monks of the said chapel on the north and his marsh of Harewurh on the south, reserving to himself passage for his animals from Hare-

[1] Two seals of yellowish wax, (1) vesica shaped, a fleur de lis; legend not deciphered; (2) oval, broken, a star-like device . . WE . . .

wurht to pasture and back, and the head of which abuts on the path leading towards Stirop[1] on the east, and on the west above the said marsh of Harewurh, with common pasture for their animals; to hold the said land and common pasture to the said monks, in frankalmoign. Warranty. Sealing clause.[2] Witnesses: Norman de Stirap' Thomas his son, Nigel Drury, Roger the clerk of Stirap', Ingram son of Reginald of the same, John Deanesle, John son of Ralph de Heselay, Hugh de *viridi* of the same, Robert Benvenu of Harewurh, William de Marny of the same, John Warde of the same. (*Ibid.*, No. E1, 2).

445. Sunday after St. Mathew the apostle, 9 Edward III [Sept. 24, 1335]. Grant by Joan, widow of Adam le Harpur of Malteby to Richard her son of a certain new house on the west side of her toft in Malteby, with all the croft belonging to the said toft; also another house by the way which leads from the vill to the mill of Malteby on the east of the said toft; also 12 acres of arable land in the field of Malteby, namely, 4 acres in the east field of which 2 lie at le Castle *lyddehat* and the other 2 in different places around Drakhowe, and 4 acres lie in the west field of which 3½ lie in one piece at Coley Well and the half acre lies at the top of the vill of Malteby in 2 strips; and 4 acres lie in the north field in one piece of ground called le North ryddyng; to hold of the grantor for the life of the said Richard, freely and in peace. Warranty. Sealing clause. Witnesses: James Liuet, lord of Hoton, Thomas son of Richard de Helonby, John Cox of Malteby, John de Helonby and John Whisteler of the same. At Malteby. (*Ibid.*, B15, 1).

446. Wednesday, SS. Simon and Jude, 12 Edward III [Oct. 28, 1338]. Release and quitclaim[3] by Richard de Crumbewell, knight to Sir Robert de Clifford of an annual rent of 6*li.* which the grantor had from his father Sir John de Crumbewell from the farms and the mills of Malteby and Staneley. Warranty. Sealing clause.[4] Witnesses: Frank de Barneby, William de Reygate, John de Lacy and William de Leysyngcroft. At Leysyngcroft. (*Ibid.*, B15, 2).

447. June 18, 1366. Notarial instrument[5] between Dom. William, rector of Maltby, diocese of York and Dom. Robert perpetual vicar of Maltby, of the one part, and the parishioners of

[1] Styrrup and Harworth, co. Notts. Humberston is difficult to identify. It is scarcely likely to be Humberston Abbey, in Lincs., and there is a Hermeston near Styrrup, which is suggestive.

[2] Heater shaped, 1½ x 1 in., Armorial seal of brownish yellow wax, broken; 2 chevrons: . . GILL'. WILLI'. DE . CHA . . .

[3] In French.

[4] Seal of red wax, diam. ¾ in.: shield of arms, a fess, over all a bend.
S' RICARDI CRVMWELL
Dorso: Une relees fait par Mons' Ric' de Crumbe-Well dune annuell rent issant du manoirs de Staneby & Malteby.

[5] Probably copy of original document; there is no evidence of seals.

Maltby, of the other, witnessing that Dom. William agrees for himself and his successors to give an annual payment to the said Robert and his successors of 4 marks to provide a chaplain to celebrate each day in the chapel of Sandbek, or instead of the 4 marks all the lords tenements and rents which the said William has and holds in the lordship of Sandbek; and Dom. Robert agrees for himself and his successors to find and supplement all the remainder of the stipend of the said chaplain from his goods; and the said William and Robert and parishioners agree that if the said lands, tenements and rents assigned for the provision of the 4 marks are not sufficient then William agrees that he and his successors shall be charged with the provision, to the true value of the said 4 marks to Robert and his successors, which true value shall be decided and agreed upon by good and lawful men. And because the seals of both parties are unknown it is sealed with the seals of John de Crakall and Richard de Clida, reverend fathers in God; the said John[1] being archbishop of York, primate of England and legate of the Apostolic see, who seal the document with the seals of their office. At Barnbrough, in the presence of the said archbishop.

John Aldfield, clerk of the diocese of York and by apostolic authority notary public and one of the special scribes of the said John, archbishop of York, who with the venerable and discreet Mag. Ralph Turnill canon of the cathedral church of Lichffeld, Gilbert de Welton, doctor of law, canon of the collegiate church of Suthwell, Dom. William de Feriby, canon of the church of York, witnessed the above written, and by the mandate of the said venerable father in God, John, archbishop of York, both inscribed it, recorded it and with his customary mark, signed it.[2] (*Ibid.*, E3, 1).

448. Sunday after St. Mathew the apostle and evangelist, 22 Richard II [Sept. 22, 1398]. Grant by Thomas de le Folde, chaplain, son and heir of John de le Estfolde near Manpasse, to Richard Goldsmyth of Tykhill, chaplain, and John de Graneby, chaplain of the free chapel of Tykhill, of a messuage and 20 acres of land and meadow with all the hedges (*hayis*) and woodland pertaining, of which the messuage and the 14 acres of land with a small piece of meadow lie together in an enclosure, together with its own hedges (*hayis*) and woodland, between the messuage of Thomas de Totill on the west and the land of William Gascwyn on the east, of which the north end abuts on the stream flowing from Westfold towards Manpasse, and the south end abuts above the field of Oulcotes; and 6 acres of land lie in the same field between the field of Styrapp' and Oulcotes on the east and the field *del* Estfolde on the west, and the southern end abuts on the common way leading from Tykhill

[1] This must be an error as the archbishop was John de Thoresby.

[2] On the left is the notary's mark; on the top of a shaft mounted on four steps a much decorated circle surrounded by leaves; Aldffeld is written on the third step; there appears to be something written on the lowest step but it is obscured.

to Oulcotes and the northern end abuts on the path leading from Manpasse to Blyth; to hold to Richard, his heirs and assigns, of the chief lords of the fee. Warranty. Sealing clause. Witnesses: John de Ewse of Sandebek, Henry Paddeley of the same, Thomas Grene of Styrapp', John de Baggeley of the same, John Alwy of the same, John Dawson of Tykhill. At Estfold near Manpasse. (*Ibid.*, E1, 3).

449. All Saints, 13 Henry IV [Nov. 1, 1411]. Grant by William Bredon, *Draper*, of Tikhill to Thomas Bilton, vicar of Tikhill and Robert Bilton esq., of a piece of toft and meadow in Tikhill and an acre of land in the fields of Tikhill; and the said piece lies in Sondreland place between the piece of land belonging to John Sandirson on the east and the land belonging to Henry Glover on the west and the said acre lies on the side of Bagelay between the land of John Aldewark on the south and the land of Henry Mason on the north; to hold with all appurtenances to Thomas and Robert, their heirs and assigns, of the chief lords of the fee. Warranty. Sealing clause.[1] Witnesses: Nicholas Coke of Tikhill, William Estfeld of the same, Walter Curry, John Legett, chaplain and John Spycer, clerk. At Tikhill. (*Ibid.*, B15, 3).

450. St. Bartholomew, 9 Henry V (Aug. 24, 1421]. Grant by Robert Lawe of Tikhill to John Huberte of Bawtre of a messuage and 12 acres of land and meadow lying separately in the field and meadows of Tikhill; and the said messuage lies in a place in Tikhill called Northgate between the messuage of William de Styrappe on the north and the messuage of the heirs of Nicholas Cake which recently belonged to John Cutsone on the south, and the east end of which abuts on the highway leading through the middle of the vill of Tikhill, and the west end on a certain path lying above the western croft of Northgate in Tikhill, and which messuage the grantor dwells in at this time; and of the 12 acres, 2 acres of land are in a place called Claycrofte, adjoining the land of Robert Morton on the west; one rood of meadow lies there at the north end of the same land next to the meadow of William de Estfeld on the west; 6 acres and 3 roods of land lie in the north field of Tikhill at a place called Spytelcrofte on both sides of a gutter (*Gutterii*) there called le Watergoyte next to the land of the said William de Estfeld on the south; 1½ acres of land lie in the same field adjoining the land of Peter Holme of Tikhill on the north; half an acre lies there next to the land of the said Peter on the south; one acre lies in the field of Willesyke next to the land of the prior of St. Oswald of Nostelle on the west; to hold to John Huberte, his heirs and assigns, of the chief lords of the fee. Warranty. Sealing clause.[2] Witnesses: William Thwyer of Tikhill, William de Styrroppe of the same, John Choppmane of the same, John Marche of the same, Richard Bolte, bailiff of Tikhill. At Tikhill. (*Ibid.*, B15, 4).

[1] Fragment of small seal of red wax, a gem, undeciphered.
[2] Seal. blob of red wax.

451. The Nativity, 2 Henry VI [Dec. 25, 1423]. Grant by Simon Reynerson to John Sandeford of Tikhill, esq., of half an acre of land lying behind Baggelay above the place called Tonfeld between the land of the same John which he lately acquired from William Haghton on the west and the meadow of Robert Thwyer called le Sybbehenge on the east, the south end of which abuts on the alder-grove called Braddekerr, and the north end on the meadow called Powreprice, which half acre the grantor acquired from Thomas Baggelay; to hold to John Sandeforde, his heirs and assigns, of the chief lord of the fee. Warranty. Sealing clause.[1] Witnesses: William Estfeld of Tikhill, Robert Coke of the same, John Lestone of the same, Walter Curry of the same, Richard Bolte, bailiff of Tickhill. At Tikhill. (*Ibid.*, B15, 6).

452. Conversion of St. Paul, 2 Henry VI [Jan. 25, 1423-4]. Grant by William Haghtone of Tikhill to John Sandeford, esq., dwelling in Tikhill, of 2 acres and a rood of land, lying separately in the south field of Tikhill; of which 1½ acres lie in three strips in the place called Godycrofte between the land recently belonging to Robert Vessy on both sides, the northern end of which abuts on the land of Thomas Smyth of Westgate, and the southern end above the land of John Grene; the acre of land lies in the place called le Longelandes in one strip between the land of Thomas Bilton, vicar of Tikhill on both sides, the western end of which abuts on le Hungrecrofte and the eastern end on the land of Robert Sowndresone of Lyndryk; the rood of land lies behind Baggeley above the place called le Tonfeld between the land of Hugh Gylle on the west and the land of the said John Sandeford which he recently acquired from Simon Raynerson on the east, the southern end of which abuts on a certain alder-grove (*alnetum*) called le Braddekerre, and the northern end on a meadow called le Powrprysse; which 2 acres and rood of land William Haghtone recently acquired by hereditary right after the death of Thomas de Lyndesay, his uncle who dwelt in Wollethwayte; to hold the said two acres and rood to John Sandeford, his heirs and assigns, of the chief lords of the fee. Warranty. Sealing clause.[2] Witnesses: William Estfeld of Tikhill, William Thwyer of the same, John Leston of the same, Walter Curry of the same, Richard Bolte of Tickhill bailiff of the same. At Tikhill.[3] (*Ibid.*, B16, 2).

453. St. Michael, 3 Henry VI [Sept. 29, 1424]. Grant by Malyna atte Gatte of Tikhill, in her widowhood to John Sandefford of Tikhill, esq., of an acre of land in 6 strips lying in the west field of Tikhill in a place called Hollebek, which lie between the stream called le Hollebek on the west and the land which lately belonged

[1] Small seal of red wax, undeciphered.

[2] Round seal of red wax, pseudo armorial. On a fess 2 roundels, beneath a chevron.

[3] Dorso: Witnesses: to the delivery of seisin: William Estfeld, William Norvsse William Walsch, John Alevn, Nicholas Romane.

to Robert Vessy of Tikhill on the east, the south end of which abuts on the stream called Hyndaghbroke, and the north end on the land of the prior of St. Oswald; to hold to the said John, his heirs and assigns, of the chief lords of the fee. Warranty. Sealing clause.[1] Witnesses: William Thwyer of Tikhill, John Leston, Robert Sowndreson, junior, Robert Sawndreson, senior, William Baddesworth, John Cutsone, all of Tikhill, Richard Bolte, bailiff. At Tikhill. (*Ibid.*, B2, 5).

454. St. Michael, 3 Henry VI [Sept. 29, 1424]. Grant by Robert Sawndresone of Tikhill, dwelling in Sondreland, to John Sandefford of Tikhill esq., of 1½ acres of land lying in 7 strips in the west field of Tikhill in the place called Hollebek, between the land of the said John which he recently acquired from Malyna atte Gatte of Tikhill on both sides, of which the south end abuts on the stream called Hyndaghbroke and the north end on the land of the prior of St. Oswald, and which once belonged to Robert Vessy of Tikhill; to hold to John, his heirs and assigns, of the chief lords of the fee. Warranty. Sealing clause.[2] Witnesses: William Estfeld of Tikhill, William Twhyer of the same, Robert Coke of the same, John Cutson of the same, John Lestone of the same, William Baddesworth of the same, Richard Bolte, bailiff of Tikhill. At Tikhill. (*Ibid.*, B2, 4).

455. St. Luke the Evangelist, 3 Henry VI [Oct. 18, 1424]. Grant by Malyna atte Gatte of Tickhill to John Sandeford of Tikhill esq., of half an acre of land lying in 4 strips in the field of Tikhill in a place called Hollebek between the land of the said John Sandefford which he recently acquired from Richard Smyth of Tikhill on the east and the land which the same John recently acquired from Robert Sawndreson, junior, on the west, the south end of which abuts on a stream called Hyndaghbroke, and the north end on the land of Robert Morton; which 4 strips once belonged to Thomas Aldewerk of Tikhill, the grantor's father; to hold to John, his heirs and assigns, of the chief lords of the fee. Warranty. Sealing clause.[3] Witnesses: William de Estfelde of Tikhill, Walter Curry of the same, Robert Sawndreson of Tikhill, junior, Robert Sawndreson of the same, senior, Robert Coke of the same, John Leston of the same, Richard Bolte, bailiff. At Tikhill. (*Ibid.*, B2, 2).

456. St. Luke the Evangelist, 3 Henry VI [Oct. 18, 1424]. Grant by Richard Smyth of Tikhill to John Sandefford of the same, esq., of 1½ acres of land in the west field of Tikhill in a place called Hollebek, lying in 6 strips between the land of the said John which he recently acquired from Robert Marche of Tikhill on the east and the land which the same John lately acquired from Malyna

[1] Small seal of red wax, a four-petalled device.

[2] Seal of red wax, between 2 sprigs of leaves and beneath a crown, the letter R.

[4] Very small seal of red wax; a four-petalled device.

atte Gatte on the west, of which the south end abuts on the stream called Hyndaghbroke and the north end on the land of Robert de Morton, all of which land once belonged to Robert Aldewerk of Tikhill; to hold to John Sandefford, his heirs and assigns, of the chief lords of the fee. Warranty. Sealing clause.[1] Witnesses: William de Estfeld of Tikhill, William Thwyer of the same, John Leston of the same, Robert Sawndresone of the same, junior, Robert Sawndreson senior, William Baddesworth, Richard Bolte, bailiff. At Tikhill. (*Ibid.*, B2, 3).

457. Purification of the B.V.M., 3 Henry VI [Feb. 2, 1424-5]. Release and quitclaim by William Haghton of Baggelay near Tikhill, and Alice, his wife, to John de Sandefford of Tikhill esq., of all right in 4½ acres and half a rood of land and half an acre of meadow lying separated in the fields of Tikhill and Baggelay; of which 1½ acres of land lie in a place called Godycrofte; 2 acres lie divided above les Longelandes; a rood and a half lie above les Baggelay buttes; a rood lies behind Bagglay above Tonfield; the said half acre of meadow lies in les Mowpassehenges as more fully described in the charter of feoffment, and which once belonged to Thomas de Lyndesay who used to dwell in Wollethwayte and which the grantors had of the gift and feoffment of Thomas Baggelay in Tikhill. Warranty. Sealing clause.[2] Witnesses: William Estfeld of Tikhill, William Thwyer of the same, John Leestone of the same, Robert Coke of the same, William Baddesworth of the same, John Grene of the same, Richard Bolte, bailiff of Tikhill. At Tikhill.[3] (*Ibid.*, B15, 5).

458. Exaltation of the Cross, 4 Henry VI [Sept. 14, 1425]. Grant by Thomas Tayllour of Tikhill, tailor, to John Sandefford of Tikhill, esq., of 4 acres and 3 roods of land lying separated in the north field of Tikhill, of which 2 acres lie near Staynton Wadde in the place called Hollebeke between the land of the said John which he recently acquired from Robert Sawndreson on the west and the land of Simon Reynersone on the east, of which the north end abuts on Simon's land and the south end on the stream called Hollebeke; and an acre and 3 roods lie adjoining the vill of Tikhill below the vill called Kynnerdwelle hille between the land of the heir of Robert de Morton on the west and the land of Alexander de Ryghelay and Rose his wife, on the east, of which the north end abuts on the grantor's land and the south end on the land of the said John which he recently acquired from Robert Marche; and one acre lies below the said hill called Kynnerdwellehill between the land of John Marche on the west and the land of William Styroppe on the east, and both ends of which abut on the meadow of John Wombwelle; to hold to John Sandefford his heirs and assigns, of the chief lords of the fee.

[1] Seal, as to preceding deed.

[2] Two small, round seals of red wax, 1) pseudo armorial, on a fess 2 roundels, beneath, a chevron; 2) a six-pointed device.

[3] Dorso: Witnesses: William Estfeld, William Walsch, William Norysse, John Aleyn, Nicholas Romane.

Warranty. Sealing clause.[1] Witnesses: William Estfeld of Tikhill, Alexander Ryghelay of the same, Robert Coke of the same, Robert Sawndresone of the same, John Leestone of the same, William Baddesworth of the same, Richard Bolte bailiff of Tikhill. At Tikhill. (*Ibid.*, B2, 6).

459. SS. Philip and James [May 1], 1427, 5 Henry VI. Grant by William de Hagthon of Bagley near Tikhyll and Alice, his wife, to Robert de Rokeley esq., of 26 acres of land and meadow and half an acre, of which the half acre lies above le Bageley, abutting between the land of Richard Grene, chaplain, on the west and the land of William Wygthorpe on the east; Item, half an acre lies there between the land of the said Richard Grene on the west and the land of William Rokysbe on the east; Item, half an acre lies there between the land of Christopher Burley on the west and east and abutting above le Heyds and Longlane on the north; Item, half an acre lies in the place called Longlands between John Cutson on the north and the demesne of Tykhyl on the south; Item, one acre lies between the said demesne on the north and the land of St. Emitats [*sic*] on the south; Item, one rood of meadow lies in Eskeryng between the land of Richard Leche on the west and le Malpus bryge on the east; Item, half an acre of meadow lies in Malpus yng between the meadow of Blessed Mary on the west and the land of the Abbot of Roche on the east; Item, 5 roods of meadow lie there between the meadow of Robert Sandforthe on the west and the abbot of Roche on the east; Item, 5 other roods of meadow lie there between the abbot of Roche on the west and the meadow of William Whyte on the east; Item, 2 acres and a rood lie in le Estsyde of le Holmes between the land of Hugh Gyll on the east and the land of William Fastyntrace on the west; Item, 3 acres of land lie there between the land of the said William on the east and the land of Hugh Gyll on the west; Item, 3 acres and a rood lie there between the land of the said Hugh on the east and the land of William Wygthorpe on the west; Item, 3 acres of land lie between the land of Hugh Gyll on the east and west; Item, one acre of meadow in the south parts of Holmes; Item, 5 acres lying there between the said Hugh Gyll on the east and the land of William Fustintrace on the west; Item, 3 acres there between the land of William Fustintrace on the east and the land of Hugh Gyll on the west; Item, 2 acres of land lying in 5 strips of which one lies between the land of William Fustintrace on the east and the land of William Twyar on the west, and the other 4 strips lie together between the land of the said William Twyar on the east and west; to hold the said land and meadow to Robert de Rokeley, his heirs and assigns, of the chief lords of the fee. Warranty. Sealing clause. Witnesses: Dom. Robert de Dewsbery chaplain, William de Twyer of Tykhyll, John de Leston of the same, William le Archar of the same, Hugh Gyll of the same. At Bageley in Tykhyll. (*Ibid.*, B16, 3).

[1] Seal of red wax; diam. ½ in., beneath a crown the letters JHO.

460. SS. Philip and James [May 1], 1427, 5 Henry VI. Grant by William de Halghton of Bagley near Tyckhyll and Alice, his wife, to Robert de Rokley esq., of 4 acres of land in Bagley Wood with all growth and undergrowth there, of which one acre lies in the east part of Bagley Wood between the pasture called Bradcar on the east and the land of Hugh Gyll on the west and which abuts above le Holmes on the south and le Tunfeld on the north; and 3½ acres lie between Hugh Gyll and Thomas Taylear on the east and the land of Blessed Mary in Benecroft on the west and abuts on le Holmes on the south and le Tunfeld on the north; and 5 acres of arable land in le Benecroft with a rood there, and the rood lies in the east part of le Benecroft between the land of Blessed Mary on both sides and abuts on le Holmes on the south and le Tunfeld on the north, and another rood lies between the land of Blessed Mary on the east and the land of Blessed Mary *de Ponte* on the west and abuts on le Holmes on the south and le Tunfeld on the north, and half an acre between the land of Blessed Mary *de Ponte* on the east and the land of Hugh Gyll on the west and abuts on the land of the grantor on both sides, and one acre between the land of Hugh Gyll on the east and Malpus lane on the west and abuts on le Holmes on the south and the grantor on the north, and a rood between the grantor on the south and the land of Robert Byrks on the north and abuts on the land of Blessed Mary *de Ponte* on the east and Malpus lane on the west, and a rood between the land of Robert Byrks on the south and le Tunfeld on the north which abuts on the land of Blessed Mary *de Ponte* on the east and Malpus lane on the west, and rood between William Twyer on the south and le Kestyguppe end on the north which abuts on the grantor's land on both sides, and half a rood between Robert Byrks on the north and le Holmes on the south and which abuts on le Holmes on the east and the grantor on the west, and half a rood at the end of the same which abuts on le Holmes on the south and Blessed Mary *de Ponte* on the north; and 9 roods lying in le Holmes of which one rood and a half lie next to Malpus lane between the land of Amisse Ratlyff on both sides which abut on le Benecroft on the north, and half an acre and half a rood lie between the said Amice Ratlyff on both sides and abut on le Malpus yng on the south and le Benecroft on the north, and a rood and a half between Amisse Ratlyff on both sides which abut on le Malpus yng on the south and le Benecroft on the north, and the other rood and a half lie between Amisse on both sides and abut on le Malpus yng on the south and Benecroft on the north, and half an acre lies between Amisse in one strip, and half a strip between half a strip belonging to Amisse on the north and Malpus yng on the south; to hold to Robert Rokley, his heirs and assigns, of the chief lords of the fee. Warranty. Sealing clause. Witnesses: [as to preceding deed]. (*Ibid.*, B16, 4).

461. Nov. 2, 9 Henry VI [1430]. Grant by William Gayte of Tikhill to Hugh Holme of Hesselay of a house (*placeam*) which

the grantor inhabits in the vill of Tikhill in the part called Sundrelande between the tenement of Richard Bolte which once belonged to Richard de Melton on the west and the tenement of Cecily, widow of Roger Piper on the east, together with 5 roods of land in the croft of the same house which lies between the land of the chaplain serving Blessed Mary of Tikhill on the west and the land of John Crosselande on the east; the southern end of which dwelling place abuts on the highway leading through the middle of the vill, and the northern end of the lands in the croft abut on the lane at Mustrellebrygges, which place and croft once belonged to Ingram del Grene of Tikhill; he also grants half an acre of land lying in a certain field of Tikhill called Estfeld between the land of William Estfeld on the west and the land of Robert Thwyer on the east, the south head of which abuts on the lane called Harellane and the north head on the land of the chaplain serving Blessed Mary in Tikhill; to hold to Hugh Holme, his heirs and assigns, of the chief lords of the fee. Warranty. Sealing clause.[1] Witnesses: William Thwyer of Tikhill, John Cutsone of the same, Richard Bolte of Tikhill, John Welynglay of the same, William Archier, bailiff of Tikhill. At Tikhill. (*Ibid.*, B15, 7).

462. Sunday after SS. Simon and Jude [Oct. 28],[2] 1436, 15 Henry VI. Indenture whereby John Hobard of Tichill grants to William Hobard, his son and Elizabeth Wyntworth, daughter of William Wyntworth late of Wyntworth, esq., and their lawfully begotten heirs, his capital messuage with appurtenances in the vill of Tikhill with all his cottages, lands, tenements, rents reversions and services which he has on the day of the making of this charter; he also grants his capital messuages with appurtenances in Kyngston on Hulle with all the cottages, dwellings, lands, tenements, rents, reversions and services which he has in Kyngston and the vill of Harttyll in Co. York; to hold to William and Elizabeth and their lawfully begotten heirs, freely and in peace, of the chief lords of the fee, with remainder in default of issue to Katherine wife of William Roche and her lawfully begotten heirs, with reversion to the grantor. Warranty. Sealing clause. Witnesses: Richard Wyntworth, John Serlby esq., John Bedford of Hull, Robert Saunderson of Tikhill, John Cutson' of the same, John Leston of the same, Richard Bolt of the same. (*Ibid.*, B15, 8).

463. May 1, 27 Henry VI [1449]. Indenture whereby John Thwynge of York, *Gentilman*, and Joan his wife, grant to Thomas Wodrove, vicar of the church of Tikhill and Thomas Awte of the same and Alice Catton of the same all those messuages lands and tenements and gardens at Bagley called Bagleyzerde, meadows rents and services with appurtenances which the grantors have in the vill and territory of Tikhill in Co. York; to hold, with all fish

[1] Seal of red wax, diam $\frac{7}{8}$, a merchant's mark, legend undeciphered.
[2] In 1436, Oct. 28, SS. Simon and Jude was a Sunday.

ponds, moors, turbaries, marshes, ways, waters and other commodities and profits belonging to the same both within and without the vill of Tikhill, of the chief lords of the fee in perpetuity, under the following condition, namely: that if Thomas, Thomas and Alice shall pay or cause to be paid to the grantors or their executors or attorneys at York 17*li.*, 4*li.* 5*s.* in equal portions, at Easter and Michaelmas in 1449, 1450, 1451, 1452, then this charter of feoffment with seisin shall remain in full force; but should the grantees fail to make any of the aforesaid payments at the specified time then the grantors may re-enter and occupy any of the said premises notwithstanding this charter. Warranty. Alternate seals.[1] Witnesses: Walter Holme, bailiff of Tikhill, Robert White, William White, William Lomberd, John Leeston, of Gunby.[2] [*Ibid.*, B16, 5).

464. Feb. 6, 1 Richard III [1483-4]. Demise by William Serlbye esq., to William Hobert of Tykhyll of 3 acres of arable land lying in 6 strips in the north field of Tykhyll in a place called Wylsykdale between the land which once belonged to John Cutson on both sides, the eastern end of which abuts on a close of Thomas Fitzwilliam, knt., and the other end extends beyond the path leading from Wylsyke towards Tykhyll; to hold to William Hobert his heirs and assigns, of the chief lords of the fee. Appointment of Thomas Norton of Tykhyll his attorney to deliver seisin. Sealing clause.[3] Witnesses: Robert Vescy of Wadworth, William Holme of Tykhyll, John Ranbye, of the same. At Tykhyll. (*Ibid.*, B15, 9).

465. April 14, 8 Henry VII [1493]. Demise[4] by William Sandford of Tikhill, the elder and William Sandford of the same, the younger to Robert Henryson, in respect of a sum of money, of 2 closes and a *litill pece of medowe* lying near Malpas between the the land of the abbot of Beauchief and the land pertaining to the Foldes and abutting on the river running to Malpas brig; to have and to occupy for the term of 7 years next following, paying yearly to William and William a rose at *missomer* if demanded; if it please Robert at any time he may *stubbe up all maner of thornes and underwode savyng oke and Esshe* growing on the close between the lane and the river, and he may carry away the same at his pleasure, with free entry and exit to the said closes and meadow for his carriage at all times. Warranty. Alternate seals. (*Ibid.*, B6, 1).

466. Jan. 2, 9 Henry VII [1493-4]. Grant by Ralph Fustenaunce of Edynstowe to Christopher Birley of Tikhill of an acre and half a rood of land lying separated in the south field of Tikhill, of which three roods lie together in the place called Godecroft between the land of John Leston on the east and the land of Blessed Mary on the west, the ends of which abut on the land of Robert

[1] Two small seals of red wax, 1) undeciphered; 2) The letter I.
[2] Dorso: Thwinge his dede to William Awt and Alice Catton.
[3] Seal of red wax, small gem, undeciphered
[4] In English.

Morton on both sides; and the other three and a half roods lie in the place called Tunfeld between the land of Hered le Drax on the east and the land of Thomas Riche on the west, of which the north end abuts above . . . le Bagley and the south end above le Bagley Carre; to hold of the chief lord of the fee in perpetuity. Warranty. Sealing clause. Witnesses: John Smyth living in the house of the brethren of the monastery (*heremitor'*) of St. Augustine of Tikhill, William Wigthorp of Tikhill, Thomas Bewis of the same. At Tikhill. (*Ibid.*, B16, 7).

467. Aug. 31, 2 Henry VIII [1510]. Indenture[1] whereby Thomas Veissy of Tykhill is assured by Clement Stanley, son and heir of Robert Stanley, late of Tykhill of a sure and sufficient estate, namely a tenement in Tykhill in the gate called Norgate, which is held by the said Thomas; to hold to Thomas from the feast of Easter next, *by thadvyce of Counsell lerned*, and Clement shall hand over all evidence and writing pertaining to the same; for which Thomas shall pay to Clement 10 marks of English money in the following manner, namely, upon the delivering of evidence 26*s*. 8*d*., at the Exaltation of the Cross next following 8 marks. The parties bind themselves in the sum of 10 marks. Alternate seals.[2] (*Ibid.*, B6, 2).

468. Aug. 31, 2 Henry VIII [1510]. Grant by Clement Stanley son and heir of Robert Stanley late of Tikhill, deceased, to Thomas Veissy of Thikhill of a messuage situated and lying in Thikhill in a place there called Norgate, between the land of Thomas Code on the south, and the common way leading towards Dancastre on the east, and abutting on the land of Thomas Twyer on the east and the lands of Nicholas Mathew on the north; to hold to Thomas, his heirs and assigns, of the chief lords of the fee. Warranty. Sealing clause.[3] At Thikhill. Witnesses: William Sanderson, Thomas Twyer, Richard Leche, John Ranby, Robert Holme, Thomas Aldewark, John Revell. (*Ibid.*, B16, 8).

469. Sept. 20, 5 Henry VIII [1513]. Release and quitclaim by Clement Stanley to Thomas Veissye of Tykhill, his heirs and assigns, of 7 acres of land lying in the north field of Tykhill, which he had of the grantor's gift. Warranty. Sealing clause. (*Ibid.*, B16, 9).

470. Oct. 6, 31 Henry VIII [1539]. Grant by Thomas Lane, son and heir of John Lane late of Tykhill, to John Turvyn of Bagleye, of 2 acres of arable land lying separated in a place called le Westfeillde in the territory of Baggleye, between the land of John Turvyn on the west and the land of the chantry (*Cantarie*) of Blessed Mary on the east and abutting on the land of the said John Turvyn towards the south and on the land of the King towards the north,

[1] In English.
[2] Small seal of red wax, a gem, undeciphered.
[3] Small oval seal of brown wax; a spray of flowers

which 2 acres John Lane, the grantor's father acquired from William Gill of Tykhill; to hold to John Turvyn, of the chief lords of the fee. Warranty. Sealing clause.[1] (*Ibid.*, B15, 10).

471. July 21, 37 Henry VIII [1545]. Grant by John Sandeford of Tykhill in co. York, gent., to Anne Vessye, daughter of Thomas Vessye of Tykhill, and William Tyas of the same, notary public, of his capital messuage lying in Tykhill in the place called Sunderland, and lately held by Robert Smyth, with all lands, meadows, pastures, closes and commons pertaining; to hold to Anne and William and their heirs to the use of the said John and Anne Vessye, of the chief lords of the fee. Warranty. Appointment of Robert Birleye of Tykhill as his attorney to deliver seisin and possession to Anne and William. Sealing clause.[2]

Per me John Sandforth.

472. Sept. 15, 37 Henry VIII [1545]. Roger North, gent., of Walkeryngham, co. Notts. grants and sells in return for a sum of money, to Thomas Justice all the lands, meadows and pastures held by the said Thomas in the fields of Wolwhayte, Staynton, and Tykell, namely, 11 acres in le Chyffe, 8 acres below le Buskeyard, 9 acres in Duramfflatte, 12 acres in Bulwell leys, 6 acres at Byrkenhed, 5 acres in Ribard Rydyng, 1½ acres in Wolnecrofte, 10 acres in Jusland, one acre in le Sandegrave hyll recently the monastery of Blythe in co. Notts. now dissolved; together with all the grantor's messuage called Carhouse and all the lands, meadows, grazings, pastures, commons and hereditaments, all in the tenure of Thomas Justice and Elizabeth his wife, parcel of the Celle of Tykell, recently of the monastery of Humberston in co. Lincoln, now by Act of Parliament suppressed and dissolved; which messuage the grantor acquired with others of the gift and feoffment of Charles Sutton esq., Richard Walby esq., and Thomas Yorke gent. by their charter made Sept. 1, 37 Henry VII, and which the said Charles, Richard and Thomas had under letters patent, being the gift of the said King Henry, and dated Aug. 25 of the same year; to hold to Thomas Justice, his heirs and assigns to the use of the said Thomas, in perpetuity, of the said King and his successors as of his manor of Braunston in co. Lincoln, in free socage, paying all accustomed services and demands. Warranty, Sealing clause.[3]

Per me Roger North.

[1] Red wax, broken, a geometric device

[2] Dorso: Seisin delivered according to the form of the charter, in the presence of Richard Smyth, John Graunt, junior, Edward Slater, Thomas Slater, Roger Aldye, Henry Smyth, Thomas Cooke and William Birleye (*Ibid* , B2, 7)

[3] Dorso: Possession and seisin delivered to Thomas Justice on Sept. 28 in the presence of Thomas Boswell, gent , Roger Hall, John Hewes, Thomas Wylson, Robert Berley, Thomas Turbyn, Brian Chester, Leonard Prockter, Thomas Lethum. (*Ibid.*, B14, 3) Seal of black wax; R.N.

Ughill (Bradfield).

473. Grant by Ralph de Uggil, John son of John of the same, Henry son of Adam of the same, to Thomas son of William de Bosco, of all that land in the wood of Uggil which lies between the land of Geoffrey de Hor' and Dungewrbroke as it is enclosed (*claudat'*), one end of which abuts on le Suannestorsike and the other above the path between Dungewr' and Bradefeld, also a piece of land called Rissiplot which is enclosed in the wood of Uggil, also a piece of land called Foxiholes lying in the wood of Uggil and enclosed there; to hold to Thomas, his heirs and assigns except religious and Jews, freely, peacefully and hereditarily, paying yearly to the grantors 3*d*. of silver for all secular services, exactions and demands, saving to the grantors all manner of profits from the waste in the woods of Uggil. Warranty. Sealing clause.[1] Witnesses: Elias de Midop', Adam son of Geoffrey de mora, John de Witeleye, William de Witelee, William son of Ervine, Adam son of Roger de mora, Richard Riuel, Adam de Schefeld. (*Y.A.S.*, Md. 244, No. 15).

474. Grant by Henry son of Adam de Uggwyll, to Thomas son of William de Bosco, his heirs and assigns, of all his land and appurtenances in the wood of Uggwyll, which William de Dymot once held, in return for a sum of money paid to him, which land abuts at one end on the water which is called Stene, and on the other on the path which leads from Dungwrthe towards Braddefeld; to hold to William, his heirs and assigns, freely, paying yearly to the grantor and his heirs and assigns 12*d*. of silver at Michaelmas for all secular services, customs, exactions, suits of court, reliefs and demands pertaining to the said lands. Warranty. Sealing clause.[2] Witnesses: Elias de Midhopp, Ralph de Aula of Wardershelf, John de Wyteley, Richard son of Maurice, William de Spina, William Brun of Braddefeld, Richard Riuell of Dungwrh, Adam de mora of Uggwill, Jonat[han] of the same, Richard the carpenter of the same, Henry son of Angr' of the same. (*Ibid.*, No. 16).

475. Sunday after the Octave of the Epiphany [Jan. 17], 1389[-40]. Quitclaim by John Reynald, chaplain, of Bradfeld, to Thomas son of William Turton of the parish of Penyston' and his heirs and assigns, of a piece of land with appurtenances which is enclosed, within the vill of Vggill, lying between the land once belonging to Adam del Side on one side and Ravenstorth on the other, which the grantor had of the gift of John Gogeson and which is called Rysschiplottes. Warranty. Sealing clause. Witnesses: William del Schagh, John Morewod, John Mall', Richard Ryuell. (*Ibid.*, No. 17).

[1] Seals 3 of dark green wax, vesica shaped; 1) a device, S'IOH'I DE VGIL; 2) a pointed device, S'RAD . . IL; 3) a cross, ✠S'HNR FIL ADE.

[2] Seal: vesica shaped green wax, broken; ✠S' HN . . . . .ADE.

Wakefield.

476. Sunday after the Purification of the B.V.M., 16 Edward I [Feb. 8, 1287-8]. Grant and quitclaim by Anabel, widow of William Ingwig, to John son of Robert of Wakefield, of all right in 3 roods of land lying above le Northegatecroftes towards the west, either by reason of her dower or through any other claim, between the land of John Cussing on one side and the land once of Hugh Chapman on the other, in return for a sum of money given to her; to hold to John, of the chief lords of the fee, freely and in perpetuity. Warranty. Sealing clause. Witnesses: Thomas Dayuile, steward of the lord Roger[1] [*sic*], Henry son of German, steward of the liberty, Thomas son of Henry, Robert de Wyuerthorp, John Cussing, Philip Damisele, German Swerd of Wakefield. At Wakefield. (*Y.A.S.*, Md. 59/24, No. 4).

477. Grant and quitclaim by Cecily de Otteley, with the assent of Hugh son of John her husband, to Mariota, wife of German le Mercer of Wakefeud, and her heirs and assigns, of all right which she has as her dower in that tenement in the vill of Wakefield which once belonged to Richard de Otteley, once her husband, of the gift of the keeper of the falcons (*falcon' pincerne*). Warranty. Sealing clause.[2] Witnesses: Sir Thomas Coke, steward of the Earl de Warenne, Richard the clerk, baillif, German le Mercer, John Wytocloff, Henry son of Robert, Ralph the dyer, Richard Duk, clerk. [*Ibid.*, No. 5).

478. Grant by Sybil and Mersoria, daughters of Richard de Otteley to Mariota, wife of German the mercer of Wakefield, and her heirs and assigns, of all their tenement in the vill of Wakefield in le Westgate, with the garden and croft and other appurtenances just as it lies between the tenement once belonging to Philip the mercer on one side and the tenement once of William le Walse on the other; to hold of the Earl de Warenne and his heirs, freely and in peace with all liberties and easements and paying yearly to the said Earl 3*d.* at the three terms ordained in the vill of Wakefield and 3*d.* to Henry, the keeper of the falcons at the same terms, for all secular services and demands. Warranty. Sealing clause.[3] Witnesses: Sir Thomas Coke, steward of the said Earl de Warrenne, Richard the clerk, bailiff of the Earl, German le Mercer, Robert le Erl, pindar of Wakefield, John Wytcloff, William the tanner, Lancelot del Clyff, Henry son of Robert, Richard Duk, clerk. (*Ibid.*, No. 6).

479. Grant by Agnes, widow of Thomas Catte, to Henry de Schulbroke, his heirs and assigns, of a messuage in the vill of Wakefield, with the messuage situated above, which lies in length

[1] It does not appear possible to identify Roger.

[2] Tongues for two seals; on the second an oval seal of white wax; a spray of leaves; legend undeciphered.

[3] Fragment of vesica shaped seal of white wax; a fleur-de-lis; . . . .RICAR.

and breadth between the house of John son of Robert on one side and the house of Robert Feryrstan on the other; to hold to Henry with all liberties and easements within and without the vill, paying yearly to the lords of the fee, 3*d*. of silver at the three terms ordained in the lands of the Earl, for all services and demands. Warranty. Sealing clause. Witnesses: William of Wakefield, German Folcoke, John son of Robert, Thomas . . illiam, Thomas son of Henry, Robert Feryrstan. (*Ibid*., No. 7).

480. Grant by William son and heir of Francis de Wodehusum, to John son of Robert of Wakefield, his heirs or to whomsoever, when or wheresoever he may wish to give, sell or assign it, of a fourth part of a burgage in the vill of Wakefield in le Westgate, between the tenement of John Cussing on the east and the tenement of Adam son of Walter on the west; to hold of Earl de Warenne, freely, peacefully and hereditarily with all appurtenances within and without the vill, as held by William of Wakefield, without reservation, paying yearly to the said Count or his heirs, 3 silver halfpennies and to Thomas called Alayn and his heirs and assigns, 2*s*. of silver at the three terms for all secular services, exactions and demands. Warranty. For this grant John gave to the grantor a certain sum of money in acknowledgement. Sealing clause.[1] Witnesses: William of Wakefield, steward of the said Earl, Robert de Wyrmthorp, John Cay, German Filkok, Robert de Phezirstan. (*Ibid*., No. 8).

481. Purification of the B.V.M. [Feb. 2], 1309 [-10]. Indenture between William of Wakefield, clerk, and Henry de Hiperum of the one part, and William Grenehod of the same, of the other part, whereby William and Henry demise and grant to William Grenehod, his heirs and assigns, a shop with a cellar in the market-place of Wakefield, which lies between the shop of a certain Peter the baker and the shop of German son of Philip, for the term of 12 years next following, in return for a sum of money given to William and Henry; to hold to William Grenehod, his heirs and assigns, paying yearly to the Earl 4*d*. of silver at the three terms. He shall maintain the premises in all things necessary both in roofing and repairing the dividing walls (*parietum*), and in all other matters until the end of the term, and at the end shall hand over the shop in good repair. The said William, the clerk, and his heirs, for the first 4 years, and the said Henry for the last 8 years, shall act as warantor for the shop and cellar, and William Grenehod shall pay to William the clerk 12d. at the end of the 4 years, and at the end of the 12 years the premises shall revert to Henry and his heirs in as good condition as when received, without contradiction from the said William. Alternate seals. Witnesses: German son of Philip, William *le taillur*, John de la Sale, Robert Wyles, William de Locwode, John Tasse, William the clerk. (*Ibid*., No. 9).

[1] Broken seal of red wax; a bird.

482. Friday after the Annunciation of the B.V.M. [Mar. 27], 1310. Grant and quitclaim by Eva, widow of Alexander le Cartewright of Wakefield, in her widowhood and lawful power, to Robert called le Hunte, her son, junior, and his heirs and assigns, of a certain tenement in Wakefield which Alexander, her husband, when living, gave to the said Robert; to hold to Robert freely [*etc.*], of the chief lords of the fee. Warranty. Sealing clause.[1] Witnesses: William de Wakefield, steward of the Earl, Henry his brother, John de Gayrgraue, German Filkoc, John de Fery, William the goldsmith, Robert Clement, German Swerd, clerk. At Wakefield. (*Ibid.*, No. 10).

483. Nativity of the B.V.M. [Spt. 8], 1312. Grant by Henry son of German the mercer of Wakefield to John son of Robert the mercer of the same, his heirs and assigns, of a certain half burgage with a garden and croft and all other appurtenances, which lies between the tenement of German son of Philip the mercer, and the tenement of Robert de Stodley, together with a certain croft which the grantor bought from John Kay and which once belonged to the tenement now of Robert de Stodley, in return for a sum of money received in acknowledgement; to hold freely and peacefully with all liberties and easements, of the chief lords of the fee. Warranty. Sealing clause. Witnesses: John de Doncastre, steward of Earl de Warenne, Henry de la Waude, head forester, German son of Philip, John Amyeus, John Kay, Robert de Wyrimthorp'. At Wakefield. (*Ibid.*, No. 11).

484. Sunday, St. Agnes the Virgin [Jan. 21], 1312[-13]. Quitclaim by Ralph Faukus to John son of Robert of Wakefield, mercer, his heirs and assigns, of all right in that croft with appurtenances which the said John once bought from Henry of Wakefield, between the croft of German Filkok and the croft of the said John. Warranty. Sealing clause. Witnesses: John de Doncastre, steward of Earl de Warenne, John Amyas, John Kay, German Filkok, Robert de Fetherston, Adam son of Laurence. At Wakefield. (*Ibid.*, No. 12).

485. Thursday the morrow of the Decollation of St. John the Baptist [Aug. 30], 1313. Grant by Robert le Hunt of Wakefield to William Pickhak, his heirs and assigns, of all that tenement with buildings upon it lying in le Kergate, between the tenement of Robert de Wyrimthorp on the south and the tenement of Roger de Mara on the north and west, in return for a sum of money; to hold to William his heirs and assigns of the chief lords of the fee, freely and in peace with all liberties and easements. Warranty. Sealing clause. Witnesses: John de Doncastre, steward of Earl de Warenne, William the goldsmith, sergeant of the liberty, John de Gargraue, John le Eril, William Wyles, Robert le Walker, William son of Robert son of Hugh, William the clerk. At Wakefield. (*Ibid.*, No. 13).

[1] Seal of white wax, diam. 1 in.; a cross; HOC SIGNO BE . . ET C.A SCO' ET . . .O.

486. Sunday before SS. Fabian and Sebastian [Jan. 19], 1314[-15]. Grant by Rose, daughter of John son of William of Wakefield, Robert Pees of Ossete, Alice his wife, Richard son of Isabel and Ellen his wife, to John son of Robert the merchant of Wakefield and Joan, his wife, their heirs and assigns, of an acre of land with appurtenances lying above the toft which once belonged to John son of William, namely between the land of John de Rauenfield on one side and the land of John son of William on the other, in return for 2 marks sterling; to hold to John and Joan, of the chief lords of the fee, freely and in peace with all liberties and easements. Warranty. Sealing clause.[1] Witnesses: Henry del Weeld, steward of Earl de Wareine, John de Gayrgraue, Thomas Alayn, William the goldsmith, Robert le Walker, Robert Swerd, German Filkoc, Thomas, his son, German Swerd of Wakefield, clerk. At Wakefield. (*Ibid.*, No. 14).

487. Saturday after Gregory the Pope, 10 Edward son of Edward [Sept. 4, 1316]. Indenture whereby Robert son of Henry de Hyperum mortgages (*inpignoravi*) to William Grenehode a certain booth in the market of Wakefield, between the booth of Peter the baker and the booth of German son of Philip, which the grantor's father Henry had quitclaimed to him, Robert, by an indenture; in return for the sum of 40*s*., payable from the Annunciation of the B.V.M., 10 Edward son of Edward March 25, 1315[-16] until the same feast, 1317[-18]. The form of this indenture being that if the said Robert or his heirs shall pay to William or his heirs 40*s*. at the said feast, then after the conclusion of 15 years during which, by an agreement between them, the said William holds the booth and cellar, then the said premises shall revert to Robert; but if the sum of money shall not be forthcoming at the said feast, then it shall be otherwise; and Robert wishes and grants for himself and his heirs that the booth and cellar shall remain to William and his heirs in perpetuity. Alternate seals. Witnesses: Henry de Walda, steward, Thomas Alayn, William de Lockewode, John de Geyrgraue, John Cussing, Peter de Acom, German Kay. At Wakefield. (*Ibid.*, No. 15).

488. Saturday before the Purification of the B.V.M. [Jan. 29], 1316[-17]. Grant by William Pykhac of Wakefield to John son of Robert the mercer of the same, and Joan, his wife and their heirs and assigns, of all his tenement with buildings in Kergate which lies between the tenement of Robert de Wyrenthorp on the one side and the tenement of Robert carpenter of Wakefield on the other, in return for a sum of money; to hold to John and Joan, of the chief lords of the fee. Warranty. Sealing clause. Witnesses: Henry del Weeld, steward of the Earl, Thomas Alayn, Robert de Wyrenthorp, William Erl, Robert le Walker, William the goldsmith, Robert Swerd, German Swerd, clerk. At Wakefield. (*Ibid.*, No. 16).

[1] Three seals of yellowish wax all rubbed and undeciphered.

489. Thursday after the Ascension[1] [May 12], 1317. Grant by Thomas de Louthe of Wakefield to John son of Robert the mercer, of the same, and his heirs and assigns, of all his tenement in Wakefield which lies in Kergate between the tenement of Juliana widow of Robert Broun on one side, and the tenement of John de Gayrgraue on the other, in return for a sum of money; to hold to John, his heirs and assigns freely and in peace, of the chief lords of the fee, with all liberties and easements. Warranty. Sealing clause.[2] Witnesses: Henry del Weeld, steward of the Earl, Thomas Alayn, sergeant of the liberty, John de Gayrgraue, Robert le Walker, John son of William Erl, Robert the goldsmith, German Swerd, clerk. At Wakefield. (*Ibid.*, No. 17).

490. Wednesday after St. Martin, 13 Edward son of Edward [Nov. 14, 1319]. Grant by Henry Poyde of Wakefield to John son of Robert of Wakefield, of all his tenement with the garden and croft which lies in the vill of Wakefield in Westgate, between the tenement of German Hodelyn on the west, and the tenement which once belonged to John Baba on the east; to hold with all appurtenances to John, his heirs and assigns, freely and in peace of the chief lords of the fee. Warranty. Sealing clause. Witnesses: German Fylcok, Henry of Wakefield, farmer (*firmario*) of the said vill. German Swerd, Richard le Wayte, Philip Damysel, Henry de Swilington, clerk. At Wakefield. (*Ibid.*, No. 18).

491. Monday before the Purification of the B.V.M. [Jan. 30] 1321[-2]. Grant by Richard Grenehode to Richard, his son, of his stall (*selda*) in the market-place in Wakefield with the tavern adjoining, which lies between the stall of William de Castelforth on the east and the stall of German Filcok on the west; to hold with all commodities and easements to Richard, his heirs and assigns, of the chief lords of the fee. Sealing clause.[3] Witnesses: John de Burton, steward of the Earl of Lancaster, German Filcok, bailiff of the liberty, John Cussing, William de Castelforth, Peter de Acom, John son of Robert, Henry Tasse, clerk. At Wakefield. (*Ibid.*, No. 19).

492. Thursday, St. Andrew, 3 Edward III [Nov. 30, 1329]. Grant by Henry de Skulbrok of Wakefield to John son of Robert the mercer, of a portion of his garden in length 12 paces towards the north from the dividing-wall (*pariete*) at the back of the north door below the new room of the said John, and in breadth 6 paces towards the east from the north gateway of the grantor's house leading into his aforesaid garden; on condition that neither the grantor nor his heirs shall be prevented by buildings erected on the piece of land

[1] Ascension day falls on a Thursday, and here the word *Jouis* appears to have been inserted in paler ink.

[2] Seal of dark green wax; diam. ⅞ in.; the Paschal Lamb; ECCE AGNVS DEI.

[3] Broken seal of white wax.

by John or his heirs, from adequate entry and exit for the carrying back and fore of their baskets (*sportis*) tubs (*cuuis*) and other necessities and from coming and going at their own free will; to hold to John, his heirs and assigns freely and in peace, of the Earl de Warenne, and paying yearly to the grantor a rose at the Nativity of St. John the Baptist for all secular services and demands. Warranty. Sealing clause.[1] Witnesses: Sir Simon de Balderston, steward of the Earl, Thomas Alayn, bailiff outside the town (*forinsecos*), John de Gargraue, Robert Goldsmyth, Robert le Roller, Adam le Hewer, Thomas le Roller, William de Lockewod, Thomas son of Laurence, John de Fery, bailiff of the said vill. At Wakefield. (*Ibid.*, No. 20).

493. Thursday after St. Dunstan, 4 Edward III [May 24, 1330]. Indenture whereby John called Hobson of Wakefield grants to Robert de Lynton and Margaret, his wife, an annual rent of 7*s*. from his tenement in the vill of Wakefield in le Westgate, which lies between the tenement of William Cussing on the east and the tenement of Henry Poyde on the west and abutts also above the tenement of the said William on the south and the king's highway on the north; to hold to Robert and Margaret and their lawfully begotten heirs, and in default of issue reversion to the grantor. Warranty. Alternate seals. Witnesses: Thomas Alayn of Wakefield, John de Geirgraue, German Kay, William de Locwode, William Cussing. At Wakefield. (*Ibid.*, No. 21).

494. Sunday after St. Thomas of Canterbury [Dec. 30], 1330. Grant by German Filkok of Wakefield to John son of Robert of the same, of a certain part of his meadow lying at his Bund croft and abutting on the land of Hugh son of Katherine, namely, that part of the meadow which lies in the same breadth with the croft of the the said John; to hold to John, his heirs and assigns of the chief lords of the fee. Warranty. Sealing clause.[2] Witnesses: Simon de Balderston, Robert de Wyrenthorp, John de Gargraue, Thomas Aleyn, John de Fery, John the clerk. At Wakefield. (*Ibid.*, No. 22).

495. Wednesday after St. Michael, 6 Edward III [Sept. 30, 1332]. Indenture whereby Henry de Ketilthorp demises to John son of Robert of Wakefield 2 acres and 3 roods of land, of which 3 roods lie in Wakefield between the land of William Cussing and the land of Thomas Filcok, and one acre lies in Stannelay in a place called le Frerecroft, and the other acre lies in the same vill of Stannelay, namely, in le Kirkefeild; to hold to Robert for the term of 14 years following the day of making these presents, and paying yearly to Henry 2*s*. of silver in equal portions at the three terms usual in the vill of Wakefield. Warranty. Sealing clause.[3] At Wakefield. (*Ibid.*, No. 23).

[1] Part of a seal of brown wax; a stag.

[2] Seal of white wax, three cups; legend undeciphered.

[3] Seal of brown wax; diam $\frac{7}{8}$ in ; three cups; ✠S'AV . . . . .CR.OI.

496. Tuesday, the Translation of St. Thomas [July 7], 1338. Appointment by Joan, widow of John son of Robert of Wakefield, of Thomas de Lepton, clerk, to deliver seisin to Robert, her son, of all the messuages, land and meadows, rents and appurtenances in the vills of Wakefield, Stanneley and Sandale, according to her grant to the said Robert. Sealing clause.[1] At Wakefield. (*Ibid.*, No. 24).

497. Thursday in Easter week [April 4], 1342. Grant and demise by Robert de Lynton to Robert son of John Hobbeson of Wakefield, of an annual rent of 7*s.* from a certain messuage in Wakefield which Adam Michel of Wakefield and Margaret, his wife, hold of the grantor, in return for a sum of money given to him by the grantee; to hold to Robert son of John, his heirs and assigns for the term of 10 years following, freely and in peace. Warranty. Sealing clause.[2] Witnesses: John de Castelforth, Thomas Bate, Thomas del Cliff, Henry del Stockes, John son of Thomas, Thomas de Lepton, clerk. At Wakefield. (*Ibid.*, No. 25).

498. Wednesday before the Apostles Philip and James [April 19], 1349. Grant by Adam son of William Filch' clerk of Wakefield to Dom Thomas de Drayton, chaplain, of an acre of land containing 5 strips which lie in breadth in the field of Wakefield in the place called Windothill between the land of John Harihill, junior, on the south and the land of John of Yorkshyre on the north; to hold to Dom. Thomas, his heirs and assigns, freely and in peace, paying yearly to Robert son of John of Wakefield, his heirs and assigns, 4*d.* yearly for all services and demands. Warranty. Sealing clause. Witnesses: John de Castelforth, Robert son of John, Thomas Erle, Thomas del Cliff, Richard de Finchedene, William Filch, John Erl. At Wakefield. (*Ibid.*, No. 26).

499. Friday after the Assumption of the B.V.M. [Aug. 21], 1349. Grant by Adam Grenehed of Wakefield to John son of Thomas Grenehed of Wakefield, his brother, of all that shop with appurtenances in the vill of Wakefield, which lies in the market-place between the shop of Robert son of John on the one side and the shop of Robert Fourbour on the other; to hold to John, his heirs and assigns, of the chief lords of the fee, freely and quietly in perpetuity. Warranty. Sealing clause. Witnesses: John de Castelford, Robert son of John, Robert de Hiperom, Robert Wolf, John Couper, John Gelleson. At Wakefield. (*Ibid.*, No. 27).

500. Wednesday after St. Luke the Evangelist [Oct. 20], 1350, 24 Edward III. Grant by John son of Thomas Grenehed of Wakefield to Robert son of John of Wakefield, of all his shop with the wine cellar (*selar' pro vino*) and with all other appurtenances in Wake-

[1] Broken seal of white wax, a spray of flowers.
[2] Small seal of brown wax, very blurred.

field which lies in that part of the vill called les Bothes, between the shop in which Robert Wolf lives and a certain lane; in return for a sum of money paid to him by Robert, which shop the grantor had of the gift and feoffment of Adam, his uncle; to hold to Robert, his heirs and assigns, of the chief lords of the fee. Warranty. Sealing clause.[1] Witnesses: Thomas del Cliff, Edward Fery, Robert Goldesmith, John de Fery, Robart Wolf, Thomas de Lepton . . . At Wakefield. (*Ibid.*, No. 28).

501. Thursday, Feb. 8, 1357[-8]. Grant by John son of Robert Gelle of Wakefield to Thomas son of Robert Jonson of Wakefield, of his shop with appurtenances in Wakefield which lies in les Flesshebothes between the shop of John de Fery on the east side and the shop of William de Sudyngton on the west; which shop the grantor had of the gift of Robert his father; to hold to Thomas freely and quietly and in peace, of the chief lords of the fee. Warranty. Sealing clause. Witnesses: Richard de Fyncheden, William de Fery, John Dykman, John Haget, Thomas de Lepton, clerk. At Wakefield. (*Ibid.*, No. 29).

502. June 3, 4 Henry VI [1426]. Indenture whereby John Thornholme esq., grants to John Qwyte of Wakefield and Joan, his wife, half a burgage with appurtenances in Wakefield which lies in that part of the vill called Westgate, between the tenement lately belonging to Thomas Megson on the west and the tenement lately of Robert Dowebyggynge on the east; to hold to John and Joan for the term of their lives or for the lifetime of the survivor, of the chief lords of the fee, and paying yearly to the grantor 10*s.* of legal English money at Martinmas and Whitsuntide in equal portions; should the rent be in arrears wholly or in part at any of the terms power to enter and distrain until satisfaction be obtained; and should the rent be in arrears for the length of 40 days after any of the terms power to enter and hold, this grant notwithstanding; and John and Joan shall keep the half burgage in as good repair throughout their lives as when they receive it. Warranty. Sealing clause. Witnesses: John Gayrgraue, William Gayrgraue, John Vauasour, John Wawan, John Sele. (*Ibid.*, No. 30).

503. June 5, 35 Henry VI [1457]. Release by John Bryan, perpetual vicar of the church of Burton Anas to Thomas Thornhom son and heir of John Thornhom of Hasthorp, esq., now deceased, his heirs and assigns, of all right in all the lands and tenements, rents and services with appurtenances in the vills of Wakefield, Stanley, Ousthorp', Dryffeld, Baynton, Foston and Brygham in co. York which the grantor and Henry Skerne of Skerne now deceased held jointly of the gift and feoffment of the said John Thornhom. Warranty. Sealing clause. Witnesses: John Constable of Halsham,

[1] Seal: small seal of white wax; in a cusped border, a shield of arms, undeciphered.

Stephen Hatefeld of Rysseby, William Ryssom of Ryssom esqs., Thomas Folkton of Ellerker, Robert Preston of Moretowne. (*Ibid.*, No. 31).

Wansford.

504. 4 Edward son of Edward [1310-11]. Grant by William de Hanlai of Wandesford, son and heir of Henry de Hanlai, to Hugh de Thornholm, his heirs and assigns, of a bovate and 2 acres of land with 1½ acres of meadow in the fields of Wandesford, of which 7 strips (*cilliones*) are in the west field and contain 3 acres lying in breadth between the land once belonging to Stephen Knot on the north and the land of Jollan Sparus on the south and which extend in length from the croft of William le Hamer towards the west as far as the headland (*forerum*) [called] Elchedi sayk, which he holds of Warin de Rale; and 4 strips of land containing 2 acres in the same field lie between the land of Jollan Sparus on the north and the land once of Walter son of Emma on the south, and they extend in length from the highway which leads towards Driffeld as far as the headland of Warin de Rale; and 5 butts of land containing 2 acres which lie in 3 places, namely, in one headland at Keldmarestal, another butt at les Langlandheudes, and 3 butts at le Brademarestal extending from le Brademarestal towards the east as far as the highway, and in breadth between the land once of Alan son of Christiana on one side and the land of Warin de Rale on the other; and 2 strips of land at Wychpildore, containing one acre which lies in breadth between the land of Warin de Rale on the north and extends in length from the highway which leads towards Driffeld towards the west as far as the meadow of the lord de Perci; and one strip of land in le Scharphow furlanges and contains one acre and lies in breadth between the land once belonging to Stephen Knot on the west and the land of Warin de Rale on the east and extends in length from the way called Scharphowgat as far as le Westker; also one headland in le Stanilandes containing half an acre which extends in length from the land once of Stephen Knot towards the south as far as the land of Thomas son of Simon which he holds of Warin de Rale; and one headland in the west field which contains half an acre, extending in length from the highway to Driffeld as far as the land of Thomas son of Simon which he holds of the said Warin; also 6 strips abutting on the croft of Robert the miller which contain 3 acres and extend in length towards the west as far as the headland of Warin de Rale, and in breadth between Warin's land on the south and the land of Robert the miller on the north; and 14 strips lie in one field on the north of the vill and contain 4 acres of land which the grantor had of the gift of John son and heir of John de Malton which he released and quitclaimed to the said Hugh with all appurtenances, and which extend from the highway on the west towards the cultivated land of Robert the miller, and in breadth between the land once of Jollan Campioun and the land of the abbot of Melsa on the north; also one acre of meadow in le Brademarescal lying between the land of Warin

de Rale on one side and the meadow once belonging to Stephen Knot on the other; and 2 pieces of the grantor's meadow in the field of Southil containing half an acre just as it lies; to hold the said bovate and 2 acres of land and 1½ acres of meadow to Hugh with all apputtenances and easements, namely, in commons, pastures, turbaries, waters and all other places, of the chief lords of the fee, freely, quietly and in peace, in perpetuity. Warranty. Sealing clause. Witnesses: Theobald de Brigham, William his son, Hugh de Patrington, of the same, Simon de Spinis of Nafferton, Mag. Roger Westiby of the same, John de Horkestowe of Wandesford, John son of John of the same. (*Y.A.S.*, Md. 59/24, No. 32).

505. Wednesday after the Circumcision [Jan. 3], 1318-[19]. Grant by John, son and heir of Roger son of Reginald de Wandesford to Hugh de Thornoholm, and Cecily his wife, and the heirs and assigns of Hugh, of a toft and half an acre of meadow in the vill of Wandesford, which toft and meadow descended to the grantor by hereditary right after the death of his father, and which had belonged to Reginald the miller; he also grants the rent from a piece of land which Robert the miller and Alice, his wife, hold of the demise of the grantor for the term of their lives, namely, the rent of 2*s*., also the reversion of the said land; similarly the rent and reversion of a piece of land which John Cotayn and Alice, his wife, hold for the term of their lives of the demise of Roger, the grantor's father, the rent of which is a clove gillyflower; to hold to Hugh with all appurtenances, of the chief lords of the fee. Sealing clause.[1] At Wandesford. Witnesses: Theobald de Brigham, Simon de Spinis of Nafferton, Robert de Lacy, John de Horkston, John Knot, John son of Stephen, Geoffrey the clerk. (*Ibid.*, No. 33).

506. Monday before Martinmas, 6 Edward III [Nov. 8, 1332]. Release and quitclaim by Jollan *ad fratres* of Wandesford to William le Proriost [*sic*] of Magna Driffeld and Agnes daughter of Hugh de Thyrnholm, his wife, and their lawfully begotten heirs, of all right in 6 strips of land with appurtenances in the field of Wandesford, which extend from the croft once belonging to Robert the miller of Wandesford in length as far as a certain strip called Warynheuedland towards the west, and in breadth between the land of Peter de Rale on the south and the land which the said Robert the miller has of William de Henlay on the north. Warranty. Sealing clause. Witnesses: William de Brigham, Simon de Spinis of Nafferton, John Knot of Wandesford, John son of Stephen of the same, Stephen Raynald of Wandesford, Robert son of Alan of the same. (*Ibid.*, No. 34).

507. Sunday before the Nativity of St. John the Baptist[2] [June 24], 1347. Indenture whereby Cecily, widow of Hugh de Thorn-

[1] Seal. Broken white wax, vesica shaped; . . .RAV
[2] The Nativity of St. John fell on a Sunday in 1347.

holm grants and demises to John Sperowe and Katherine his wife, of Wandesford, an annual rent of 6*s.* from a messuage and an acre of land in Brigham which John Couhird holds of Cecily, for the term of his life; and to hold to John and Katherine, their heirs and assigns from the feast of the Nativity of St. John the Baptist, 1347, for the full and complete term of the three years next following, and which is payable at Martinmas and Whitsuntide in equal portions, in return for a certain sum of money received by Cecily; if the rent should be in arrears, power to John and Katherine to enter the messuage and distrain until satisfaction is obtained. Warranty. Alternate seals. Witnesses: William de Brigham, Edmund Cante, Robert de Wadnesford, John Fi . . . . . At Brigham. (*Ibid.*, No. 35).

508. April 10, 8 Henry VI [1430]. Grant by John Thorneholm to Robert Conestable, lord of Flaynborgh, Robert Mownteney, Robert Rudestane and William Skyeryn, of his manor of Thorneholm in Wandesford, 5 roods of land in Brygham and a bovate in Wandesford and 5 roods in Skyeryn with all appurtenances; to hold to the grantees, their heirs and assigns, of the chief lords of the fee. Warranty. Sealing clause. Witnesses: Robert Hilton, knt., William Brigham esq., John Richardson of Wanysforth. At Wandesforth. (*Ibid.*, No. 36).

509. April 26, 8 Henry VI [1430]. Indenture whereby Robert Conystable, lord of Flaynborgh, Robert Mownteney, Robert Rodestane and William Skyeryn grant and confirm to Thomas son of John de Thorneholme, and son and heir of Margaret wife of the said John, and Constance, daughter of Stephen de Thorppe, wife of the said Thomas, the lands [*as in the preceding deed*]; to hold to Thomas and Constance and their lawfully begotten heirs, and in default of such issue remainder to, 1) John and Margaret, parents of the said Thomas, and their lawfully begotten heirs, 2) William de Thorneholme, brother of the said John, and his lawfully begotten heirs, 3) the right heirs or assigns of the said John. Alternate seals.[1] Witnesses: Robert Hilton, knt., John Conystable esq., William Brygham esq., Henry Skyeryn, John Stabiler, John Richardson. At Wandesforth. (*Ibid.*, No. 37).

Warlaby.

510. Tuesday after All Saints [Nov. 7], 1307. Indenture whereby Robert de Garton of Northaluerton, merchant, binds himself to Nicholas son of Roger Sparuer of Warlouby, in the sum of 20*s.* sterling, payable yearly to the said Nicholas, his heirs and assigns in equal portions at Martinmas and Whitsuntide. If it should happen that the grantor and his heirs hold the fourth part of that meadow called le Smal Engs in the territory of Warlouby with which

[1] Tongues for 4 seals. Small seals of red wax on 1, 2, 4; (1) a hound couchant; (2) a stag's head; (4) a star above a crescent.

the said Nicholas enfeoffed the grantor, as is more fully contained in his charter, beyond the full term of 10 years from Whitsuntide 1308, then the said Nicholas may enter and distrain until he obtains full satisfaction for any rent and arrears. Alternate seals.[1] Witnesses: Dom. Roger Latour of Warlouby, chaplain, John Latour of the same, Richard son of Nicholas de Northaluerton, Thomas son of Ranulf de Brunton', John de Hamby. At Northaluerton. (*R. Lee, Esq.*).

511. Sunday after St. Margaret the Virgin [July 21], 1308. Grant by Roger the chaplain, son of Roger Latour of Warlouby, to Robert de Garton, of Aluerton', merchant, of the fourth part of all the mill of Warlouby which he had of the gift of William Pouring of Otterington, to hold to Robert, his heirs and assigns, of the chief lords of the fee, freely, quietly and in peace, with all liberties and easements in perpetuity. Warranty. Sealing clause.[2] Witnesses: Nicholas son of Alexander de Northaluerton, Ralph Fischer, Robert Dibelot, Robert Gykel of the same, Nicholas Sparuer of Warlouby, William de Werleton of the same, John Lassell of the same, John de Lythe of Morton'. At Northaluerton.[3] (*Ibid.*).

512. Grant by Nicholas son of Roger Speruer of Warlouby to Robert de Garton of Aluerton', merchant, of a fourth part of that meadow in the territory of Warlouby called le Smale Eng which came to the grantor by inheritance after the death of Roger, his father; to hold to Robert, of the chief lord of the fee, with all liberties and easements, paying yearly a rose in the season of roses if demanded, for all secular services and demands. Warranty. Sealing clause.[4] Witnesses: Dom. Roger Latour of Warlouby, chaplain, John Latour of the same, Richard son of Nicholas de Aluerton', Thomas son of Ranalf de Bruntton, John Hamby. (*Ibid.*).

513. St. Edmund the archbishop [Nov. 16], 1353. Indenture whereby Nicholas de Garthton leased and demised to Sir Roger de Hewyk, knt., all his part of the water mill of Warlaby with appurtenances, for the full term of 18 years next following; to hold to Sir Roger, his heirs and assigns, paying yearly to Nicholas and his heirs 10*s*. sterling in equal portions at Whitsuntide and Martinmas; should the rent be in arrears for 3 weeks power to Nicholas to enter and retain until full satisfaction is obtained. Warranty. Alternate seals. Witnesses: William Lasseles of Warlaby, Thomas Lasseles of the same, Thomas Caber of Kyrkeby Wysk, William de Kyrkeby of Thyrtoft and John Zol of Norhtalretone. At Warlaby.[5] (*Ibid.*).

[1] Seal of white wax; undeciphered.

[2] Seal of white wax; undeciphered.

[3] Dorso: Carta Rogeri capellani fil' Rog' Latoure fact' Roberto de Garton de quart' parte molend' de Warlauby.

[4] Seal of white wax, diam. $\frac{1}{2}$ in.; undeciphered.

[5] Dorso: Indent' N. de Gartona fact' Roger de Hewik de tot' parte sua molend' de Warlawby ad term' xviij annorum. Warlauby.

Wheatley (Ilkley).

514. Saturday after the Purification of the B.V.M. 12 Edward [Feb. 5, 1283-4]. Notification[1] by Anthony (*Antoigne*) de Lucy, Richard de Kirkebride, Benet de Pappecastre, Thomas de Hardegill, that on the Saturday after the Purification of the B.V.M. Richard de Wetley came before them and stated that he had safely and in good order (*ferme et estable*) all the goods which were agreed upon between Peter de Middilton and himself, and he had made feoffment of his lands with the exception of those which Peter holds of him, and he maintained all things arranged by them in the letters which passed between them when the said Richard was in prison. Sealing clause.[2] At Cardoill. (*Y.A.S.*, Md. 59/24, No. 38).

515. Grant and confirmation by Richard son of Robert de Whetely to Peter son of William de Middleton, of all the lands, tenements, rents and services with appurtenances which he had after the death of Robert, his father, in the vill and territory of Wheteley; to hold to him, his heirs and assigns in perpetuity, of the chief lords of the fee. Warranty. Sealing clause.[3] Witnesses: Thomas de Hoton, John de Skelton, Richard de Denton, Richard de Hoton, John Lespenser, Reginald Le Pulter of Carlisle. (*Ibid.*, No. 39).

516. Grant and confirmation by William son of Adam de Skybdon to Sir Adam de Middelton, of all the lands and tenements, rents and services which he has or may have in Whetelay after the death of Beatrice, widow of Thomas de Vlskelf, his grandmother; to hold to Sir Adam, his heirs, of the chief lords of the fee. Warranty. Sealing clause. Witnesses: Walter de Middleton, Robert his son, Peter son of William de Middelton, Patrick del Stede, Thomas de Scalwra.[4] (*Ibid.*, No. 40).

517. Sunday, Martinmas, 8 Edward son of Edward [Nov. 11, 1314].[5] Grant and quitclaim by Richard son of Robert de Whetley to Sir Adam de Middelton, of all right in a messuage and 10 acres of land with appurtenances in Whetley, which messuage and land is called le Campioland. Warranty. Sealing clause, Witnesses: Sirs Robert de Plumpton, Mauger le Vauasur, knt., Walter de Middel-

[1] In French.

[2] Tongues for 4 seals cut from the bottom of the deed: (a) red wax, diam. $\frac{7}{8}$ in., in a cusped border a shield of arms; three lucies; (b) red wax, broken: below a spray of flowers, a shield of arms; a cross fusilly; . . . . . . .IDE.

[3] On one tongue two seals; a) vesica shaped, of red wax; $1\frac{1}{4}$ x 1 in.; haloed figure of Christ with a staff in the left hand and the right uplifted in blessing a kneeling figure, legend undeciphered; b) small round seal of brown wax; probably a sheaf of wheat; legend undeciphered.

[4] Endorsed: Carta Will' fil' Ad' del Hauck

[5] In 1314 Martinmas fell on Monday.

ton, William Mauleuerer, John de Caylly, Thomas de Preston. At Middelton.[1] (*Ibid.*, No. 41).

518. Friday before Palm Sunday, 9 Edward son of Edward [April 2, 1316]. Release and quitclaim by John de Whetlay, living in York, to Sir Adam de Middelton, of all right in all the lands and tenements, rent and srevices which the said Sir Adam has in Whetlay and Stubbum near Ilkelay. Sealing clause. Witnesses: Robert de Plumpton, Mauger le Vauasour, Henry de Hertelyngton, knts., Walter de Burlay, Robert, his son, William son of William Mauleuerer, William de Castelay, Thomas de Scalwra, William de Colyn, John de Cailuy, Thomas de Preston, Robert de Neuby, clerk. At Stubbum. (*Ibid.*, No. 42).

519. Monday before the Ascension, 14 Edward son of Edward [May 25, 1321]. Indenture whereby Richard de Whetlay leases to Peter son of Richard de Midelton the messuages, tofts, land, meadow and pasture with appurtenances which he has in Whetlay, with the exception of a messuage, 9 acres of land and half an acre of meadow and pasture for his own animals; he also grants *housbote* and *haybote* from his woods of Whetley; to hold to Peter and his heirs, of Richard during the grantor's lifetime, quietly and in peace, with all liberties and easements, paying yearly to Richard 20*li.* at Martinmas and Whitsuntide in equal portions, and to the lord of Ilkeley 16*s.* 4½*d.* on behalf of the said Richard, and to the chief lords of the fee the due and accustomed services; and should the said Peter alienate the land to anyone, or if the rent should be in arrears for 15 days, Richard may enter and at his will hold the goods and chattels in the said tenements until the rent and arrears are fully paid. Warranty. Alternate seals.[2] Witnesses: Sirs Peter de Middelton, Mauger le Vauesur, Robert de Plumpton, knts., Patrick de Marton, Robert de Burley, Thomas de Scalwra. At Whetley. (*Ibid.*, No. 43).

520. [1322]. Grant by John son of Nicholas de Caluy and Agnes his wife, to Sir Peter de Middleton, knt., of their messuage, land wood with all appurtenances which they have in the vill of Weteley, of the demise of Thomas de Preston; to hold to Sir Peter for their lifetime, of the chief lords of the fee, paying yearly for them for the first 8 years 38*s.* 4*d.* to the said Thomas, in equal portions at Whitsuntide and Martinmas, and after the said 8 years, 10 marks at the same times; beginning at Whitsuntide, 15 Edward son of Edward [May 30, 1322]. Sealing clause.[3] Witnesses: Sirs Robert de Plumton, Henry de Hertlington, knts., Thomas de Scalwra, Peter de Stede. (*Ibid.*, No. 44).

[1] Endorsed: Fait aremembre q' le dit Sir Adam ad grante a le dit Richard par son escrıt q' quiel hour q'il ly paye xv libr'. Il lui revandra la terre avant dite et noun pas autrement.

[2] Small seal of red wax; a sheaf of wheat; legend undeciphered.

[3] Tongues for two seals, fragment of yellow wax on the first.

521. April 26, 44 Edward III [1370]. Indenture[1] witnessing that whereas Sir Nicholas de Middleton, knt., has granted to Sir Brian de Stapelton and William de Holme iuxta Paule, and their heirs, an annual rent of 40 marks from all his lands and tenements in Draghton, Whetelay, Mensyngton, Dyghton, Lynton, Whitwell, Fenton, Thornore and Gesyngton,[2] at the two terms, namely Whitsuntide and Martinmas, in equal portions, as appears in a charter concerning the said annual rent, granted to them by the said Sir Nicholas; nevertheless, the said Sir Brian and William agree and grant for themselves and their heirs, that if Auyce, the wife of Sir Nicholas should survive him, and after his death be impleaded (*enplede*) of the manors of Stubbum,[3] Midelton, Scalwra, Ousteby[4] and Askwyth, or any parcel of them, and if her estate should be set aside or void as a result of entry or recovery by the heirs of the said Sir Nicholas, or any other, then the said annuity of 40 marks shall be in force and strength, but if otherwise then it shall lose its power and be annulled for always. At Helagh. Sealing clause.[5] (*Ibid.*, No. 45).

522. Monday after Whitsunday, 12 Henry IV [June 1, 1411]. Indenture whereby Nicholas de Middelton, knt., grants to Thomas de Scalwra of Whetelay a messuage with 10 and 8 acres of land and meadow with appurtenances in Whetelay, which John de Scalwra once held of the grantor and which lie between the messuage of John de Scalwra on the north and the messuage of the lord of Ilkley on the south; he also grants another messuage and 7 acres of land and meadow lying on the east side of Whetelay which Agnes de Scalwra once held of him; to hold with all liberties and easements to Thomas, his heirs and assigns, of the chief lords of the fee, in exchange for a messuage and a croft with appurtenances in Middelton which once belonged to Richard de Scalwra, Thomas's father, which the said Thomas granted to Sir Nicholas in perpetuity. Alternate seals.[6] Witnesses: Richard de Redemane, Henry Vauasour, knts., Robert de Lyndelay, John Faukes, William Faukes. At Whetelay. (*Ibid.*, No. 46.)

523. Monday after Whitsunday, 12 Henry IV [June 1, 1411]. Indenture whereby Nicholas de Middelton, knt., grants to Thomas de Scalwra of Whetelay, his heirs and assigns, an annual rent of 9*s*. from all the lands and tenements recently belonging to the said Thomas in Middelton, until the grantor or his heirs shall give security

[1] In French.

[2] Grassington.

[3] Stubham, parish of Ilkley.

[4] Scalwray, hamlet in Middleton, par Ilkley; Austby in Nesfield.

[5] Seals: two of red wax, both good impressions; a) diam 1 in., broken at the edges; in a cusped border a shield of arms; a lion rampant to the dexter. b) diam. 1 in , in a cusped border a shield of arms, 3 bars, on a quarter, a chaplet; SIGILLUM.WILLILMI.D.HOLME.

[6] Seal: blob of red wax; the letter R.

to Thomas or his heirs in respect of 8*s*. worth of land or rent in Whetelay or any other suitable place [*the last* 5 *words interpolated above the line*]; under the following conditions, namely, that if the said annual rent should be in arrears either wholly or in part for as long as 40 days after either of the two terms, Whitsuntide and Martinmas, then it shall be lawful for Thomas to enter and distrain on all lands in Middelton until full satisfaction is obtained, and if the rent should be in arrears for half the year, power to Thomas to enter, retain and peacefully posses the lands until Nicholas or his heirs render full satisfaction. Alternate seals. Witnesses: [*as to the preceding deed*]. (*Ibid*., No. 47).

Whitby.

524. Jan. 21, 8 Elizabeth, 1565[-6]. Grant[1] by George Conyers of Whitbie, esq., to Leonard Conyers, his son, gent., Christopher Lepton, esq., Robert Rookbie and Robert Yoward, gent., of all his goods, moveable and fixed, of his *shyppe* with all the furnishings thereto belonging, also all his leases and rights in the same; with the exception of his lease of Staynescar with certain goods and chattels which he has there, namely, 8 oxen, 4 . . . .[2] *whaynes* . . . and *plewys and the corne upon the grownde with all reddy swoen;* he also grants the reversion of his lease of Bagdale closes with *tethe* corn of Dunsley and Newsum granted to his son, Nicholas Conyers, with the exception also of 10 *qwyes* appointed in his will to Meriall . . . . ; he also grants all the moneys derived from Thomas Balland, clerk, as a result of the grantor's judgement against him; to hold to Leonard, Christopher, Robert and Robert, their executors and assigns, in perpetuity. Sealing clause.[3] George Conyers. (*R. Lee, Esq.*).

Miscellaneous.

525. Saturday the eve of Palm Sunday, 12 Edward III [April 4, 1338]. Ralph de Normanuille and Henry de Scorby, collectors of the wool tax in co. York, both within the liberties (*libertates*) and without, to Walter de Haukesworthe and Peter de Marthelay, greeting. It is decreed by the King in these terms: 'Edward, by the grace of God, to his elect, Ralph de Normanuille, knt., and Henry de Scorby, greeting; be it known that since the prelates, counts, nobles, magnates and commonalty of the realm at the present parliament at Westminster, called on the morrow of the Purification of the B.V.M. [Feb. 3], in consideration of the difficulty of the times, have granted to us, for the defence of our realm and the holy church of the same, as well as for our other lands and places which by right

[1] In English.
[2] Document badly stained
[3] Sealed and delivered in the presence of Roger Lee, John Postgate, parson of Smeton.

of our crown have lately increased and on account of which and the necessary military service (*expeditionem*), have occasioned the expenditure of a great (*excessiua*) sum of money, half of their wool now shorn, to the amount of 20,000 sacks as a subsidy for the maintenance of the aforesaid operations; therefore we appoint you, either severally, or together, to collect without fraud or deceit, half the wool now shorn, from the said prelates, abbots, priors, counts, barons, knights and merchants and of all others of whatsoever condition in the aforesaid county, as well in the liberties as without, excepting only the district of Crauen, in such a way that the said wool shall be at the ports of Kyngeston super Hulle and St. Botolph before the feast of Easter next following, or at the said feast, and all and singular the wool of the said county, except the parts stated, shall be had under forfeiture of the wool and all their other goods and chattels, and there shall not be any disturbance nor shall any impede either or both of you in any way in the collection of the aforesaid wool; and those who may be found obstructive or rebellious against the collection of the said wool, or who may conceal their wool or cause any delay, shall from time to time, without further writ or intimation be so punished that the punishment shall fall also on the rest as an example for such rebellious action, and moreover, their lands and tenements, goods and chattels shall on account of their disobedience be seized into our own hand; and as often and when it shall seem desirable to one or both of you, the collection of the wool and the carriage of the same to the said ports may be deputed to others whom you know of, for the greater expedition of the same'. Wherefore, on behalf of the king we command you and in our place appoint you, severally or together, to make the collection, to the use of the said king of half the wool in the wapentake of Skyrak, in the said county, as well within the liberty as without, and to deliver to us in writing the names of all from whom you receive wool, to York in the octave of Easter next following. Letters patent at York.[1] (*Farnley Hall Muniments*, No. 14).

[1] Two seals of red wax:)1) broken, a standing figure, possibly an angel; (2) oval; a shield of arms below three fleur de lis, a fess between two bars

APPENDIX

Original Text. No. 366.

Frontispiece.

Hec est conuencio facta inter dominum Johannem de Lascy, Comitem Lincolnie et Constabularium Cestrie ex una parte et dominum Rades de Duffeld militem et Emmam vxorem suam ex altera. videlicet quod predictus Johannes de Lascy concessit dictis Rades et Emme vxori sue et heredibus suis sexaginta acras terre in Fippin' mensuratas per perticam viginti pedum quarum decem sunt de bosco stanti, et quinquaginta de coopicio, iuncto dicto bosco stanti in Fippin' versus Pouelington'. Et pro hac concessione quietum clamauerunt predicti. Rades et Emma vxor eius pro se et heredibus suis dicto Johanni et heredibus suis . totum ius et clamium quod habuerunt uel habere potuerunt ipsi uel heredes sui in predicto bosco de Fippin' et in Almholm'. saluis predictis Rades et Emme uxori sue et heredibus suis et hominibus suis duobus chiminis. vno incipiente ad Cuwik per mediam culturam ipsius domini Johannis de Lascy usque ad sudcampum ad capud de Almholm' versus orientem et alio chimino se extendente inter boscum quod predictus dominus Johannes eis superius concessit et boscum suum usque ad sudcampum versus occidentem . latitudinis duarum perticarum. Hanc autem conuencionem warantizabunt predicti Rades et Emma uxor eius contra omnes gentes tam contra homines suos liberos quam contra alios. Hanc autem conuencionem fideliter tenendam . utraque pars affidauit. In huius autem rei testimonium utraque pars sigillum suum alterius rescripto apposuit. Hiis testibus. Dominis Henrico de Notingham . persona Rowell'. Ada de Nereford'. Johanne de Crigel' sen[escallo]. Thoma de Polington'. Henrico de Goldhal'. Magistro Rogero de Bodham. Waltero de Ludham. Waltero de Hauuill'. Michaeli de Tanett'. Osberto clerico et aliis multis.

Tag for seal; seal missing.

Indented cut on the word *cyrographya.*

The date of this document must be between 1232 when John de Lascy became earl of Lincoln, and 1240 which was the year of his death.

John de Crigleston is not recorded by Richard Holmes in his list of stewards in Vol. I of *The Pontefract Chartulary.* Fippin is marked as Phippin parks on the 1 inch Ordnance Survey, and lies to the east of Pollington. It also appears on a later deed in the same series,[1] where John de Lynlay is described as the keeper.

1 *Yorkshire Deeds,* ix, p. 160.

INDEX

Place names, when identified, are indexed under their modern spelling. Field-names, local names and unusual words are printed in italics.

An asterisk (*) indicates that the name occurs in more than one document on the same page, or in a single document and a footnote. A hyphen indicates that a name occurs more than once within the pages specified. The letter *n* indicates that the name occurs only in a footnote.

Made in the USA
Las Vegas, NV
27 March 2021

20275618R00142